WALKING THE MUNROS

Volume Two:
Northern Highlands and the Cairngorms

ABOUT THE AUTHOR

Steve Kew made his first solo climb at the age of 11 in the Lake District when he pioneered an interesting route from his campsite in Grasmere to the summit of Helm Crag; he has been hooked on mountains ever since. He attended a beginners' rock climbing course in 1970 and immediately returned to do the intermediate and advanced courses. Since then he has climbed and walked extensively throughout Britain; in the Alps he has done many of the classic 4000m peaks such as the Matterhorn, Nadelgrat and Monte Rosa traverse and has been on several trekking and climbing trips to the Nepal Himalayas and the Karakoram. He lives in southwest Scotland where he is a member of the Galloway Mountain Rescue Team and Chairman of the Stewartry Mountaineering Club. His previous writing includes three other books, many articles for newspapers and magazines and radio drama for the BBC. This is his first guidebook.

WALKING THE MUNROS

Volume Two:
Northern Highlands and the Cairngorms

by
Steve Kew

CICERONE

2 POLICE SQUARE, MILNTHORPE, CUMBRIA LA7 7PY
www.cicerone.co.uk

© Steve Kew 2004
ISBN 1 85284 403 5

A catalogue record for this book is available from the British Library.

ACKNOWLEDGEMENTS

I am grateful to the Ordnance Survey for permission to base my own maps and measurements on the OS 1:50,000 series, and to Lucy Histed and Hazel Clarke for helpful suggestions on creating the maps and organising the guide.

I am also indebted to the staff of the Gaelic College in Sleat – Sabhal Mòr Ostaig – for invaluable help with Gaelic names and pronunciations. Any mistakes or oddities in the handling of these names in the text, however, is entirely my own fault.

Thanks also are due to Jean Etherington for helping to keep track of where I was on my travels, and also to the numerous youth hostel wardens and local police with whom I left details of routes.

I am also grateful to Graham Mitchell for big-hearted help with the text.

The short quote from the *Song of Duncan Ban Macintyre* in the section on Beinn Dorain comes from a translation by Angus Macleod, published by Oliver and Boyd for the Scottish Gaelic Texts Society, 1952, and with acknowledgements to this book, if only for an extraordinary description of a female red deer drinking a mouthful of the water in a little burn on the east side of Beinn Dorain called *Allt na h-Annait*.

Above all, this is for Tink, who was with me every step of the way.

Maps are based on Ordnance Survey ® material, licence number PU100012932.

ADVICE TO READERS

Readers are advised that while every effort is taken by the author to ensure the accuracy of this guidebook, changes can occur which may affect the contents. It is also advisable to check locally on transport, accommodation, shops, etc.
The author would welcome information on any updates and changes. Please send to the author care of Cicerone Press, 2 Police Square, Milnthorpe, Cumbria LA7 7PY

Front cover: Corrag Bhuidhe pinnacles from Sgurr Fiona

CONTENTS

Maps
Area covered by the Guide 9
Area Map 6 10
Area Map 7 11
Area Map 8 12
Area Map 9 14
Area Map 10 16
Area Map 11 17

Introduction 19

Cairngorms Braemar
Route 1
Beinn a' Bhuird, Ben Avon
(Leabaidh an Daimh Bhuidhe)...................39

Route 2
Beinn Bhreac, Beinn a' Chaorainn 43

Route 3
Beinn Mheadhoin..46

Route 4
Derry Cairngorm, Ben Macdui,
Carn a' Mhaim..48

Route 5
The Devil's Point, Cairn Toul, The Angel's
Peak (Sgor an Lochain Uaine) 54

Route 6
Beinn Bhrotain, Monadh Mor.....................57

Cairngorms: Glen Ey
Route 7
Carn an Fhidhleir, An Sgarsoch 60

Route 8
Carn Bhac, Beinn Iutharn Mhor 63

Cairngorms: Coylumbridge
Route 9
Bynack More, Cairn Gorm 67

Route 10
Braeriach 71

Cairngorms: Glen Feshie
Route 11
Mullach Clach a' Bhlair 75

Route 12
Sgor Gaoith 79

Monadhliath
Route 13
A' Chailleach, Carn Sgulain, Carn Dearg.....81

Route 14
Geal Charn..84

Loch Laggan
Route 15
Creag Meagaidh, Stob Poite Coire
Ardair, Carn Liath 86

Route 16
Beinn a' Chaorainn, Beinn Teallach 90

Glenfinnan
Route 17
Sgurr nan Coireachan, Sgurr Thuilm............92

Route 18
Gulvain (Gaor Bheinn) 96

Loch Lochy
Route 19
Meall na Teanga, Sron a'
Choire Ghairbh 99

Glen Dessarry
Route 20
Sgurr nan Coireachan, Garbh Chioch
Mhor, Sgurr na Ciche 102

Route 21
Sgurr Mor 106

Glen Quoich
Route 22
Gairich 109

Route 23
Gleouraich, Spidean Mialach 110

Route 24
Sgurr a' Mhaoraich....................................113

Knoydart
Route 25
Luinne Bheinn, Meall Buidhe...................115

Route 26
Ladhar Bheinn 119

Hourn
Route 27
Beinn Sgritheall 122

Glen Shiel
Route 28
The Saddle, Sgurr na Sgine........................125

The South Shiel Ridge
Route 29
Creag a' Mhaim, Druim Shionnach,
Aonach air Chrith, Maol Chinn-dearg,
Sgurr an Doire Leathain, Sgurr an
Lochain, Creag nan Damh 130

The Five Sisters of Kintail
Route 30
Sgurr na Ciste Duibhe, Sgurr na
Carnach, Sgurr Fhuaran............................135

Route 31
Ciste Dhubh, Aonach Meadhoin,
Sgurr a' Bhealaich Dheirg, Saileag 139

Route 32
A' Chralaig, Mullach Fraoch-choire 143

Route 33
Carn Ghluasaid, Sgurr nan
Conbhairean, Sail Chaorainn.....................146

Route 34
Beinn Fhada, A' Ghlas bheinn...................149

Glen Affric
Route 35
Mullach na Dheiragain, Sgurr nan
Ceathreamhnan, An Socach 153

Route 36
Mam Sodhail, Carn Eige,
Beinn Fhionnlaidh.....................................157

Route 37
Tom a' Choinich, Toll Creagach 162

Strathfarrar/Mullardoch
Route 38
An Socach (Glen Elchaig)..........................164

Route 39
An Riabhachan, Sgurr na Lapaich,
Carn nan Gobhar 167

Route 40
Sgurr na Ruaidhe, Carn nan Gobhar,
Sgurr a' Choire Ghlais, Sgurr 171
Fhuar-thuill

Monar
Route 41
Bidein a' Choire Sheasgaich,
Lurg Mhor 174

Route 42
Sgurr Choinnich, Sgurr a' Chaorachain 178

Route 43
Maoile Lunndaidh 181

Route 44
Moruisg, Sgurr nan Ceannaichean............184

Coulin
Route 45
Maol Chean-dearg.....................................186

Route 46
Beinn Liath Mhor, Sgorr Ruadh 189

Isle of Skye
Route 47
Sgurr nan Gillean 194

Route 48
Am Basteir, Bruach na Frithe 198

Route 49
Sgurr a' Mhadaidh, Sgurr
a' Ghreadaidh 202

Route 50
Sgurr na Banachdich 206

Route 51
Sgurr Dearg (The Inaccessible
Pinnacle), Sgurr Mhic Choinnich..............209

Route 52
Sgurr Alasdair...215

Route 53
Sgurr Dubh Mor, Sgurr nan Eag................218

Route 54
Bla Bheinn 222

Torridon
Route 55
BEINN ALLIGIN – Tom na Gruagaich,
Sgurr Mhor...225

Route 56
LIATHACH – Spidean a' Choire Leith,
Mullach an Rathain....................................229

Route 57
BEINN EIGHE – Ruadh Stac Mor,
Spidean Coire nan Clach............................234

Kinlochewe
Route 58
Slioch 238

The Fannaichs
Route 59
A' Chailleach, Sgurr Breac,
Sgurr nan Each, Sgurr nan Clach Geala,
Meall a' Chrasgaidh 241

Route 60
Beinn Liath Mhor Fannaich, Sgurr Mor,
Meall Gorm, An Coileachan......................245

Route 61
Fionn Bheinn...249

Strathvaich
Route 62
Am Faochagach..251

Wyvis
Route 63
BEN WYVIS – Glas Leathad Mor.................254

Fisherfield/Letterewe
Route 64
Ruadh Stac Mor, A' Mhaighdean,
Beinn Tarsuinn, Mullach Coire Mhic
Fhearchair, Sgurr Ban, Beinn a'
Chlaidheimh..257

An Teallach
Route 65
Sgurr Fiona, Bidein a' Ghlas Thuill............264

Conival (Freevater)
Route 66
Eididh nan Clach Geala, Meall nan
Ceapraichean, Cona' Mheall,
Beinn Dearg...268

Route 67
Seana Bhraigh...272

Inchnadamph
Route 68
Conival, Ben More Assynt 275

Strath Vagastie
Route 69
BEN KLIBRECK – Meal Nan Con 279

Strath More
Route 70
Ben Hope...282

Appendix 1: Bibliography..........................285
Appendix 2: Contact Details 286
Appendix 3: Index of Munros...................288
(alphabetical)
Appendix 4: Index of Munros...................296
(by height)

Map Symbols

△   Munro summit

○   Munro Top

Road

Track

Railway

Route

Alternative route

Rivers

Lake/sea

Contours:
For the sake of simplicity only four contours have been used. They are intended to indicate the general shape of the hills and to include prominent features such as summit ridges. Because of the height of the Munros varies considerably (between 915m and 1344m) these contours may designate differing heights from map to map.

Direction of grid (north) and scale in kilometres

0km   1km
Scale
N

ⓅParking

■   Buildings/habitation

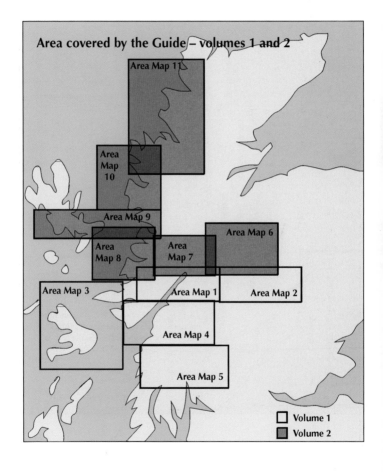

Area covered by the Guide – volumes 1 and 2

Area Map 11

Area Map 10

Area Map 9

Area Map 8

Area Map 7

Area Map 6

Area Map 3

Area Map 1

Area Map 2

Area Map 4

Area Map 5

☐ Volume 1
■ Volume 2

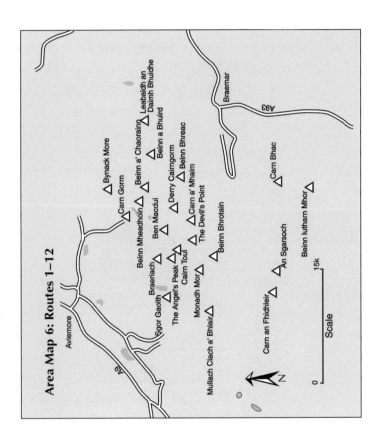

Area Map 6: Routes 1–12

Aviemore

A9

Sgor Gaoith △

Braeriach △

The Angel's Peak △
Cairn Toul △

Monadh Mor △

Mullach Clach a' Bhlair △

Carn an Fhidhleir △

Beinn Mheadhoin △

Ben Macdui △

△ Carn Gorm

△ Bynack More

Beinn a' Chaorainn △

Leabaidh an
Daimh Bhuidhe

Beinn a Bhuird

△ Derry Cairngorm
△ Beinn Bhreac

△ Carn a' Mhaim
The Devil's Point

△ Beinn Bhrotain

△ An Sgarsoch

Beinn Iutharn Mhor △

△ Carn Bhac

Braemar

A93

N

Scale

0   15k

10

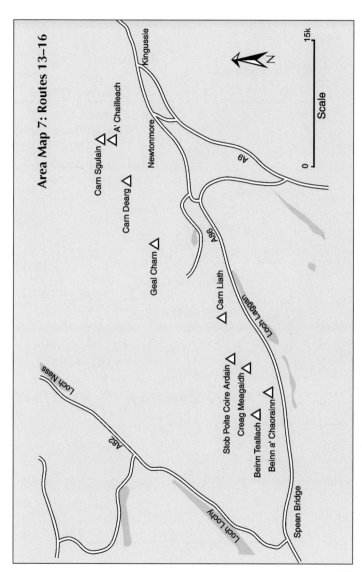

Area Map 7: Routes 13–16

Carn Sgulain
A' Chailleach
Carn Dearg
Geal Charn
Newtonmore
Kingussie
Carn Liath
Stob Poite Coire Ardain
Creag Meagaidh
Beinn Teallach
Beinn a' Chaorainn
Loch Laggan
Loch Ness
Loch Lochy
Spean Bridge
A9
A86
A82

N
Scale
0   15k

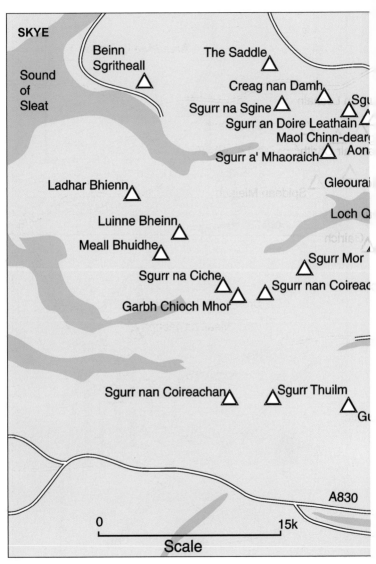

SKYE

Sound of Sleat

Beinn Sgritheall △

The Saddle △

Creag nan Damh △

Sgurr na Sgine △

Sgurr an Doire Leathain △

Maol Chinn-dearg

Sgurr a' Mhaoraich △

Ladhar Bhienn △

Luinne Bheinn △

Meall Bhuidhe △

Sgurr na Ciche △

Garbh Chioch Mhor

Sgurr nan Coireac

Sgurr Mor △

Sgurr nan Coireachan △

Sgurr Thuilm △

| 0 | 15k |

Scale

A830

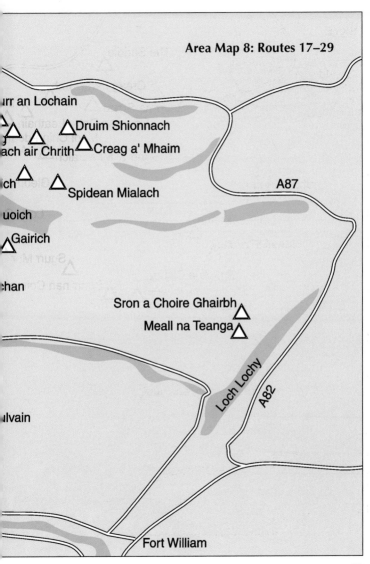

urr an Lochain

Druim Shionnach

ach air Chrith

Creag a' Mhaim

ich

Spidean Mialach

uoich

Gairich

chan

Sron a Choire Ghairbh

Meall na Teanga

A87

Loch Lochy

A82

ulvain

Fort William

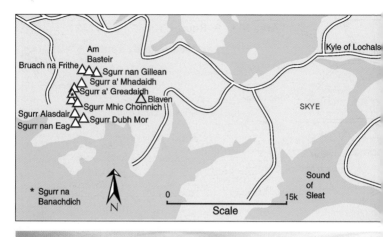

Am Basteir
Bruach na Frithe
Sgurr nan Gillean
Sgurr a' Mhadaidh
Sgurr a' Greadaidh
Blaven
Sgurr Mhic Choinnich
Sgurr Alasdair
Sgurr Dubh Mor
Sgurr nan Eag

* Sgurr na Banachdich

Kyle of Lochals

SKYE

Sound
of
Sleat

0   15k
Scale

N

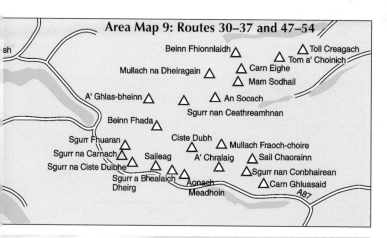

Area Map 9: Routes 30–37 and 47–54

sh

Beinn Fhionnlaidh △   △ Toll Creagach

△ Tom a' Choinich

Mullach na Dheiragain △   △ Carn Eighe

△ Mam Sodhail

A' Ghlas-bheinn △   △   △ An Socach

Sgurr nan Ceathreamhnan

Beinn Fhada △

Sgurr Fhuaran △   Ciste Dubh

Sgurr na Carnach △   △   △ Mullach Fraoch-choire

Sgurr na Ciste Duibhe △   Saileag   A' Chralaig △ Sail Chaorainn

Sgurr a Bhealaich   Aonach   △ Sgurr nan Conbhairean

Dheirg   Meadhoin   △ Carn Ghluasaid

A87

An Teallach from Summit of Ruadh Stac Mor (Route 65 from Route 64)

15

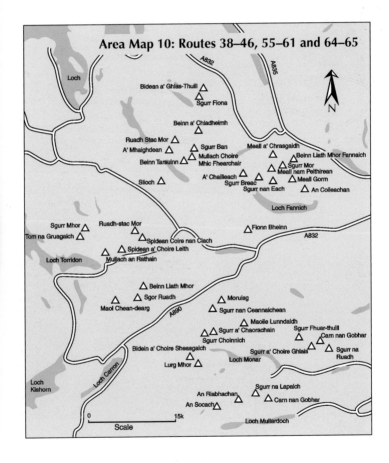

Area Map 10: Routes 38–46, 55–61 and 64–65

N

Loch

A832

A835

Bidean a' Ghlas-Thuill △

Sgurr Fiona △

Beinn a' Chladheimh △

Ruadh Stac Mor △

Meall a' Chrasgaidh △

A' Mhaighdean △   △ Sgurr Ban   Beinn Liath Mhor Fannaich △

Mullach Choire   △ Sgurr Mor

Beinn Tarsuinn △△ Mhic Fhearchair   Meall nam Pelthirean △

A' Chailleach △   △ Meall Gorm

Slioch △   Sgurr Breac △   Sgurr nan Each △   △ An Coileachan

Loch Fannich

Sgurr Mhor △   Ruadh-stac Mor   △ Fionn Bheinn

Tom na Gruagaich △   △ Spidean Coire nan Clach   A832

△ Spidean a' Choire Leith

Loch Torridon   Mullach an Rathain

Beinn Liath Mhor △

Sgor Ruadh △   △ Moruisg

Maol Chean-dearg △   △ Sgurr nan Ceannaichean

△ Maoile Lunndaidh

△△ Sgurr a' Chaorachain   Sgurr Fhuar-thuill △   Carn nan Gobhar △

Sgurr Choinnich   Sgurr a' Choire Ghlais △   Sgurr na Ruadh △

Bidein a' Choire Sheasgaich △   Loch Monar

Loch Kishorn   A890   Lurg Mhor △

Loch Carron   Sgurr na Lapaich △

An Riabhachan △   Carn nan Gobhar △

An Socach △   Loch Mullardoch

0   15k

Scale

16

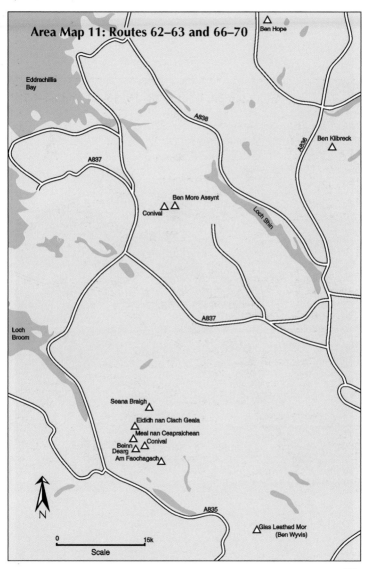

Area Map 11: Routes 62–63 and 66–70

Eddrachillis Bay

Ben Hope

A838

A836

Ben Klibreck

A837

Ben More Assynt

Conival

Loch Shin

A837

Loch Broom

Seana Braigh

Eididh nan Clach Geala

Meal nan Ceapraichean

Beinn Dearg

Conival

Am Faochagach

A835

Glas Leathad Mor (Ben Wyvis)

N

0   15k

Scale

East ridge of Carn Eige

INTRODUCTION

There are 284 Munros – that's a lot of cheese sandwiches. It's a lot of blisters, too, and sweat and tired muscles and wet socks. But think of the positive side. Doing the Munros will take you to places of quite extraordinary beauty that you would never otherwise have seen; places that inspire awe, reflection and sometimes fear. The pleasures awaiting the Munroist are many and varied. Navigating your way through the primeval wonderland of Scotland's mountain landscapes will put the rest of your life into a new perspective. There will be moments of great satisfaction, often in the midst of adversity; moments when you have unforgettable encounters with wildlife, and moments when friendships are forged through shared experience.

Climbing the Munros can also give you a richer understanding of the forces that have shaped this great landscape, and an appreciation of the lives of those hardy creatures and plants that depend upon it for their existence. It will perhaps introduce you to some of the great stories of Scottish history that have been played out in the Highlands. If you are lucky it might even give you a greater understanding of your own inner strengths and weaknesses, a discovery of where your own limits lie and a chance to stretch yourself beyond them. There is a lot to be gained from walking the Scottish hills.

So why is there a need for this new guide to the Munros when there are other more lavishly illustrated guides on the market? The answer became clear to me when I saw walkers carrying scribbled route descriptions and crumpled photocopies with them on walks. Big, hardback guidebooks are fine for a coffee table, but they can't be slipped into your back pocket and taken with you where they're really needed. This guide, with its waterproof jacket, can be taken on your walk, and gives a full, clear and up-to-date route description.

Let's be honest about it: doing the Munros is not as hard as it once was. The logistics are much easier now, for a start; within the lifetime of one generation many of the Highland roads have become wider, straighter and faster. Where once you had to wait until morning for a ferryman to arrive and take one or two cars across at a time, now there is a bridge. There are also more people walking the hills; routes are well established and danger points better understood. A good safety net is also provided by mountain rescue teams across the country in the event of things going wrong. Route-finding is also much easier than it used to be, with a network of paths on most of the major hills where thousands of others have gone before. But – and it is a big but – climbing the Munros is still an adventure; one that will grip you and give you a fund of memories to last a lifetime. And when the weather turns bad there is just the same need as ever there was for sound judgement, fortitude and navigational skill to bring you safely home.

The qualities required of the Munroist are not technically or even physically as demanding as those, say, of the rock climber or the high-altitude mountaineer (unless the routes are being done in winter conditions, in which case they can become a serious and arduous mountaineering undertaking). But a certain doggedness is nevertheless needed – the perseverance to see through a huge task – plus the skill and courage to navigate in conditions that can change all too

rapidly in the Scottish hills. And this is not to mention a willingness to get wet, cold, shrouded in mist and buffeted by storms. If you only venture out when the sun is shining on the tops it may take more than one lifetime to complete the round.

Some people may deride those who are working through the Munros, as if the act of ticking them off a list somehow corrupts an otherwise pure experience of mountaineering. In my experience the opposite is true. By accepting the challenge of doing them all you open yourself up to a host of new experiences, and you find yourself in a variety of mountain situations that you might never have otherwise experienced. Besides this, of the many accomplished and aspiring Munroists I

Beinn Bhreac from the Derry Dun (Route 2)

On the descent of Sgurr na Sgine (Route 28)

know, I can think of none who confine their hillwalking just to the peaks that are on the list. I know of none who have not felt enriched by trying to complete the round.

THE MUNROS

What exactly are the Munros? I don't propose here to retell the history of this select group of hills. Suffice to say that Sir Hugh Munro's great idea of

21

climbing all the 3000ft mountains in Scotland has for over a century captured the imagination of everyone who loves mountains. In the popular imagination the Round of Munros includes all the hills that are over 3000ft in height. Once you start climbing them, however, you quickly realize that this is not the whole story. There are many points where the land rises above 3000ft but is not regarded as a separate hill; or where it clearly is a separate hill, but it has still not been accorded the status of a Munro.

Sir Hugh's original list, drawn up in 1891, was rather different from the most recently updated version. Some revisions have taken place as a result of improvements in mapping. Sir Hugh, for example, rather conveniently believed that the Inaccessible Pinnacle was lower than Sgurr Dearg and so it was not originally listed as a Munro. Even today the latest satellite mapping techniques may reveal that the accepted heights of hills is wrong (usually only by the odd metre). The Munro summit of Ben a' Chroin had to be redefined a couple of years ago because what was previously thought to be a lower Top nearly 1km away was found to be 1m higher than the classified summit. Similarly the respective heights of Beinn a' Chaorainn's three summits have recently been revised, and Ben Nevis itself is now officially 1m lower than it was a few years ago.

Successive revisions of the list by the Great and the Good have sought to declassify some hills and upgrade others, not just because their respective heights have been reassessed but also

Creag a' Mhaim (centre right) across Loch Loyne (Route 29)

on the basis of their 'character' or 'remoteness', or whether it was felt that readers ought to be directed to one rather than another. There is not always an obvious logic to the hills that are in or out of the list at any moment in time, and the list has been revised so often that it is in some danger of being discredited. The last revision came in 1997, and on the current list there are 284 Munros and 227 tops.

Despite all the argument and lack of clarity about what makes a hill a Munro, and despite the all-too-frequent revisions, there is no doubting the fact that the underlying idea of the list makes sense to most people; it always has made sense and it probably always will. The list stands for something meaningful both to the hillwalker and to the public at large, and that something involves the idea that the Munros are all the highest hills in Scotland.

USING THE GUIDE

This guide is published in two volumes: volume one covering the southern Munros and volume two the northern peaks. In general the routes in volume two are listed from south to north. First listed are routes in the northern Cairngorms, then those on the northern side of Glen Spean/Glen Spey, and finally from Glen Finnan working northwards all the way up to Ben Hope. The 'area maps' at the front of the book place the Munros in their local context, and the overview map of Scotland locates them within the country as a whole.

Some of the Northern Munros, such as those in Fisherfield and Letterewe, are particularly remote; some, most notably those on the Cuillin of Skye, involve scrambling on rock. Such demands may be new to the average hillwalker, and it is incumbent on them to make sure that they have the necessary judgement and skills to cope safely with these challenges (two useful mountain skills books are recommended in 'Difficulty', below).

The guide contains a special intro-duction to the Munros in the Cairngorms and to those on the Isle of Skye; this is to highlight the particular dangers that arise for hillwalkers in these areas. The introductions, which

Sgurr an Lochain from Sgurr an Doire Leathain (Route 29)

23

Sgurr na Lapaich from Glen Strathfarrar (Route 39)

most Munros fall naturally into distinct pairs or small groups. Sometimes, however, this natural grouping of hills can make for a very long route if done in one outing. Usually these longer routes, such as the Lochnagar circuit or the Ben Lui hills, can be broken down into shorter walks if required, and whilst several long routes are described here in full, suggestions are made (where appropriate) about how to tackle them in a number of shorter outings if preferred.

Each route is prefaced by a box containing information to help you in planning your ascents.

MOUNTAIN NAMES AND PRONUNCIATIONS

All the mountain names have been taken in the form that they appear on the current 1:50,000 OS maps, although it is clear that there could be alternative spellings for many of them. Spellings on the maps sometimes appear in their Gaelic form, for example 'bheinn' and 'mhor', and sometimes in anglicized versions of Gaelic words, such as 'ben' and 'more'. For the sake of consistency I have kept faithful to the OS spellings, even where these appear to be wrong.

Suggested meanings and pronunciations have been given at the start of each route for the names of all the peaks, drawing on a variety of sources. The origin of mountain names is often complex and sometimes obscure. Whilst the majority of Scottish

immediately precede the Cairngorm routes and Skye routes, should be read before attempting any walks in those areas.

The routes described are often the most popular ones for each hill; usually these are also the most direct and obvious ways up. Like most walkers I have a preference for circuits rather than returning by the route of ascent, and these have been given where appropriate. Some alternatives to the described route are indicated. There may be 'better' ways up some of the hills, but the distances involved in reaching them can be a strong disincentive to their use.

Some Munros are isolated and have to be climbed on their own, but mountain names are of Gaelic origin, some owe more to Norse, Pictish, Scots or English influence. Some names may contain elements of more than one language – Bla Bheinn on Skye, for example, is often held to derive from 'bla', a Norse word meaning 'blue', and 'bheinn', the Gaelic word for mountain, although there are others who feel that Bla comes from the Gaelic 'blath', meaning 'flowers'. Many Munro names have more than one possible derivation.

Pronunciations, too, are far from fixed and certain, and it would be wrong to be too dogmatic about them. I have tried to give a simple phonetic rendition of each pronunciation so that a modern English speaker can readily understand it. But this is not a simple task: many of the names may have Gaelic roots, but over time they have been corrupted into words that are no longer recognisably Gaelic. Ben Chonzie, for example, may have its origin in the Gaelic word 'còineach', meaning moss, but there is no letter z in the Gaelic alphabet, and the name as it appears on maps today is no more recognisable to a Gaelic speaker than it is to an English speaker.

Putting these names into phonetic spellings presents other difficulties too. Gaelic has a number of sounds which have no equivalent in English, for example the Gaelic sound 'ch' (as in the word 'loch') is always a soft sound produced in the back of the throat, not the harder English sound of 'lock' or the 'ch' sound produced in the front of the mouth (as in 'chalk'). Moreover Gaelic has distinct regional differences in pronunciation, and in some areas where Gaelic is no longer spoken the local pronunciations of mountain names may not accord with

Ladhar Bheinn from Loch Hourn (Route 26)

received wisdom about the 'correct' pronunciation.

Many people regard it as a form of vandalism to change old names in any way, and whilst I have a lot of sympathy with this view I am also aware that language can never be frozen in time. The historical evidence shows clearly that, like all other place names, the names of Munros have changed and evolved over time. There is nothing inherently wrong with modern usage bringing new changes to these words. There is no one period in history to which the 'correct' pronunciation should be attributed.

MAPS

The maps accompanying each route are based on the 2002 editions of the Ordnance Survey 1:50,000 series maps. With the notable exception of one or two areas, such as the Black Cuillin on Skye, this is the scale of map that I personally prefer for climbing the Munros, and it is widely recognized as being a suitable scale of map for the hillwalker. The box at the start of each walk also makes reference to the relevant OS Explorer maps, which some people might prefer. These 1:25,000 maps give much more detail, which can be advantageous at times, but it can also complicate the process of routefinding – particularly on steep ground where a lot of contours are packed very close together, or in areas where there is a lot of exposed rock. Sometimes more than one map is needed to cover the walk in question. Munros are listed on the covers of the Explorer maps in which they appear, but unfortunately some of these lists

Beinn Tharsuinn (centre) from Bidean a' Choire Sheasgaich (Route 41)

are currently inaccurate. Some hills that are not officially Munros have been accorded Munro status; others that are Munros have not been listed. No doubt this will be rectified in future editions of these maps.

The 'area maps' referred to in the box at the start of each route correspond to those at the start of the book; these are designed to give a broad view of where each Munro lies in relation to major roads and also to neighbouring Munros. The overview map of Scotland accompanying these area maps shows the location of each area within Scotland as a whole.

The sketch maps accompanying each route description are designed to assist in planning route-finding. Although they are drawn to scale based on the OS 1:50,000 series maps, they are not intended to be a replacement for the OS maps for the purposes of navigation, and it is strongly recommended that the appropriate OS map is carried at all times. Harvey also make an excellent series of maps for some of the areas described.

If you are using different maps, an older edition of the OS maps, you should bear in mind that spot heights and names may vary from those in the text.

GRID REFERENCES

As an aid to navigation, grid references have been given for summits and for other key features and descent points on all the routes. These are all 10-figure

readings taken on the walk itself with a GPS. Whilst GPS readings can sometimes be inaccurate by 50m or more, they are usually much more accurate than this and are nearly always close enough for hillwalking purposes. (In a number of recent mountain rescue exercises small canes were planted in rough ground in a mountain area of several square miles and were found without much difficulty from their grid reference using a GPS, even in poor visibility.) The next generation of GPSs is likely to be even more accurate and reliable. Many walkers now carry a GPS and it can be a useful navigational tool, especially if you need to establish your exact position in poor visibility. This does not obviate the need for a map and compass, however, and great care needs to be taken if you are navigating from one waypoint to another in poor visibility, as a straight line between the two may well take you over a cliff.

DISTANCE AND ASCENT

The distances given in the information box at the start of each walk are always from the car park and back to the car park unless otherwise stated. The ascent for each route includes the cumulative height gained over undulating ground.

DIFFICULTY

Climbing any Munro involves a degree of difficulty. A fair level of fitness, an

The Black Cullin from Bla Bheinn (Sgurr nan Gillean distant right) (Route 47)

ability to navigate using a map and compass in poor visibility and an understanding of the mountain environment are all necessary qualities for anyone attempting to climb a Munro, and it is assumed that anyone using this guide will have these minimum skills.

In certain walks, additional skills are required for activities such as scrambling on rock, dealing with exposure or crossing rivers. Notes on 'difficulty' appear in the preface to such walks. However, the absence of any mention of specific problems does not imply that a walk is necessarily 'easy' or to be taken lightly. The usual grading system for scrambling has been used, that is from grade 1 for relatively simple scrambles to grade 3 for relatively hard ones.

There are certain ranges of Scottish mountains that pose special difficulties or dangers for the walker or climber and I have written special introductions for the Munros on the Isle of Skye,

The following books may be useful for developing mountain skills:

- Terry Adby and Stuart Johnston, *The Hillwalker's Guide to Mountaineering* (Cicerone Press, 2003)
- Eric Langmuir, *Mountaincraft and Leadership* (Scottish Sports Council – SportScotland, 1995).

and for those in the Cairngorms, to highlight these dangers. These area observations (which both occur in Volume 2) precede the relevant routes and should be read before attempting any of the walks in these areas.

TIMES

Approximate route times are given in the information box for each route. These have been worked out using an adapted version of Naismith's rule, combined with common sense and my own experience of the character of the route. Some walkers will consistently achieve faster times; others will be slower. It really doesn't matter which, except on very long routes where you may run the risk of benightment if you take too long. Above all, every effort has been made to be consistent so that each walker can get used to the values given in relation to their own speed. Bear in mind that the times given do not include elements for stoppages, lunch breaks, etc, which should be added on.

PARKING AND STARTING THE WALK

Details are given in the walk information box about the best places to park for each walk and how to access the hill from these points. It should be borne in mind, however, that approved places for parking are more liable to change than other aspects of a route, and you should be prepared for possible local changes. In a similar vein getting from the road onto the hill frequently takes walkers through a fringe of forest or through farms or other habitation where the preferred line of access may change from time to time. Please ensure that you follow local signs.

ACCOMMODATION AND CAMPSITES

The nearest youth hostel is given in the information box and, where appropriate, the nearest Independent Hostel. It should be noted, however, that there are some routes, for example in Glen Clova and Glen Esk, where the nearest hostel is a very considerable distance away. For most routes the box also gives the nearest centre where hotels or bed and breakfast accommodation can

be found. Occasionally a specific hotel is named if it is the only accommodation in the immediate vicinity of the route.

An indication of where the nearest campsites are has also been given for each route. Unfortunately campsites seem to come and go with some rapidity. 'Wild camping' is generally accepted in remote areas well away from the road, so long as the usual rules about rubbish and waste disposal are observed; but the practice of roadside camping – which is currently widespread – is strongly frowned on by landowners, local councils, the police and others.

ACCESS

The Land Reform Act (Scotland), which was passed by the Scottish parliament

Bla Bheinn from Loch Cill Chriosd (Route 54)

in 2003, greatly clarifies the issue of access to Scottish mountains, most of which are privately owned. Whilst it bestows a general right of access to the walker, it does not change the need for considerate behaviour in terms of closing gates, protecting stone dykes, taking home litter and respecting both the livestock and wildlife that live in the hills. Nor does it change the need to avoid conflict with other users. In fact, these responsibilities have been built into the bill in the form of a Code of Access, along with the requirement that walkers shoulder responsibility for their own safety. Details can currently be viewed on www.snh.org.uk.

There are critical times in the life of upland estates when particular care should be taken. These include the lambing season from March to early summer, and the stalking season – which for stags is from July to October (the latter part of this period is the most critical time for many estates) and for hinds is from late October to mid-February. The shooting season for grouse runs from 12th August to mid-December.

Certain estates in the recent past have not welcomed walkers at all, particularly during the stalking season, and there have been one or two well-publicized battles over access. Some estates do not welcome dogs at any time, and most estates insist that if dogs are brought onto their land they are kept on a lead. Dogs are rarely welcome during the lambing season. Fortunately the vast majority of estates

> ### Hillphones scheme
> This scheme provides hillwalkers in a number of areas in upland Scotland with daily information about deer-stalking activities. Recorded messages indicate where stalking is taking place and which walking routes will be unlikely to affect stalking, and give a forecast of stalking activity over the next few days. The messages are generally updated by 8am each day and are charged at normal call rates. Walks in areas covered by the scheme have the hillphones number in the 'Access' section of the box at the start of each route. For further information contact www.hill-phones.info

now have an enlightened view about public access and many subscribe to the hillphones scheme (see box) or put up notices and maps at the start of walks to assist walkers. Some estates have even constructed car parks specifically for the use of hillwalkers.

Whilst most estates like walkers to ring the factor's office or head stalker to discuss their routes before venturing onto the hill during the stag-stalking season, many are happy for walkers to come even at this time of year, providing they stick to the popular routes. Generally speaking, walkers would be advised to keep to ridges and high ground rather than to move through corries. There is less likely to be a conflict at weekends than midweek. On Sundays no shooting at all takes place. If in any doubt try ringing the relevant contact number for advice, but bear in mind that estate offices are not always manned throughout the day.

Co-operation isn't always straightforward: stalkers – the gillies – often don't know in which area they will be working until the morning of the day in question, and contacting them at that time may not be possible. Estates owned by the National Trust for Scotland, such as those in Torridon and Glencoe, do not impose restrictions on responsible access. Every effort has been made in this guide to give up-to-date contacts for every walk (see 'Access' in the box at the start of each walk), but it should be remembered that, just like other sorts of property, estates do sometimes change hands. For smaller estates where the contact may be a stalker's home number, both the person and the phone number can change fairly often.

A number of routes are accessed by crossing railway lines, and at the time of writing Network Rail are proposing to close some 600 unattended railway crossings to the public on the grounds of safety. There have occasionally been accidents involving walkers crossing railway lines, and walkers should make sure that they cross only at designated places or have the necessary permission to cross from Network Rail. Future Munroists should

be aware that new legislation in this area might necessitate changes to the start of some walks.

PATHS

The passage of many feet has left paths on most of the popular routes, and in some places on the lower slopes these paths are robustly constructed. Many walkers may prefer not to travel on such paths, but it should be remembered that constructed paths are there to prevent unnecessary erosion in a fragile landscape. They also limit the disturbance to nesting birds and other wildlife. In some of the walks in this guide you are strongly urged to keep to the described route; this may be because of the particular vulnerability of certain landscapes or to avoid conflict with other land users such as stalkers and shooters at particular times of the year. Path repair and management projects are not there to make the walking easier but to protect the quality of the mountain landscape and its ecology. On the other side of the coin, the Munroist should never assume that there will be a path – particularly on the higher slopes – or that, if there is, it can be easily followed. Anyone who has such an expectation will be quickly disillusioned.

Throughout the guide a distinction is drawn between roads, tracks and paths. 'Road' is used to indicate a tarmacked public road. 'Track' is used

Bha Bheinn from Silgachan (Route 54)

Corrag Bhuidhe buttress – An Teallach (Route 65)

There are hills which lie so far from any public road that the use of a bike to approach the hill along a forestry track or estate road can save many hours of walking. Opinion is split on whether or not this is a good thing. Some people prefer the long walk in. The National Trust has been trying to encourage a pedestrian approach: in some cases – for example in the Mar Lodge Estate in the Cairngorms – by digging up some of the estate roads and turning them back into footpaths.

My own view is that the wilderness character of remote areas needs to be strenuously protected from vehicular access and other sorts of development. There seems to be little restraint even today on the creation of new private roads in Scotland's fragile wilderness areas; but as long as there is a road leading to the hill, used by estate workers and their clients in their heavy four-by-fours, I can see no valid reason why a bike should not be used on it too. Whatever one's position on this, there is widespread agreement that mountain bikes should not be taken beyond these tracks onto footpaths.

to denote a forestry road or a private estate road or landrover track where the public does not have a right of vehicular access and where the road surface is usually rough (sometimes very rough), but where a bike could perhaps be used. 'Path' is used to denote a constructed footpath, or one that has formed over time by the passage of many feet. Bikes should not be taken on these. Some paths are startlingly obvious features cutting brashly across the countryside; others may be almost non-existent.

BIKES

The use of mountain bikes by hill-walkers on estate roads has become very widespread in the Highlands.

LEAVING WORD

Walkers should always leave word with someone about their intended route and expected time of return. Youth hostels throughout the Highlands have specially printed route cards. These can be filled in and left with the hostel in case you have an accident. Police stations throughout the area have similar forms, and in hillwalking areas the police are usually very helpful to walkers. They are, after all, the first point of contact if a mountain rescue team has to be called out. In preparing this book I did all the Munros solo and frequently left details of where I was going at local police stations.

Bear in mind, though, that many of the smaller police stations in the Highlands – even in major climbing centres like Braemar – are not manned every day. Always speak to an officer just to be sure, otherwise the scribbled note you put through the letterbox describing your proposed route may not be picked up for several days. It may be better to contact one of the larger regional stations such as Fort William or Inverness. These are always manned and many of the staff will be knowledgeable about routes and well versed in rescue procedures should the need arise. It is of course essential that if you leave a route card with someone, you must return or ring them up to let them know you have got back safely. Mountain rescuers never mind going onto the hill to search for someone in trouble, but they do not take kindly to searching for someone who has gone home and forgotten, or simply not bothered, to tell anyone that they got back. The time and effort that go into such searches is often considerable.

In the event of an emergency, contact the local police or ring 999 and be prepared to say where the emergency has arisen, with a grid reference if at all possible. If you are carrying a mobile phone bear in mind that in large parts of the Highlands it is not possible to get a signal. Your best chance of getting a signal in many mountain areas may be high up on the summits, or dial 121 on your mobile and you will be connected via any available network.

WHEN TO GO

This guide has been written with the summer walker in mind. Summer conditions will usually prevail between May and September, although deep-lying snow can last into the summer in some high places, affecting the safety of otherwise 'easy' routes. 'Winter' storms are not

Beinn Dearg from the col

Eas Mor waterfall (Routes 50, 51)

uncommon in May or September – I have been caught out by snow in June! You should always obtain an up-to-date weather forecast from one of the many specialized forecast services before venturing into the Scottish hills. Avalanche warnings for specific areas are available on the internet at: www.sais.gov.uk.

In winter conditions many routes may not be possible without strong all-round mountaineering experience. Navigation becomes more difficult, simple scrambles can become technical climbs, daylight is short and deteriorating weather can quickly lead to arctic conditions. Whilst a covering of snow can greatly add to the beauty and atmosphere of these mountains, remember that paths, cairns and other markers can quickly be obliterated; corniced ridges, snow-drifts and iced-up rock can make simple summer routes slow and fraught with danger. The Scottish hills should never be underestimated.

Enjoy them safely. Happy climbing!

THE CAIRNGORMS: INTRODUCTION

There is no agreed and definitive boundary to the mountains known as the Cairngorms (Routes 1–12). The name comes from two mountains which were both originally called An Carn Gorm. One of these, now known as Cairn Gorm, is at the centre of the Scottish ski industry; the other is now known as Derry Cairngorm. The widespread use of the collective name 'Cairngorms' to describe the range of hills around these two peaks seems to have started in the 19th century and grown in the 20th century, displacing earlier names such as Am Monadh Ruadh, 'the red mountain land', or Mounth.

Some people hold that the Cairngorms embrace only those hills that lie between the Dee and the Spey, although this would exclude hills such as Lochnagar, which many people think of as being part of the Cairngorms. Peter Drummond, in his book *Scottish Hill and Mountain Names,* describes how the use of the Cairngorms as a generic name has gradually 'spread out like a ripple in a pond to become the name of the whole range'. Other writers have used 'the Cairngorms' to refer to all of the mountains lying to the east of the A9, and the new Cairngorm National Park would have largely embraced this idea were it not for last-minute political shenanigans. As it stands, the national park's boundary includes the Lochnagar hills, but cuts meaninglessly right across the middle of hills such as Carn Bhac, Beinn Iutharn Mhor, The Cairnwell and others.

The range is also known, particularly in atlases, as the Grampians, although this is not a locally used name today. The Grampians is another very vague appellation. Some sources use it just to refer to the mountains that lie to the south of Braemar; the British Geological Survey uses it to refer to a much bigger area that includes Ben Nevis.

I am aware that this matter of names bothers some people greatly, and I have no particular axe to grind in this matter, but for the purposes of this book I have referred to the Cairngorms fairly loosely to include all the ranges that surround Braemar; this includes the Lochnagar hills, the Glenshee hills and the other hills to the immediate south of Glen Dee. My reason for doing this is quite simple: from a hillwalker's point of view all these hills share a great deal in terms of their geology, their flora and fauna and, more importantly for the walker, the nature of their topography and the weather patterns that affect them.

Walking in the Cairngorms can be a very serious undertaking, even in summer, and it is essential that your fitness, skills and preparation are up to scratch. Many of the summits are very remote, involving very long outings and an absence of quick escape routes. The rolling, high-level plateaux can leave the walker exposed to the worst of the elements for much longer than in other ranges where there are fast descents to the valley. It is important to bear in mind that the times given for walks are guidelines only and do not include time for lunch breaks and other stops. Some parties might find that these times are much faster than they can easily manage, and all parties should allow a generous extra margin for breaks, mishaps and unforeseen delays. The use of a bike on the long estate roads is recommended, where possible, to shorten the day.

Navigation in these hills is frequently more demanding than in other areas, since the rounded and indeterminate nature of much of the terrain means that there may be very few obvious features to work from, often over very great distances. In white-out conditions this can become a nightmare, but even in the summer months – when the weather is bad and visibility is poor – navigation can be extremely difficult, and the consequences of a mistake can be serious.

The other characteristic that these hills share is the weather. There is something about the position of these hills, combined with their topography, that attracts some of the worst weather that Britain has to offer. True, in the summer months there is often less rainfall here than in Scotland's western and northern ranges, but extreme winds can howl over these hills at any time of year; in winter the conditions can be truly Arctic. Map reading in such conditions can be virtually impossible, so it would help to know your route as thoroughly as possible before setting out, including checking escape routes and noting key bearings. It is also important to check the weather forecast with one of the specialized mountain weather services before setting out. Always be prepared to postpone a walk if the weather or the forecast is not good.

ROUTE 1

Beinn a' Bhuird (1197m), Ben Avon

(Leabaidh an Daimh Bhuidhe) (1171m)

Pronunciation: *Bine yuh Voordge;*
Ben Arn; Labby un Dive Vooyuh
Translation: *Table Mountain; Mountain*
of the River Avon; Bed of the Yellow Stag

Distance:	36km (of which 14km can be covered by bike on estate tracks)
Ascent:	1210m
Time:	10hrs 10mins (about 2hrs 15mins less if a bike is used on the estate track)
Difficulty:	see the general introduction to the Cairngorms (above)
Maps:	OS sheets 36 and 43; Explorer map 404; Area Map 6
Parking:	off-road at Keiloch (a new car park is planned for Keiloch, possibly with a small charge for parking)
Start:	along estate road past Keiloch and Invercauld House
Hostel:	YHA Braemar; independent Ballater
B&B/hotel:	Braemar; Ballater
Camping:	Braemar; Ballater
Access:	Invercauld Estate, tel: 013397 41224 or 013397 41227

This tough, long route makes an excellent circuit, with superb views on a clear day from Beinn a' Bhuird over the rest of the Cairngorms. The huge plateau that gives Beinn a' Bhuird its name is well appreciated from the southern flanks of Ben Avon. Isolated granite tors stand up like a series of strange growths on the smooth surface of these mighty hills, giving them the appearance of some distant planet, and many a climber, caught in deteriorating conditions, has learnt the hard way that this is not a place to be underestimated.

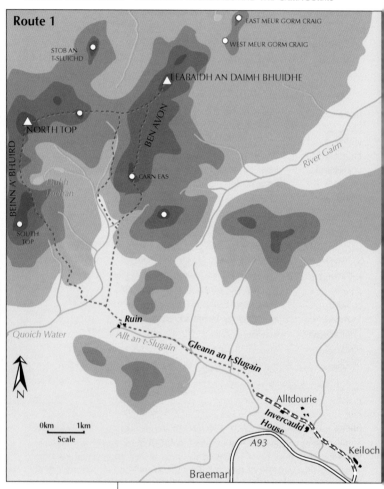

Route 1

EAST MEUR GORM CRAIG

WEST MEUR GORM CRAIG

STOB AN T-SLUICHD

LEABAIDH AN DAIMH BHUIDHE

BEN AVON

River Gairn

NORTH TOP

BEINN A' BHUIRD

Dubh Lochan

CARN EAS

SOUTH TOP

Ruin

Quoich Water

Allt an t-Slugain

Gleann an t-Slugain

Alltdourie

Invercauld House

A93

Keiloch

Braemar

N

0km   1km
Scale

From Keiloch, walk or cycle along the track past Invercauld House and Alltdourie into Gleann an t-Slugain. The track is signposted to Glen Quoich until ½km past Alltdourie, where the track divides; the left

This walk lies at the eastern end of the Cairngorm massif. Like many of the Cairngorm routes it is both long and arduous, taking you into harsh, uncompromising landscape. The use of a bike on the estate track at the start and end of the walk can save valuable time and is strongly recommended.

branch leads to Glen Quoich, and the right branch to the Slugain. The going gets progressively rougher the further you go, until a flat green apron is reached nestling in a little valley (beyond which the Landrover cannot go). Leave your bike here and continue on foot on a good footpath; this leads past the ruins of Slugain Lodge to the high upper valley of the Quoich Water.

The main path, which leads up the Glas Allt Mor to the Sneck (the col at the top), is left at 11607 95833 for a path which crosses the Quoich Water, then winds through the heather and climbs around the steep little nose of Carn Fiaclach. It stays on the western side of this ridge and climbs steadily along it before reaching its crest higher up, then veers left again near the top to avoid the stones on the upper slopes. It is further than it looks – or perhaps it just feels further than it is. Eventually you pass between the south top and the prominent granite tor of Point 1179, and soon the high ground of the ridge is reached as you traverse around the impressive crags above the Dubh Lochan, a climber's playground. These dramatic scenes on your right are matched by a sensational view to your left over the entire range of the Cairngorm hills. The North Top of **Beinn a' Bhuird** is marked by a cairn at 09230 00611 (5hrs 15mins; about 1hr 10mins less if a bike is used on the estate track).

Continue east-northeast past (or over) a craggy minor top, then descend steeply down a badly eroded sandy path to the col known as the Sneck (at 11852 01000). In poor visibility you should stay well to the left (north) of this path, as there are many false 'runs' that lead down to the Glas Allt Mor (an escape route leads down this valley, via a good path, in a fairly direct line to the Allt an

*Looking across the
Sneck to Ben Avon*

t-Slugain). From the col it is a straightforward climb onto
Ben Avon. The summit is a substantial granite tor set back
about 1½km to the northeast (Leabaidh an Daimh
Bhuidhe). Scramble up to the top of the tor at 13194
01835 (6hrs 30mins; less if a bike is used).

You could return via the path running back down the
Glas Allt Mor from the Sneck, but a pleasanter way to
complete the route is to head south, passing over the next
hill – Carn Eas – at point 1089, then descend quite
steeply at first down the southern slopes of that hill. There
is a high corrie here, which should be avoided as its back
wall is very steep, but on either side of it are ridges where
the angle is much easier. Descend over heather to join
the main path just beyond a little tributary burn and
follow this back past Slugain Lodge to the track.

ROUTE 2

Beinn Bhreac (931m),

Beinn a' Chaorainn (1082m)

Pronunciation: *Bine Vrack; Bine uh Chooereen*
Translation: *Speckled Mountain; Mountain of the Rowan*

Distance:	32km (of which at least 12km can be cycled)
Ascent:	840m
Time:	8hrs 35mins (about 1hr 20mins less if a bike is used to Derry Lodge)
Difficulty:	see the general introduction to the Cairngorms (above)
Maps:	OS sheets 36 and 43; Explorer map 403; Area Map 6
Parking:	car park at Linn of Dee
Start:	footpath from back of car park (if walking), or private track from the road (if cycling)
Hostel:	YHA Braemar or Inverey; independent Spittal of Glenshee
B&B/hotel:	Braemar
Camping:	Braemar; wild camping at Derry Lodge
Access:	National Trust for Scotland, Mar Lodge Estate, tel: 013397 41669. Normally no restriction on access at any time of year

This long walk takes you across the vast plateau at the heart of the Cairngorm and returns along Glen Derry through a beautiful area of ancient Caledonian pine forest.

Walk or cycle to Derry Lodge and continue into Glen Derry, staying on the right-hand (east) side of the Derry Burn. Follow the track to a high point in the trees at 04542 94990. It is possible to cycle to this point at present, although this may not always be the case as the National Trust's intention is to turn the track back to moorland with just a footpath in its place. A faint path starts here up the hillside through trees and heather, and

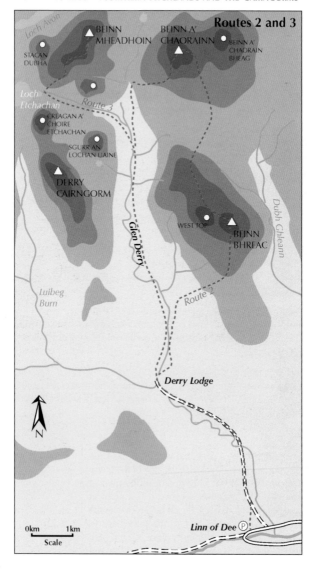

Beinn Bhreac from the Derry Burn

if you can find this path it makes the going a lot easier. Climb across the moorland to a narrow col between Meall an Lundain and Beinn Bhreac, then follow the line of the ridge up to the rounded, stony eastern top of **Beinn Bhreac**, which is its highest point at 05868 97067 (3hrs 30mins; about 40mins less if a bike is used on the track).

Beinn a' Chaorainn looks to be only a few hundred metres from here, but it is actually nearer to 5km. The going is firm and easy to start with as you bypass or cross Beinn Bhreac's western top, then head on to Craig Derry. But soon the ground becomes wet and peaty, although there are enough stones in the peat to make progress fairly easy. The best line follows the high ground, zigzagging from Craig Derry to Moine Bhealaidh, then making for the stony southeast ridge of **Beinn a' Chaorainn**. Climb this more easily to the summit cairn at 04515 01351 (5hrs; about 40mins less if a bike is used).

Descend southwest over granite boulders to the steep enclosing slope that drops down to the Lairig an Laoigh. If you try to descend too soon, this slope is rocky, scree covered and uncomfortably steep. The easiest line drops down due west from 03750 00500. Once here, all difficulties are over and the prominent path can be followed back along Glen Derry. If you used a bike beyond Derry Lodge, turn uphill to the left at a metal bridge and follow the path and track back to the foot of Meall an Lundain, where you started the ascent. If you walked from Derry Lodge, the pleasantest way back is to cross the metal bridge and follow the path back along the west bank of the river.

ROUTE 3

Beinn Mheadhoin (1182m)

Pronunciation: *Bine Veeyann*
Translation: *Middle Mountain*

Distance:	32km (of which 15km can be cycled)
Ascent:	800m
Time:	8hrs 35mins (about 1hr 50mins less if using a bike)
Difficulty:	see the general introduction to the Cairngorms (above)
Maps:	OS sheets 36 and 43; Explorer map 403; Harvey's Superwalker map Cairn Gorm; Area Map 6
Parking:	car park near Linn of Dee
Start:	along footpath from back of car park (if walking) or along estate road (if cycling)
Hostel:	YHA Braemar or Inverey; independent Spittal of Glenshee
B&B/hotel:	Braemar
Camping:	Braemar
Access:	National Trust for Scotland, Mar Lodge Estate, tel: 013397 41669. Normally no restrictions on access at any time of year

Beinn Mheaddhoin is a hidden hill that nestles right in the middle of the Cairngorms, as its name suggests. It is often climbed from the north, but this approach involves rather more descent and reascent than the route described here. The approach from the south via Glen Derry may be slightly longer but it is also easier.

From Linn of Dee walk or cycle to Derry Lodge and continue into Glen Derry. The estate track to the east of the river can be cycled for a further couple of kilometres at the time of writing, although this is one of the tracks that the National Trust is planning to restore to moorland. The footpath on the west side of the river offers a pleasanter approach through the trees. The two tracks join just beyond a footbridge, and a well-trodden path then follows the river, dividing higher upstream where the right-hand branch heads into the Lairig an Laoigh. The left-hand branch veers round past the Coire Etchachan bothy and climbs up to the black waters of Loch Etchachan.

Just beyond the outflow of this loch, climb a steep gravel path onto **Beinn Mheadhoin**'s main ridge. The scenery on this broad ridge is reminiscent of a prairie from the Far West, with a pavement of broken granite slabs set in gravel and sand with short, tufted grass sprouting through intermittently. All the scene needs is a few cacti and a man on a horse... Pass a number of small, weathered granite tors until a large square-set tor is reached, larger and higher than the rest. It seems impregnable as you approach, but a short scramble up the far side takes you to the summit at 02459 01683 (4hrs 55mins; less if using a bike).

Return by the route of ascent.

ROUTE 4

Derry Cairngorm (1155m), Ben Macdui (1309m), Carn a' Mhaim (1037m)

Pronunciation: *Derry Cairngorm; Ben Macdui; Karn er Vime*
Translation: *Wooded Blue Hill; (probably)*
Hill of the Sons of Dubh (or Duff); Cairn of the Pass

Scotland's second highest mountain, Ben Macdui, lies appropriately in the very heart of this remote and unforgiving range of hills. Reaching it from any direction involves a long but satisfying walk. Although there is no technical climbing or scrambling on this walk, there is much rough terrain to cover high on the mountains. This, plus the distance involved, makes it quite a tough outing.

From the Linn of Dee walk or cycle to Derry Lodge along the private track and cross the Derry Burn at the footbridge. The day can be shortened by cycling, or perhaps by camping in the meadows at Derry Lodge and using this as a base for the three or four long routes that start from here. Once you have crossed the Scots pine meadows and passed through a small enclosure via two

Distance:	32km (of which 11km can be cycled)
Ascent:	1340m
Time:	9hrs 20mins (1hr 20mins less if a bike is used to Derry Lodge)
Difficulty:	see the general introduction to the Cairngorms (above)
Maps:	OS sheet 43; Explorer map 403; Harvey's Superwalker map Cairn Gorm; Area Map 6
Parking:	car park at Linn of Dee
Start:	footpath from car park or, if cycling, along estate track from road
Hostel:	YHA Braemar or Inverey; independent Spittal of Glenshee
B&B/hotel:	Braemar
Camping:	Braemar
Access:	National Trust for Scotland, Mar Lodge Estate, tel: 013397 41669. Normally no restrictions on access at any time of year

Ben Macdui from Braeriach summit

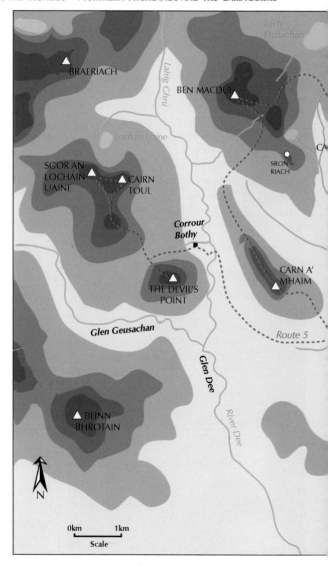

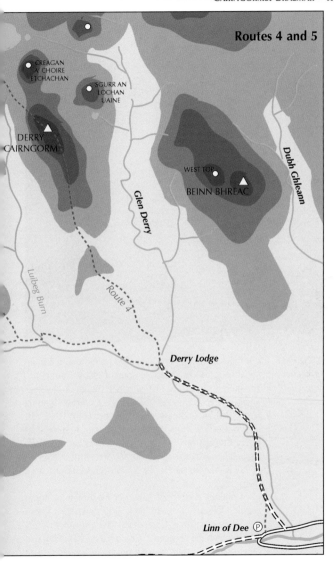

Routes 4 and 5

CREAGAN
A' CHOIRE
ETCHACHAN

SGURR AN
LOCHAN
UAINE

DERRY
CAIRNGORM

WEST TOR

BEINN BHREAC

Dubh Ghleann

Glen Derry

Luibeg Burn

Route 4

Derry Lodge

Linn of Dee ℗

Carn a' Mhaim and the Lairig Ghru from Braeriach

stiles, the climbing starts in earnest up the Creag Bad an t-Seabhaig, the southeastern spur of Derry Cairngorm. The path is obvious at first, although higher up it sometimes gets lost amongst the stones. Continue gaining height steadily and pass over, or round, Point 1040, just before the final stony climb to the conical summit of **Derry Cairngorm**. There are actually two cairns on the summit a few metres apart, but the first of these appears to be the higher at 01749 97986 (2hrs 30mins from Derry Lodge).

Continue north-northwest over the jumble of stones capping Derry Cairngorm, then drop down to a grassy col below Creagan a' Choire Etchachan. It is not necessary to climb the Creagan a' Choire Etchachan, which in other company might be a Munro itself. Instead pass to its left (west) and then veer round to the southwest above the steep crags of Coire Sputan Dearg. A clearly defined path appears, which leads gently along the cliff tops until it turns west at 999 988 to reach the summit of **Ben Macdui**, just beyond the ruins of the old bothy. The summit is crowned by a large cairn and trig point at 98903 98930, as well as by various other impromptu stone structures (4hrs 5mins from Derry Lodge).

There is a pleasant descent to Glen Luibeg down the southeastern spur of the hill – the Sron Riach – but a third Munro of the day is beckoning within easy reach. From Ben Macdui's stony summit go west-southwest for about 1km until the incipient Allt Clach nan Taillear is crossed at 99648 98643. The descent can then be made down the spur that runs to the southeast of this burn. The hillside here is a vast jumble of stones and boulders, and the way through these is not always obvious. Descend with care to the col at the northern end of Carn a' Mhaim's long, sharp ridge. Sharp ridges are an unusual feature in these parts and this one provides pleasant and easy walking along the narrow rocky edge until the summit is reached at 99464 95181, marked by a small cairn (5hrs 50mins from Derry Lodge).

A more workmanlike cairn sits atop **Carn a' Mhaim**'s southeastern summit ½km further on at 99842 94947, but this is not as high as the main top and the path bypasses it. The descent from here to the valley goes straight down the southeast spur, dropping quite steeply to the prominent track that skirts around the base of the hill. Follow this to the Luibeg Burn. It may be possible to cross this burn where the track meets it at the ruins of the old bridge, but a short diversion upstream to the new Luibeg Bridge will probably be necessary, as this river can carry a lot of water. Once across, a major path, recently reconstructed, leads back to Derry Lodge.

ROUTE 5

The Devil's Point (1004m),
Cairn Toul (1291m), The Angels'
Peak (Sgor an Lochain Uaine) (1258m)

Pronunciation: Kayrn Tool; Sgor un Lochan You-annya
Translation: Devil's Point is a euphemism
for the original Gaelic, meaning 'Devil's penis';
Peak of the Barn; Pinnacle of the Green Lochan
(better known as the Angels' Peak)

Distance:	38km (of which 11km can be cycled)
Ascent:	1380m
Time:	10hrs 55mins (about 1hr 20mins less if cycling to Derry Lodge)
Difficulty:	see the general introduction to the Cairngorms (above)
Maps:	OS sheet 43; Explorer map 403; Harvey's Superwalker map Cairn Gorm; Area Map 6
Parking:	car park at Linn of Dee
Start:	footpath from back of car park or, if cycling, along estate track from road
Hostel:	YHA Braemar or Inverey; independent Spittal of Glenshee
B&B/hotel:	Braemar
Camping:	Braemar
Access:	National Trust for Scotland, Mar Lodge Estate, tel: 013397 41669. Normally no restrictions on access at any time of year

From Derry Lodge cross the bridge over the Derry Burn and follow the path along Glen Luibeg to the Luibeg Burn. Cross this at the new bridge and return to the path that skirts around the southern flanks of Carn a' Mhaim to reach the southern end of the Lairig Ghru. Once you are in the Lairig Ghru you soon leave the main path and cross a short wet section of peat bogs to reach a metal

The massive plateau of the northern Cairngorms is split in two towards its western end by a single deep valley – the Lairig Ghru. To the east of this valley rise the shadowy giants of Creag an Leth-choin, Cairn Lochan, Ben Macdui and the long ridge of Carn a' Mhaim. To its west a series of steep cliffs falls from the summits of another range of giants that include the Devil's Point, Cairn Toul and Braeriach. Reaching these grand but remote hills is yet another long and demanding day if starting from Linn of Dee, albeit a thoroughly worthwhile one.

Time can be saved by cycling to or camping at Derry Lodge. Alternatively Corrour Bothy, at the foot of the Devil's Point at the southern end of the Lairig Ghru, makes a convenient base for this and other hills.

The Devil's Point from Carn a' Mhaim

Lochain Uaine from the flanks of Cairn Toul

bridge over the River Dee and, just beyond it, Corrour Bothy. From the bothy climb steeply up to the col below the **Devil's Point**. The footpath here was reconstructed in 2002 right up to the col. From the col it is an easy walk to the summit, bearing southeast along a boulder-strewn path to reach the summit cairn at 97612 95123 (3hrs 30mins from Derry Lodge).

After admiring the breath-taking views of Beinn Bhrotain and Glen Dee, return to the col and then climb steadily up to Cairn Toul's southern top. The obvious path keeps close to the edge but passes through the worst of the jumbled boulders. There is a better line further west that avoids these, but it is much easier to find and follow in descent than ascent. There are good views of Cairn Toul's main top across the Coire an t-Saighdeir. From the cairn on the southern top there is a short drop before climbing again over more blocks and boulders to **Cairn Toul**'s main summit. There are two cairns on top. Pass the first and continue to the second, which is about 150m further on along a stony ridge, at 96323 97227. This is the highest point (5hrs from Derry Lodge).

The Angels' Peak, Sgor an Lochain Uaine, is only just over 1km from the summit of Cairn Toul and really has to be bagged while you are here. Descend over more boulders and stones to a sandy col above the Lochan Uaine at 95752 97328 (Sgor an Lochain Uaine), then climb easily to the **Angels' Peak**, which does indeed command heavenly views to the north and west across the Allt a' Gharbh Choire, taking in the Falls of Dee, Braeriach and the central well of the Lairig Ghru. The summit cairn is at 95425 97692 (5hrs 30mins from Derry Lodge).

After photographs have been taken, return to the sandy col then turn southeast, skirting around the flanks of Cairn Toul to regain the col between it and its southern top. This is an easy traverse with few boulders to cross until the col is reached. From here it is a straightforward task to regain the southern top of Cairn Toul and follow the outward path back to Corrour Bothy and eventually to Derry Lodge.

ROUTE 6

Beinn Bhrotain (1157m),

Monadh Mor (1113m)

Pronunciation: *Bine Vrotteen; Monnath More*
Translation: *the Hill of the Brodan*
(the fabled hound or mastiff); Big Mountain

This is yet another long outing, this time at the western end of the range, giving fine walking over rough terrain in some very remote country. Compared with some of their illustrious neighbours, these two hills have relatively few ascents.

From Linn of Dee walk or cycle along the private track to the White Bridge. Cross the bridge and immediately turn right along the southwest bank of the River Dee. The

Distance:	37km if returning via Glen Geusachan; 32km if returning by route of ascent (in total 16km can be cycled)
Ascent:	1010m if returning by Glen Geusachan; 1300m if returning by route of ascent
Time:	9hrs 15mins (about 2hr 25mins less if using a bike on the estate track, but add about 1hr if returning via Glen Geusachan)
Difficulty:	see the general introduction to the Cairngorms (above)
Maps:	OS sheet 43; Explorer map 403; Harvey's Superwalker map Cairn Gorm; Area Map 6
Parking:	car park at Linn of Dee
Start:	follow private track along north side of the Dee
Hostel:	YHA Braemar or Inverey; independent Spittal of Glenshee
B&B/hotel:	Braemar
Camping:	Braemar
Access:	National Trust for Scotland, Mar Lodge Estate, tel: 013397 41669. Normally no restriction on access at any time of year

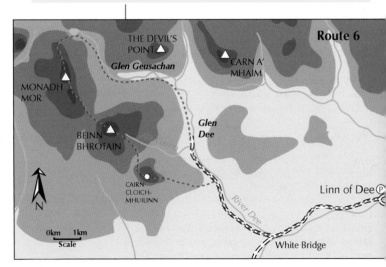

track can be cycled right up to the eastern flanks of the
mountain, but it gets rougher the further you go. Be
prepared for a bumpy ride. When you get to a bend in
the track to the southeast of Carn Fiaclach Beag, take to
the heathery hillside and climb to the south of this rocky
little knob. Continue on the same line, passing just south
of the next outcrop – Carn Fiaclach. Ahead of you rises
the steep stony cone of Carn Cloich-mhuilinn, and whilst
it is possible to avoid the summit itself, passing to its
northeast, little is gained by doing so and it is pleasanter
to go straight over the rocky, cairned top. Drop down the
stony northwest slopes on the other side and cross a little
plateau before tackling the final grassy flanks of **Beinn
Bhrotain**. A rib on the south side of the Coire an
t-Sneachda provides an easy way up. The broad, stone-
covered summit has a number of cairns, the highest of
which contains a trig point at 95413 92278 (4hrs
15mins; less if using a bike).

The western side of this hill is similar in character to
Carn Toul, and a huge jumble of boulders has to be
crossed as you drop down to the narrow col at Point 975
(94748 92704). From here climb steeply at first, but
more easily, onto **Monadh Mor**'s long summit ridge. Pass

*The River Dee and
Beinn Bhrotain from
the Devil's Point*

the cairn at its southern top to reach the highest point at 93865 94220 (5hrs 15mins; less if using a bike).

The quickest route to return by is the route of ascent, even though this requires the reascent of Beinn Bhrotain. To descend via Glen Geusachan continue along the ridge for another ½km or so, to 93750 94979, then descend to the northeast towards the southern end of Loch nan Stuirteag, passing to the north of a line of crags. A short, steep descent is then made to the infant Geusachan Burn, and from here the burn is followed on its west and south sides back to its confluence with the River Dee and thus back to the track. The path along this section is at best intermittent, and the country to be crossed is rough and, in places, wet. Eventually better ground arrives, and once the track is reached it is a simple task to return to Linn of Dee by the outward route.

CAIRNGORMS: GLEN EY

ROUTE 7

Carn an Fhidhleir (994m),

An Sgarsoch (1006m)

Pronunciation: *Karn ern Eeleth; Un Sgarshoch*
Translation: *The Fiddler; Place of Sharp Rocks*

These two remote hills lie a very long way from civilization, but a good track from Linn of Dee to Geldie Lodge makes access to them relatively easy. If you are making the long walk-in this will indeed be a long and tiring day, however the Landrover track can be covered very quickly on a bike as far as Geldie Lodge and this will shorten the day considerably.

From the large car park at Linn of Dee (you should not park at the bend just above the bridge) follow the track

Distance:	42km (16km from Geldie Lodge; 13km each way from Linn of Dee to Geldie Lodge)
Ascent:	940m
Time:	11hrs from Linn of Dee (about 3hrs 30mins less if using a bike on the estate track)
Difficulty:	see the general introduction to the Cairngorms (above)
Maps:	OS sheet 43; Explorer maps 394 and 387; Area Map 6
Parking:	car park at Linn of Dee
Start:	follow private track along north side of the Dee
Hostel:	YHA Braemar or Inverey; independent Spittal of Glenshee
B&B/hotel:	Braemar
Camping:	Braemar
Access:	National Trust for Scotland, Mar Lodge Estate, tel: 013397 41669

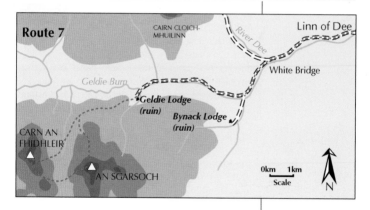

along the River Dee to the White Bridge (which is actually red). Cross this bridge and follow the Geldie Burn all the way to the ruins of Geldie Lodge. The track is a bit rough in places but is easily negotiable by mountain bike. Near the lodge there are three rivers to cross at fords: at the first, the Allt Dhaidh Mor, the ford is too deep for a bike but there is a good crossing point just a little

An Sgarsoch from the southeast end of Carn an Fhidhleir

downstream. At the second, the Geldie Burn, the ford is again quite deep but there is a crossing point just upstream. The third is crossed more easily. Bikes should be left at Geldie Lodge but a good footpath, recently reconstructed, continues from here around the foot of Scarsoch Bheag. From the end of this path a less obvious path continues across the Allt a' Chaorainn and then through peat bogs to the eastern flanks of Carn an Fhidhleir. The trouble with this path is that it leads you to the steepest part of the hill. It can be climbed without too much difficulty to emerge just to the south of the stone-capped summit, but some people might prefer a slightly wetter crossing of the peat bogs further north to make the ascent by the north ridge. Either way brings you to the small summit cairn of **Carn an Fhidhleir** at 90467 84170, with its airy views across the Cairngorm hills (2hrs 30mins from Geldie Lodge).

Head down the broad southeast ridge to the outlier at Point 906. You don't need to climb this, but traverse around it and then descend grass slopes quite steeply to the peaty col. The worst of the peat hags can be bypassed to the left (north), but they are not as bad as they look from above. From the col climb steadily up the west ridge of **An Sgarsoch** to its throne-like cairn at 93335 83659 (4hrs from Geldie Lodge).

As you start the descent down the north-northwest ridge the mountain's name seems suddenly appropriate; however, the stony summit is soon left behind for grass and heather. Pass to the west of Scarsoch Bheag to regain the footpath back to Geldie Lodge.

ROUTE 8

Carn Bhac (946m),

Beinn Iutharn Mhor (1045m)

Pronunciation: *Karn Vack; Bine Yoo-ern Voar*
Translation: *Peat Bank; Big Sharp-edged Hill*

Distance:	33km (16km from Altanour Lodge)
Ascent:	1050m
Time:	9hrs 15mins (about 1hr 45mins less if using a bike to Altanour Lodge)
Difficulty:	see the general introduction to the Cairngorms (above)
Maps:	OS sheet 43; Explorer map 387; Area Map 6
Parking:	parking area at start of private road, Inverey
Start:	along private track that starts opposite houses
Hostel:	YHA Braemar or Inverey; independent Spittal of Glenshee
B&B/hotel:	Braemar
Camping:	Braemar
Access:	National Trust for Scotland, Mar Lodge Estate, tel: 013397 41368

These hills are set in remote wilderness country and give all the appearance of being seldom visited. The Landrover track along Glen Ey allows a bike to be taken as far as the atmospheric ruins of Altanour Lodge, which greatly shortens the day; but even so this is rough walking country, largely lacking in paths, and it should not be underestimated, especially in poor weather.

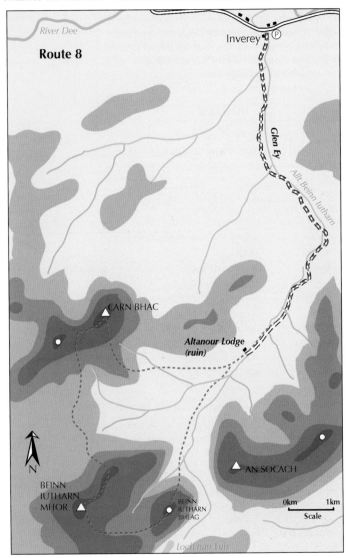

From Altanour Lodge a very rough Landrover track continues up the hillside for about 2km, and this can be followed to its end on the broad moss and heather-covered south ridge of **Carn Bhac**. Continue up this ridge to the top, where rough quartzite stones cap the summit at 95099 83240 (1hr 40mins from Altanour Lodge).

The way to Beinn Iutharn Mhor from here is barred by a sea of peat bogs that give Carn Bhac its name. These cannot be completely avoided. The best course is to go west-southwest along the ridge of Carn Bhac to the minor top at Point 920, where an ill-defined spur leads south to a wide col. A little further along this ridge, beyond Point 920 towards Carn a' Bhutha, are the remains of an old stone building in a position of such remoteness and altitude that the imagination can't fail to be stirred by its appearance. Descending to the col is pleasant and easy at first over soft grass, but the problems soon arrive in the form of deep peat hags and pools which must somehow be crossed. If you traverse too far to the left or right you run the risk of dropping down below the col and having to climb back up to it.

Once this obstacle has been successfully negotiated the next one becomes apparent. The steep scree-covered slopes of the Big Sharp-Edged One have now to be climbed. Do not go into the corrie on the right where the headwalls are very steep. Instead climb straight up from the col. There are signs that people have made the ascent at various points along this flank. The right-hand end of the wall, before it curves round into the corrie, may be the best line of attack. Once you are onto the ridge proper things become easy for a while, and a pleasant walk brings you up to the **Beinn Iutharn Mhor** summit cairn at 04570 79270 (3hrs 40mins from Altanour Lodge).

If the weather is favourable and you are still feeling strong, it is possible to continue on to Carn an Righ and Glas Tulaichean before descending, but bear in mind that this will add over 500m of vertical ascent to the route, in addition to the extra 8 or 9km of walking (an extra 3hrs 15mins). (These two summits, together with nearby An Socach, are covered in volume 1 of this guide.)

To descend from Beinn Iutharn Mhor there are two or three possibilities. Perhaps the easiest is to go the full length of the ridge and drop down its northeast spur. It is steep at the bottom, where there is deep heather to cross, but the difficulties are fairly short-lived. This route brings you to the west bank of the Allt Beinn Iutharn. Another possibility is to descend south to the col between Beinn Iutharn Mhor and Mam nan Cairn and then follow the burn down the valley to the northeast. This is wet and rough in places. Some deer tracks on the valley sides may help, but most of them will take you the wrong way if you follow them too far.

The usual return route, and probably the best, is to drop south to the col below Mam nan Carn, then traverse around this hill to reach the stony col between it and Beinn Iutharn Bheag. You have another 100m of climbing to do this way, but out of the blue a path appears to help you on your way. Pass the cairn on Beinn Iutharn Bheag's summit at 06498 79057 and continue to another small cairn at 06753 79430, which marks the top of the descent (the path by now has once again vanished). The north side of Beinn Iutharn Bheag is quite steep, especially at the top. There are two ribs, not really recognizable as ridges – one to the west and one to the east. The one to the west is the safe way down, though it does not come into sight until after you have started the descent. In poor weather this can be an intimidating line to follow. Work your way down through the heather and cross the burn, then follow it back to Altanour Lodge.

CAIRNGORMS: COYLUMBRIDGE

ROUTE 9

Bynack More (1090m),

Cairn Gorm (1245m)

Pronunciation: Binnack More; Cairn Gorm
Translation: Big Chimney-pot or (possibly) Big Cap; Blue Cairn

Distance:	15km
Ascent:	1320m
Time:	6hrs 10mins
Difficulty:	see the general introduction to the Cairngorms (above)
Maps:	OS sheet 36; Explorer map 403; Harvey's Superwalker map Cairn Gorm; Area Map 6
Parking:	Coire na Ciste car park
Start:	across moorland from the car park
Hostel:	YHA Loch Morlich; Aviemore
B&B/hotel:	Coylumbridge; Aviemore
Camping:	Coylumbridge; Glenmore Forest
Access:	Ranger's Office, tel: 01479 861703 Abernethy Forest Reserve, tel: 01429 821409. Normally no restrictions on access at any time of year

The northern corries of Cairn Gorm are areas of great despoliation by man – there are ski tows, tracks, buildings, huge car parks and a mountain railway to boot. It is hard to avoid these things in any ascent of Cairn Gorm, and yet when the ski tows and buildings have been left behind this is still a fine mountain. Perhaps the best approach is from the south or east, and this is possible when combined with the ascent of Bynack More as described here.

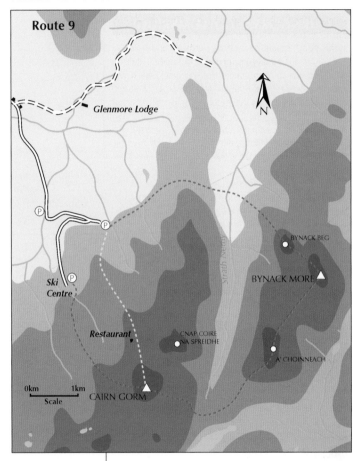

Start from the lower car park at the foot of Coire na Ciste and head across rough heather moorland to a low point on the skyline, just south of Point 737 and to the right of a small plantation (now felled but still clearly visible on the hillside). From the col a gully drops down to the east into Strath Nethy. Follow this down, keeping to either of the enclosing ridges – the gully itself is steep, wet, vegetated and full of awkward rocks. Cross the Garbh Allt at the bottom. The river flows in two separate streams at this point, separated by boggy ground, and both are easy to cross. Clamber up the slope of thick heather on the other side until the vegetation becomes less dense and a sandy path materializes, making progress easier. Cross over Bynack Beg to the col below Bynack More at 03749 06623. From here it is an easy climb over bouldery ground to the rocky summit of **Bynack More**. The cairn, which is not immediately obvious, is near the southern end of the castellated summit ridge at 04192 06319 (2hrs 40mins).

Continue south past a series of granite tors that stand out along the south ridge above the Barns of Bynack like serrations on the spine of an ancient dragon, then turn southwest across a rather wet col, before pushing on over A' Choinneach at 03210 04824. Drop down easily on the other side of A' Choinneach over stony and bouldery ground to reach The Saddle at 01836 03312. This wonderful vantage point in the very heart of the Cairngorm massif offers a vista of crags and Munro summits across the black waters of Loch Avon that is one

Granite tors on Bynack More

69

Descending to the Saddle with Ben Macdui in distance behind Loch Avon

of the finest to be had. Cross The Saddle and look for a path that rises diagonally up the hillside to the north-northwest. (It is visible as you descend from A' Choinneach.) Follow the path past the steep slabs at the foot of **Cairn Gorm**'s southeastern flanks then, when these are cleared, head straight up due west to the summit cairn and weather station at 00516 04060 (5hrs 10mins).

The quick way back to the ski centre in Coire Cas goes down through the boulders past a cairned top at the top of the Fiacaille a' Choire Chais (99911 03999), then follows a constructed path back to the road. Alternatively, either of the enclosing ridges of Coire na Ciste can be followed directly back to the lower car park, thereby avoiding at least some of the tourist hordes.

ROUTE 10

Braeriach (1296m)

Pronunciation: Bray-ree-erch
Translation: Dappled Neck

Distance:	21km
Ascent:	1200m
Time:	6hrs 10mins
Difficulty:	see the general introduction to the Cairngorms (above)
Maps:	OS sheet 36; Explorer map 403; Harvey's Superwalker map Cairn Gorm; Area Map 6
Parking:	lower car park (about 2km below the Coire na Ciste car park)
Start:	cross road to start of footpath
Hostel:	YHA Loch Morlich; Aviemore
B&B/hotel:	Coylumbridge; Aviemore
Camping:	Coylumbridge
Access:	Rothiemurchus, tel: 01479 810477. Normally no restrictions on access for the route described at any time of year

Leave the car park by a path through trees to the south, then cross the road and follow the path on the other side down to a bridge over the Allt Creag an Leth-choin. Go over the bridge and continue on this heavily constructed

Braeriach is a wonderful mountain, hard to reach from any direction, guarded by spectacular cliffs and dominating the western Cairngorm massif. It can be approached from Glen Feshie, perhaps by combining it with Sgor Gaoith, in a very long day, or from Glen Einich via Coire Dhondail. The shortest and most popular ascent (described here) is from the northeast, starting from the 'Sugar Bowl' car park at a sharp bend in the road just below the two ski-centre car parks.

path for 3km across moorland to the Chalamain Gap. Pass through the jumble of big boulders in the gap, then

To the north of the Lairig Ghru

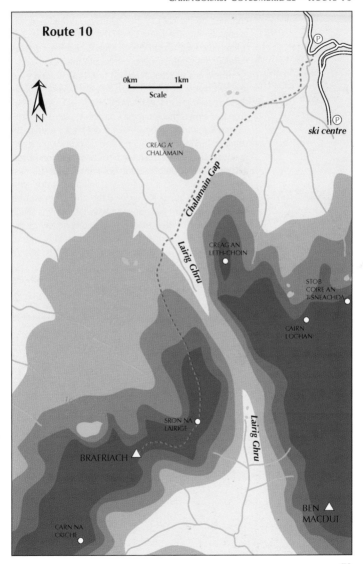

Route 10

0km   1km
Scale

N

P

P
ski centre

CREAG A'
CHALAMAIN

Chalamain Gap

Lairig Ghru

CREAG AN
LETH-CHOIN

STOB
COIRE AN
T-SNEACHDA

CAIRN
LOCHAN

SRON NA
LAIRIGE

Lairig Ghru

BRAERIACH

BEN
MACDUI

CARN NA
CRICHE

continue on the path to the southwest, dropping down eventually into the Lairig Ghru. The ascent of Braeriach follows the long north ridge of Sron na Lairige, so cross the river and start the steep climb onto this ridge.

There is a substantial path at first, until boulders are reached higher up on the ridge. Clamber over the boulders to easier ground and pass by or over the two tops of Sron na Lairige. This is typical Cairngorm plateau: stone-scattered rounded summits which offer easy walking in summer, but tricky navigation when visibility is poor and major problems in the white-out of winter storms. Drop a short distance into the col beneath **Braeriach**'s east ridge and from here it is an easy climb almost due west to the summit along the edge of the cliffs above Coire Bhrochain. There are superb views along this edge looking across to Ben Macdui, the southern end of the Lairig Ghru and the dramatic northern crags of Carn Toul and Angels' Peak. The cairn is at 95318 99892 (3hrs 55mins).

Return by the same route.

CAIRNGORMS: GLEN FESHIE

ROUTE 11

Mullach Clach a' Bhlair (1019m)

Pronunciation: *Mooluch Clach uh Vlarth*
Translation: *the Peak of the Stony Plain*

Distance:	23km (of which 12km can be cycled)
Ascent:	740m
Time:	6hrs 30mins (about 2hrs less if a bike is used as far as Carnachuin)
Difficulty:	see the general introduction to the Cairngorms (above)
Maps:	OS sheet 43; Explorer map 403; Area Map 6
Parking:	roadside where public road ends, at Tolvah
Start:	continue south along private track
Hostel:	YHA Aviemore; independent Glen Feshie
B&B/hotel:	Aviemore
Camping:	Aviemore; Coylumbridge
Access:	Glenfeshie, tel: 01540 651361 or 01540 651212; see note on bridge at Carnachuin, below

From a navigational point of view this is one of the easiest of the Caingorm Munros, so long as the hill is in summer condition. The featureless plateau of the Mounth has been cut by a Landrover track that passes within a few metres of the summit.

Leave the car at the end of the public road, just beyond a small wooden bridge and walk or cycle to Carnachuin, where there is a sagging wooden bridge across the River Feshie. Apart from the first 100m the private track from Tolvah to Carnachuin is a high-quality tarmac road which passes through the best scenery in this lovely glen. Leave

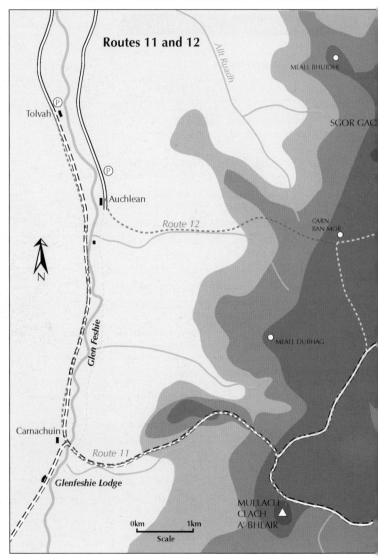

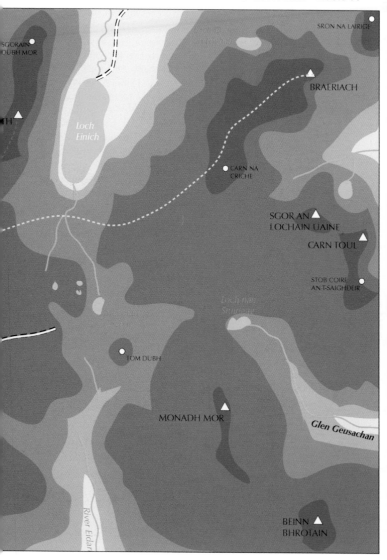

The traditional approach to this hill is from Auchlean on the east side of Glen Feshie. This is a good starting point if one wishes to include Sgor Gaoith in the day's itinerary, in which case start up the path to Carn Ban Mor and then go north-northeast to Sgor Gaoith. From there it is a long walk across the moor to reach Mullach Clach a Bhlair. However this simpler way to climb the hill starts not from Auchlean but from Tolvah, on the west side of Glen Feshie.

Note: The bridge at Carnachuin is starting to buckle badly and it looks as if its days are numbered. (It would be a good idea to check on its status with the estate before setting out.) If it goes altogether and is not replaced, access to this route is possible from Auchlean on the east side of the River Feshie. A path heads south from Auchlean alongside the river, then passes through a plantation to reach the Scots pine meadows on the route described below.

Mullach Clach a' Bhlair from the northwest

your bike at Carnachuin and cross the bridge, then pass through some lovely Scots pine meadows, staying on the Landrover track as it climbs steeply up above the Allt Coire Chaoil. There are good views at one point across the steep-sided gully of Coire Garbhlach. Shortly after the plateau is reached the track divides. Take the right fork, which passes a couple of hundred metres from the

summit of **Mullach Clach a' Bhlair**. An incised path takes you from the track to the top at 88291 92690. (If you miss the path in a pea soup, a secondary Landrover track a few yards further on leads almost up to the cairn.) On a clear day there are views across the plateau to Braeriach and Beinn Bhrotain (3hrs 45mins walking from Tolvah; significantly less if using bike to Carnachuin).

ROUTE 12

Sgor Gaoith (1118m)

Pronunciation: Sgor Gayee
Translation: Windy Peak

Distance:	16km
Ascent:	830m
Time:	4hrs 30mins
Difficulty:	see the general introduction to the Cairngorms (above)
Maps:	OS sheet 36; Explorer map 403; Area Map 6
Parking:	car park just beyond the end of the public road in Glen Feshie
Start:	along private track to start of footpath near Auchlean
Hostel:	YHA Aviemore; independent Glen Feshie
B&B/hotel:	Aviemore, Coylumbridge
Camping:	Coylumbridge
Access:	Glenfeshie, tel: 01540 651361 or 01540 651212

On the western fringe of the Cairngorms the high plateau comes to a fairly gentle conclusion, dropping down over heather-clad slopes to Glen Feshie. Sgor Gaoith is one of two Munros on this part of the plateau and this hill has something of a split personality. Viewed from most angles it is little more than an unassuming grassy bump on a skyline of gentle undulations, but there is another side to this hill – for to its east it bares granite teeth and plummets down in a headlong dive to the dark waters of Loch Einich some 600m below.

Flanks of Braeriach from Sgor Gaoith

Start at the car park about 1km north of Auchlean and walk along the private road to a path on the left signposted to Carn Ban Mor. Follow this substantial path uphill through the plantation and through a gate to reach the open hill. The path continues up the hillside, passing just a few hundred metres from the summit of Carn Ban Mor. Leave the path where it divides at a little cairn (89267 96843) and head just east of north, passing over the gentle dome of Carn Ban Mor to the little pointed eminence of **Sgor Gaoith**. Suddenly a huge gash in the plateau becomes visible as Gleann Einich comes into view and the other side of Sgor Gaoith's character is revealed. The summit cairn is at 90300 98954, perched high above the loch (3hrs).

Return by the same route unless continuing on to Mullach Clach a' Blair or Braeriach, either of which is quite feasible from here to make a longer outing.

MONADHLIATH

ROUTE 13

A' Chailleach (930m), Carn Sgulain (920m),

Carn Dearg (945m)

Pronunciation: Uh Chalyok; Karn Skoolern; Karn Jerrack
Translation: the Old Woman; Hill of the Basket; Red Hill

Distance:	24km
Ascent:	1080m
Time:	7hrs 15mins
Maps:	OS sheet 35; Explorer map 402; Area Map 7
Parking:	parking area at end of public road above Newtonmore
Start:	follow footpath behind parking area
Hostel:	YHA Aviemore; independent Newtonmore or Laggan Bridge
B&B/hotel:	Newtonmore, Kingussie
Camping:	Newtonmore
Access:	Glenbanchor, tel: 01540 673606

To the north of the River Spey the hills rise to their greatest prominence around Creag Meagaidh. To the east of this, above Newtonmore, are three hills which are less frequently visited and have a rather more remote feel than their illustrious neighbours.

Start at the parking area where the public road ends and a private track begins. A footpath leads north, skirting a plantation, then climbs alongside the Allt a' Chaorainn. After about 2km a small cairn marks the point where a path leads down to a bridge over the river. Cross here, then continue upstream on the west bank. After a further

81

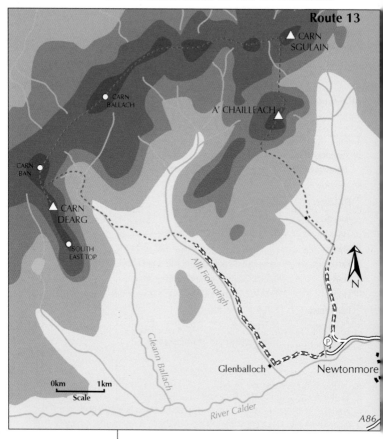

To climb these three hills together (as described here) makes for quite a long day. The alternative is to climb A' Chailleach and Carn Sgulain in one outing and do Carn Dearg on another day. Although Carn Sgulain could be approached from the east, the most usual approach for all three hills – and the easiest – is from the end of the minor road that heads up the valley of the River Calder from Newtonmore, and from here they form a natural circuit.

½km, head northwest over heather and grass to reach the remains of a tin bothy. A path continues north-northwest to the peaty moorland south of **A' Chailleach**. There is a short dip before the final easy climb to the summit cairn at 68117 04177 (2hrs 15mins).

Continue north to the sharply incised valley of the Allt Cuil na Caillich. The path gets lost in peat bogs as you descend. Climb sharply up the other side and continue to the round summit of **Carn Sgulain**. There is a small cairn at 68301 05806, but the true summit is a little further on at 68435 05880 (2hrs 55mins).

Now comes the long, high-level traverse to Carn Dearg. It is some 7km in total with five or six minor tops to pass en route, many of them with their own small cairns. Although the landscape here is mostly flat and featureless, a line of metal fence posts runs almost the whole way, greatly easing navigation in poor weather. There are one or two wet bealachs to cross early on, but most of this section offers easy walking. When Meall na Creughaich is reached the ground becomes stony, and at the summit of Carn Ban the line of fence posts has to be abandoned as it heads off to Sneachdach Slinnean. Descend Carn Ban south over scree to a wide col, then climb the final slope along the edge of **Carn Dearg**'s steep east face to the summit cairn at 63569 02393 (5hrs 10mins).

There is no easy descent from Carn Dearg without returning to the col and dropping down to the northeast on easy grass slopes, taking care to avoid the small crags to the south of this line. Follow the east bank of the Allt Ballach as it winds through peat hags and pools. If you stay close to the river the going is easy. After about 2km leave the river and head east across peat and heather moorland to a gap between the long southern spur of Meall na Ceardaich and Creag Liath. A clear path appears at the bottom of this incised little valley and this is followed to a wooden bridge over the Allt Fionndrigh. Soon the path becomes a track, which leads easily back to your starting point.

ROUTE 14

Geal Charn (926m)

Pronunciation: *Geeya Charn*
Translation: *White Hill*

Distance:	13km
Ascent:	640m
Time:	3hrs 30mins
Maps:	OS sheet 35; Explorer map 401; Area Map 7
Parking:	roadside parking area by the Garva Bridge to the west of Laggan
Start:	cross bridge and follow track, then footpath
Hostel:	YHA Aviemore; independent Laggan Bridge or Newtonmore
B&B/hotel:	Laggan; Newtonmore
Camping:	Newtonmore
Access:	tel: 01528 544222

To the east of the Creag Meagaidh National Nature Reserve there is a break in the high hills where the young River Spey flows through the Sherramore Forest. The next hill in the chain is Geal Charn, which lies some distance from any other Munro, such that it can't easily be linked up to make a longer day.

In total there are no fewer than 19 hills called Geal Charn in this part of Scotland, so if you're leaving details of where you're walking be sure to specify which one of the 19 you're on. Four of these Geal Charns are on the Munro list and this one, being gently contoured on its southern and western flanks, is probably the easiest of the four.

Cross the Garva Bridge over the River Spey and follow a farm track across a metal bridge over a tributary burn – the Feith Talagain – a short distance to the north. A track,

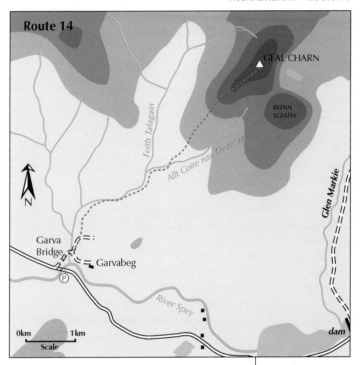

then a path, follows the line of this burn until it reaches the Allt Coire nan Dearcag. Climb alongside this for a few hundred metres before crossing it to ascend the broad southwest ridge. There is a clear path up this heathery ridge, though its start is a little elusive. The path is by no means essential, however; just stay close to the crest of the ridge, which is fairly easy-angled throughout. Once the angle levels out at the top by a small cairn, continue over a gently undulating plateau for a further ½km to **Geal Charn**'s large summit cairn at 56143 98757 (2hrs 10mins).

Return by the route of ascent. In poor visibility don't be misled by the many lines across the summit plateau, which could be confused with paths.

LOCH LAGGAN

ROUTE 15

Creag Meagaidh (1130m), Stob Poite Coire Ardair (1053m), Carn Liath (1006m)

Pronunciation: *Krayk Meggy;*
Stob Poytya Korrer Arder; Karn Leeya
Translation: *Crag of the Bog;*
Peak of the Pot of the High Corrie; Grey-green Cairn

Distance:	20km
Ascent:	1190m
Time:	6hrs 55mins
Maps:	OS sheet 34; Explorer map 401; Area Map 7
Parking:	car park off A86
Start:	private track then footpath past Aberarder
Hostel:	YHA Loch Lochy, Glen Nevis; independent Roy Bridge, Tulloch
B&B/hotel:	Roy Bridge
Camping:	Roy Bridge
Access:	Scottish Natural Heritage Creag Meagaidh National Nature Reserve, tel: 01528 544265. Normally no restrictions on access at any time of year, but dogs not allowed at any time

Starting from the car park at Aberarder, walk past the visitor centre and continue up the valley of the Allt Coire Ardair where downy birch, silver birch, oak and hazel are beginning to flourish. The boggy path has been boarded for long sections to protect the vegetation and to make the going easy for the walker. As you progress into the upper valley the huge cliffs of Coire Ardair – one of the great winter playgrounds of the ice climber – come into

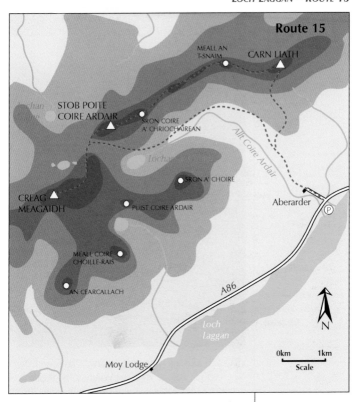

The National Nature Reserve of Creag Meagaidh was one of the first areas in the 1980s in which a major attempt was made to drastically reduce the numbers of grazing sheep and deer. As a result of the culls that followed, and the subsequent management policies, many native tree and wild flower species that had been virtually wiped out in this area have begun to thrive here once again. With this enrichment of the habitat the range of insects, birds and other wildlife has grown substantially. The three Munros in this group, dominated by Creag Meagaidh, offer dramatic scenery and a fine high-level walk that can be tackled in many different ways.

Lochan a' Choire and the Window on Creag Meagaidh

view. Pass the dark waters of Lochan a' Choire and climb the steep scree slope up to the Window, the incised col between Creag Meagaidh and Stob Poite Coire Ardair. From the back of this col a path leads up over the north-eastern flanks of **Creag Meagaidh** onto the huge bare summit plateau. The plateau is crossed in a curving line until a massive cairn is reached at 42330 87757. It would be easy in mist to mistake this for the summit, but this is Mad Meg's Cairn – a curiosity of obscure origin – and the summit cairn lies a few hundred metres further on at 41846 87536 (3hrs 10mins).

Retrace your steps to the Window then climb easily up its far side to **Stob Poite Coire Ardair**. There are a couple of small cairns marking high points on the top, but the summit is at 42898 88849 (3hrs 50mins).

Once you are on top of the ridge the long, high-level traverse begins, following the line of the Allt Coire Ardair, but high above it to the north. The crest of this ridge is followed all the way round to Carn Liath, passing easily over a number of small tops. A line of rusty fence posts marks the correct line for much of the way. Each time the posts seem to have stopped another one looms out of the mist like an old friend calling you on (I'm told that there isn't always a mist here, but I remain to be convinced). Cross Point 1051 and descend to the north-east above Coire a' Chriochairein, then veer east to climb the cairned Point 991 at 44798 89917. From here, a sharp little descent to a col leads up to Point 963. Next, cross easy ground to another minor top, Meall an t-Snaim, at 969m. At last the big grey-green, scree-covered bulk of **Carn Liath** beckons you on, and its summit is reached without difficulty at 47232 90323 (5hrs 10mins).

To descend, come back a couple of hundred metres across the stony southwest ridge of Carn Liath, then descend over scree to reach the hill's southern ridge. A faint path leads down, becoming more obvious the lower it goes. Just before the ridge ends in the lump of Na Cnapanan, follow the path down to its right (west) through heather to rejoin the main trail along the valley floor at 47300 88330. The last section of the descent path is becoming heavily overgrown and is getting difficult to follow.

There are two alternative ascent/descent routes on Creag Meagaidh. One crosses Puist Coire Ardair from the summit plateau and follows the ridge to the rounded top of Sron a' Ghoire, then drops down the western slopes of this hill along the line of a small burn, the Allt Beallach a' Ghoire, to cross the Allt Coire Ardair at a bridge above Aberarder. The other, less convenient for a circuit, starts at Moy – about 8km southwest of Aberarder on the A86 – and climbs over Creag na Cailliche, the rocky nose of Creag Meagaidh's south-west ridge, which it then climbs on a steadily rising, curving line to the summit.

ROUTE 16

Beinn a' Chaorainn (1052m),

Beinn Teallach (915m)

Pronunciation: *Bine uh Chooereen; Bine Chyalloch*
Translation: *Mountain of the Rowan Tree;*
Mountain of the Forge (or Fireplace)

Distance:	15km
Ascent:	1160m
Time:	5hrs 15mins
Maps:	OS sheet 34; Explorer maps 401 and 400; Area Map 7
Parking:	roadside on A86
Start:	along private forestry track
Hostel:	YHA Loch Lochy; independent Tulloch Station
B&B/hotel:	Roy Bridge; Spean Bridge
Camping:	Roy Bridge
Access:	tel: 01397 712602

This fairly short walk takes you over the two most westerly Munros of the great chain that extends along the north side of the Glen Spean/Glen Spey valley. Beinn a' Chaorainn's long summit ridge gives fine views of Creag Meagaidh's western slopes. Climbed together the two hills offer a natural circuit starting from Roughburn on the A86, just a short distance northeast of the Laggan dam.

Start along the private track through the forest and after 1½km take a turning on the left. The quickest way onto the hill is to follow a very narrow forest ride marked by a small cairn about 100m beyond this turning. This leads uphill to the right. It can be very boggy at first, but after a short distance you emerge onto open hillside. Skirt to the left around the rocky western flanks of Meall Clachaig and climb onto the ridge, which leads directly up to

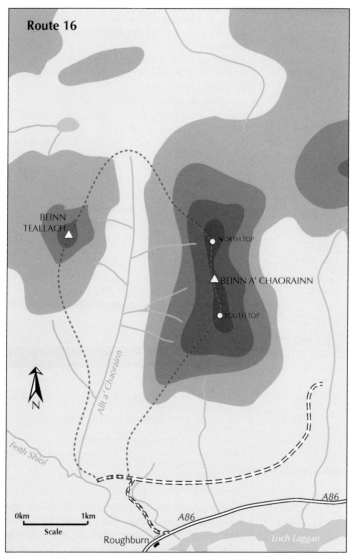

Beinn a' Chaorainn's summit. The ridge offers easy, pleasant walking. Until very recently the southern peak of Beinn a' Chaorainn, at 38639 84510, was taken to be the highest point. Recent mapping has shown that the middle top at 38605 85052 is in fact marginally higher at 1052m (2hrs 15mins).

Continue along the broad, grassy ridge over the middle and north peaks (both cairned) before descending directly to the peaty col below **Beinn Teallach**'s northeast ridge. This knobbly ridge is then climbed without difficulty to the summit. At the top the first cairn you reach, at GR 36135 85978, is sometimes cited as the highest point, but a second bigger cairn is reached a short distance further on, at 36020 85909, and this appears to be slightly higher (4hrs 5mins).

Descend the broad, grassy ridge to the south, making sure you are not drawn by the angle of slope towards the more clearly defined southwest ridge. Drop easily down to the Allt a' Chaorainn by the corner of the plantation and for a few hundred metres follow this boulder-filled burn, which is then crossed to reach a stile. This leads on to the forestry track and thus back to the road.

GLENFINNAN

ROUTE 17

Sgurr nan Coireachan (956m),

Sgurr Thuilm (963m)

Pronunciation: *Skoor nern Korrachun; Skoor Hoolum*
Translation: *Peak of the Corrie; Peak of the Hill*

Start from the car park just off the A830 by the River Finnan and follow the long private road on the west bank of the river. Pass under the viaduct, which is a fine sight with steam trains on it again, as there now are in the summer

Distance:	21km (of which 10km can be cycled)
Ascent:	1300m
Time:	7hrs 35mins (about 1hr 20mins less if a bike is used to Corryhully)
Maps:	OS sheet 40; Explorer map 398; Area Map 8
Parking:	parking area off A830 at start of private track
Start:	along private road to Corryhully
Hostel:	YHA Glen Nevis; independent Fort William
B&B/hotel:	Glenfinnan; Fort William
Camping:	just north of Fort William
Access:	Glenfinnan, tel: 01397 722203

The extraordinary rock-sculpted landscape of the Rough Bounds of Knoydart comes to its southern limit at these two Munros. The traverse of both peaks makes a fine excursion with some excellent ridge walking, glorious views, and a taste of the hundreds of square miles of rough, wild landscape, almost untouched by man, that lie to its north.

Whilst both of these hills could be accessed from the north via Loch Arkaig, by far the most usual approach (described here) is from Glenfinnan in the south, where Bonnie Prince Charlie first landed in Scotland and raised the Jacobite standard. The ridge can be traversed in either direction, although the descent is probably easier from Sgurr Thuilm.

months. Harry Potter fans will have an interest in this: it was the location for a celebrated scene in one of the films. At Corryhully the tarmac runs out and the track that continues from here is quite rough. The Allt a' Choire Charnaig, which has to be crossed, can carry a lot of water, but there are big stepping-stones across it. Once the nose of the long south ridge of Sgurr nan Coireachan is passed, where the track reaches a high point, a path leads off up the eastern flank of the ridge. A small cairn marks its start. Follow this path

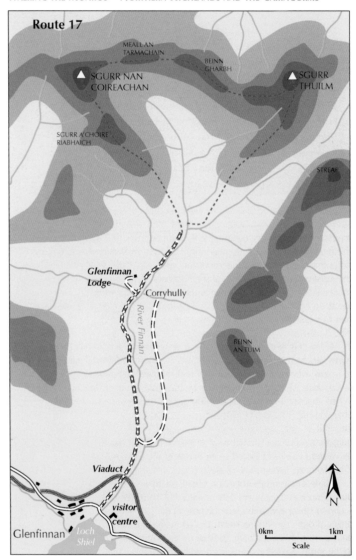

Route 17

MEALL AN TARMACHAIN

BEINN GHARBH

SGURR NAN COIREACHAN

SGURR THUILM

SGURR A'CHOIRE RIABHAICH

STREAP

Glenfinnan Lodge

Corryhully

River Finnan

BEINN AN TUIM

Viaduct

visitor centre

Glenfinnan

Loch Shiel

N

0km   1km

Scale

*Glenfinnan Viaduct
Gulvain from*

onto the crest of the ridge and gain height steadily until the steep, prominent peak of Sgurr a' Choire Riabhaich is reached. The path veers round to the southwestern side of this peak and climbs steeply, returning to the crest of the ridge before the top. Once the top of this peak is reached, the worst of the climbing is over and the scenery becomes more wild and rocky. Continue on for about 1km to reach the stone enclosure and trig point at the summit of **Sgurr nan Coireachan** 90294 87994 (3hrs 45mins; less is if a bike is used).

From this point on, the ridge switchbacks over numerous little tops. There is a path, which is not hard to follow even in poor visibility, and there are old metal fence posts along the ridge to further aid navigation. When the final slopes of **Sgurr Thuilm** are reached, abandon the fence posts and head north to the summit. This hill is much grassier and more rounded than its neighbours (with the exception of the rocky ramparts on its western side). The summit cairn is at 93910 87971 (5hrs 20mins; less if a bike is used).

To descend, head south to a broad col then climb up a short way to gain the crest of the south west ridge – Druim Coire a' Bheithe – and follow this all the way down, dropping off to the south just before its end. This path can get quite muddy. Follow the track below back to the starting point.

ROUTE 18

Gulvain (Gaor Bheinn) (987m)

Pronunciation: Gulvain
Translation: Great Rough Hill;
Gaor Bheinn means literally 'filthy mountain'

Distance:	21km (of which roughly 13km can be cycled)
Ascent:	1170m
Time:	7hrs (about 1hr 45mins less if a bike is used)
Maps:	OS sheets 40 and 41; Explorer maps 399 and 391; Area Map 8
Start:	track leads in front of houses to a gate on east side of the Fionn Lighe
Parking:	lay-by on A861 a few metres from its junction with the A830
Hostel:	YHA Glen Nevis
B&B/hotel:	Corpach; Fort William
Camping:	Camaghael (near Victoria Bridge)
Access:	Fassern Estate, tel: 01397 772288 or 01397 722217

A long, rough approach, followed by a stiff climb and a long ridge-walk, brings you to the summit of this shy peak, which is quite stoutly defended by its southern top.

From the A830 follow the track round to the right in front of the houses. Pass through a gate and stay on the estate track for 6½km to a wooden bridge over the Allt a' Choire Reidh. Gulvain begins to appear in front of you as you progress along the track, but it seems to take a long time to get any nearer. It is possible to cycle to this point on a mountain bike, although the track gets progressively rougher the further you go. A short distance beyond the Allt a' Choire Reidh the main track veers round to the left and a fainter trail heads off right. This trail to the right is

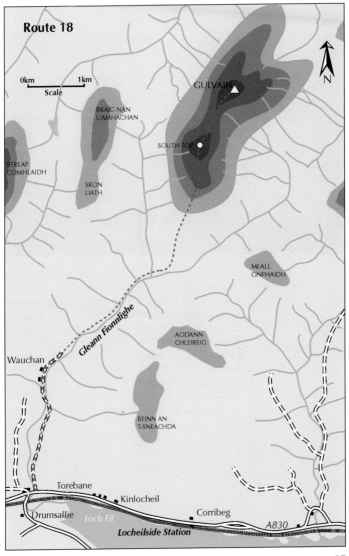

Route 18

0km   1km
Scale

N

STREAP
COMHLAIDH

BRAIG NAN
UAMHACHAN

SRON
LIATH

GULVAIN

SOUTH TOP

MEALL
ONFHAIDH

Gleann Fionnlighe

AODANN
CHLEIREIG

Wauchan

BEINN AN
T-SNEACHDA

Torebane

Kinlocheil

Drumsallie

Corribeg

Loch Eil

A830

Locheilside Station

Gulvain from south summit

in fact the start of a path which leads fairly steeply up Gulvain's southern ridge. Some 730 vertical metres have to be climbed without a break to reach the first top and it is quite a grind. From this top, cross hillocky ground to reach the trig point on the south summit at 99679 86446. There is a good view from here along the next part of the ridge to **Gulvain**'s summit. Drop down over stony ground quite sharply to the northeast and cross the narrowing ridge to the final climb. There is a substantial cairn on top at 00273 87565 (4hrs 20mins; less if a bike is used).

Return by the route of ascent.

ROUTE 19

Meall na Teanga (917m),

Sron a' Choire Ghairbh (935m)

Pronunciation: *Miaowl nuh Tyenga; Stron a Horrer Girreth*
Translation: *Hill of the Tongue; Nose of the Rough Corrie*

Distance:	18½ km (of which 7km can be cycled)
Ascent:	1190m
Time:	6hrs 25mins (up to 1hr less if a bike is used on forestry track)
Maps:	OS sheet 34; Explorer map 400; Area Map 8
Parking:	roadside at end of the public road (small charge levied by farmer)
Start:	along forestry track to the southwest
Hostel:	YHA Loch Lochy; independent Fort William
B&B/hotel:	Laggan; Fort William
Camping:	Faichem, Invergarry; A82 north of Spean Bridge
Access:	Stalking Scotland, tel: 01349 864080 (for Sron a' Choire Ghairbh); Lochiel Estate, tel: 01397 712709 (for Meall na Teanga)

Park at the end of the public road at Kilfinnan at the northern end of Loch Lochy. There are a few parking spaces quite close to the gate where the private track starts, but some people prefer to leave vehicles where the tarmac runs out, just before Kilfinnan farm is reached. At either place the farmer makes a small charge for leaving vehicles. Walk or cycle along the forestry track, taking the upper branch when the track divides. At the start of the Cam Bhealach a signpost marks the point where the track (and bikes) are left behind.

A good path climbs up, through trees at first then over open ground, to reach the col at the top. The two

Bonnie Prince Charlie's fugitive companion, Major Glenaladale, describing part of their journey southwest down the shores of Loch Lochy refers to 'terrible mountains on the right'. The highpoints of these terrible mountains are Meall na Teanga and Sron a' Choire Ghairbh.

These hills do often seem to have a dark and brooding character when seen across Loch Lochy. However they present no difficulties to the modern hillwalker and they can even perhaps be counted amongst the easiest of Munros. Both hills can be approached from Gleann Cia-aig in the southwest, but they are more usually climbed from the northeast, as described here.

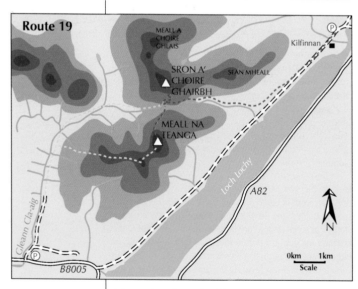

Route 19

MEALL A CHOIRE GHLAIS

Kilfinnan

SRON A' CHOIRE GHAIRBH

SEAN MHEALL

MEALL NA TEANGA

Loch Lochy

A82

Gleann Cia-aig

B8005

0km   1km
Scale

N

Munros lie either side of this col. To the south **Meall na Teanga** is reached by a path which skirts around the grassy northern flanks of Meall Dubh. From the col between that hill and Meall na Teanga it climbs Teanga's

grassy north ridge. The path can be followed virtually all the way, with just a short break when it peters out briefly towards the top of the ridge. Pass the first cairn to reach the summit further on at 22045 92492 (3hrs 35mins).

Return to the col on the Cam Bhealach then climb the zig-zag path up to the north onto **Sron a' Choire Ghairbh**. This path peters out a short way below the grassy summit ridge. Follow the broad ridge round to the summit cairn at 22250 94552 (4hrs 45mins).

Descend by the route of ascent.

Meall na Teanga from the south

GLEN DESSARRY

ROUTE 20

Sgurr nan Coireachan (953m),

Garbh Chioch Mhor (1013m),

Sgurr na Ciche (1040m)

Pronunciation: *Skoor nern Korrachun;*
Garav Cheeyerch Voar; Skoor nuh Keechya
Translation: *Peak of the Corries;*
Big Stony Breast; Peak of the Breast

Distance:	26km
Ascent:	1440m
Time:	8hrs
Maps:	OS sheet 33 or 40; Explorer map 398; Area Map 8
Parking:	at the end of the public road at the west end of Loch Arkaig
Start:	follow private track from parking area
Hostel:	YHA Loch Lochy; Glen Nevis
B&B/hotel:	Spean Bridge
Camping:	A82 near Spean Bridge
Access:	Glendessarry, tel: 01397 712406

If you like your hills wild, rough and remote you'll really enjoy this route. In poor weather, especially in winter, it is a serious undertaking on account of the nature of the terrain and the distance from any roads. However its popularity has left a fairly clear path along almost the whole route, which considerably eases the difficulty of navigation through this rocky wilderness.

From the end of the public road, continue on the private track past Glendessarry (which fell victim to fire in 2003) to Upper Glendessarry. The use of bikes on this estate track is discouraged. Just before Upper Glendessarry is reached, leave the track and cross a stile which is signposted to Sourlies Bothy and Inverie. This is an ancient right of way. The path heads along the north side of a spruce plantation, and after a couple of kilometres crosses the Allt Coire nan Uth. A few metres beyond this burn a small but distinct path heads north up the southern ridge of **Sgurr nan Coireachan**. The real character of this walk is established on this ridge – particularly higher up – where frequent rocky outcrops are scattered randomly across the hillside. Progress is quite easy, however, if you can keep to the little path that leads all the way to the top. Pass the first summit cairn at 93396 95525 and drop down a short way before climbing to a second, higher top at 93307 95815 (3hrs 35mins).

In clear weather the complexity of the hills to the west can now be fully appreciated. Go west over a little nose then descend quite steeply to a col between Sgurr nan Coireachan and the Garbh Chioch Bheag. A path can be followed all the way. From the col a stone wall

Looking east along Garbh Chioch Mhor's east ridge

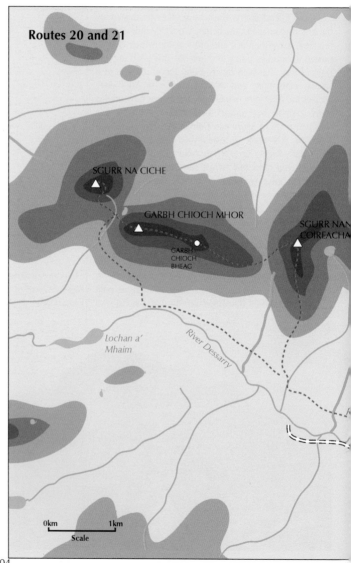

Routes 20 and 21

SGURR NA CICHE

GARBH CHIOCH MHOR

GARBH
CHIOCH
BHEAG

SGURR NAN
COIREACHA

Lochan a'
Mhaim

River Dessarry

0km   1km
Scale

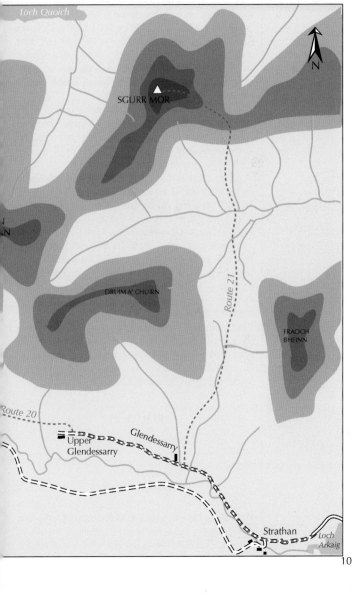

105

can be seen rising high onto the ridge. One can't help but wonder at the lives of the men who built it. The path stays mostly to the left (south) side of the dyke and, after a steep climb onto Garbh Chioch Bheag, traverses the wonderful rocky switchback of the ridge over a couple of minor tops to reach the final cone of **Garbh Chioch Mhor** at 90984 96087 (4hrs 55mins).

Continue westwards along the ridge until it drops steeply to the little col beneath **Sgurr na Ciche**. The views from just above this col are stunning, revealing the awesome nature of the Knoydart landscape in all its rocky complexity. Cross the col and climb to the left of the craggy face that confronts you. A path leads round to a little gully on the south side of the summit. Climb up over boulders (the path stays mostly to the right of these) until the summit ridge is reached. From here it is only a short distance to the summit cairn at 90236 96669 (5hrs 35mins).

Retrace your steps to the col then descend a steep little gully to the southwest, which has the feel of a steep-sided gorge in places. When you emerge from this gully, veer round to the left (southeast) and traverse beneath the silver-grey crags of Garbh Chioch Mhor. The path is somewhat indistinct here, but head for GR 90504 95625, where a small burn begins on the edge of a broad bealach. Follow this burn down over rather wet grass until the path joins the main trail from Inverie to Glendessarry. This takes you back to the plantation, where you rejoin the outward route.

ROUTE 21

Sgurr Mor (1003m)

Pronunciation: *Skoor More*
Translation: *Big Peak*

Walk along the estate track to Glendessarry (at the time of writing this lodge has been destroyed by fire). After crossing the Allt na Feithe, but just before you reach the

Distance:	18km
Ascent:	1240m
Time:	6hrs 10mins
Maps:	OS sheet 40; Explorer map 398; Area Map 8
Parking:	west end of Loch Arkaig at end of public road
Start:	follow private track from parking area
Hostel:	YHA Loch Lochy; Glen Nevis
B&B/hotel:	Spean Bridge
Camping:	A82 near Spean Bridge
Access:	Glendessarry, tel: 01397 712406

This is another rugged and fairly remote hill that can only be accessed easily from the western end of Loch Arkaig.

Sgurr Mor (centre) and Gairich (left) from the east top of Luinne Bheinn

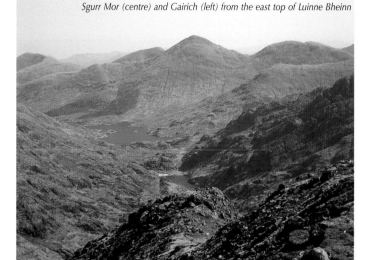

lodge, turn uphill, passing through a gate, and follow a path up to the wide col between Fraoch Bheinn and Druim a' Chuirn. Do not be tempted to follow the Landrover tracks, which go all the way into Glen Kingie following a line of posts. They will lead you astray through some very wet ground. Once on the col the path crosses and recrosses the meandering Allt na Feithe, then it swings across to the east side of the col before skirting round the nose of the northwest ridge of Fraoch Bheinn.

At this point, leave the path and descend over watery meadows to the River Kingie, which now has to be crossed. There are many good crossing places when the water level is low. One such place is marked by wooden posts at GR 97417 96277. If the river is in spate, however, it may be necessary to go further upstream.

If you have to go more than 1½ km to find a crossing, it would probably be better to join the path on the north side of the burn and follow this to the west, then north, to reach the col on the southwest side of Sgurr Beag. Then climb this minor top and continue northeast to Sgurr Mor. (This detour will add time, distance and an extra 140m of vertical ascent to the day. Allow an extra 1hr 30mins.)

Assuming the river can be crossed without trouble, climb steeply up the grassy slopes to the col between Sgurr Mor and Sgurr an Fhuarain at 97519 97599. Don't be drawn too far to the west into the corrie immediately beneath Sgurr Mor as there is no direct access to the summit from here. From the col there is a path along the main ridge which rises steadily to the summit cairn of **Sgurr Mor** at 96535 98033 (3hrs 45mins).

Return by the same route.

ROUTE 22

Gairich (919m)

Pronunciation: *Garreech*
Translation: *Roaring*

Distance:	15km
Ascent:	870m
Time:	4hrs 45mins
Maps:	OS sheet 33; Explorer map 399; Area Map 8
Parking:	parking area at the dam at east end of Loch Quoich
Start:	cross dam to footpath
Hostel:	YHA Loch Lochy
B&B/hotel:	Invergarry; Tomdoun
Camping:	Invergarry
Access:	Kingie, tel: 01809 511261

This fairly easy route climbs the long east ridge of Gairich, starting along the Druim na Geid Salaich, from the eastern end of Loch Quoich. This is the only practicable approach for this hill, unless one makes a long walk-in from the western end of Loch Arkaig and crosses the River Kingie to reach a steep path on the western flanks of Gairich Beag.

From the parking area cross the dam, or cross the river just below it, to reach a footpath heading south through wet ground initially for nearly 3km. When the path drops down to meet another path at the edge of a pinewood plantation, turn left for 100m, then right onto the eastern end of the Druim na Geid Salaich ridge. (You can cut off the corner here by continuing uphill instead of turning

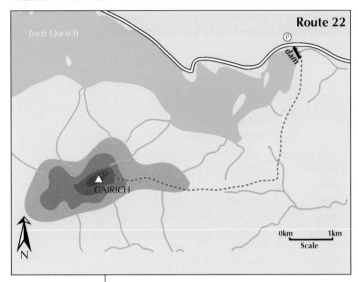

left.) Once you are on the main ridge just follow the path westwards over Bac nam Foid to the foot of **Gairich**'s steep eastern face. The path looks as if it's heading off up Glen Kingie to the south of the hill, but it comes right back and tackles the steep face directly, zig-zagging cleverly around crags until the summit cairn is reached at 02596 99571 (3hrs 5mins).

Return by the route of ascent.

ROUTE 23

Gleouraich (1035m),

Spidean Mialach (996m)

Pronunciation: *Glorich; Speedyan Meealloch*
Translation: *Peak of the Roaring; Peak of the Louse*

Start by an estate sign which indicates the route. There is a good path from the road that winds steadily up the

Distance:	12km
Ascent:	1170m
Time:	4hrs 50mins
Maps:	OS sheet 33; Explorer map 414; Harvey's Superwalker map Kintail; Area Map 8
Parking:	roadside by Loch Quoich at 02919 02995
Start:	follow footpath opposite parking area
Hostel:	YHA Loch Lochy
B&B/hotel:	Invergarry; Tomdoun
Camping:	Invergarry
Access:	tel: 01809 511220

This is a pleasant and straightforward circuit with views over Loch Quoich on one side and the hills of the south Shiel ridge on the other.

southwest ridge of Gleouraich. In fact it is possible to follow this path for most of the way. At the point where the north ridge tumbles away from the main hill, the path changes direction for the final few hundred metres to **Gleouraich**'s cairned summit at 03949 05331 (2hrs).

To complete the traverse, continue in a generally easterly direction, dropping gradually to the col below the next top (Point 1006). Climb up to this top then drop again, more steeply, to another col. From here the going is easy, passing around the edge of **Spidean**'s impressive northern corries. Pass a cairned minor top at 06229 04412 and continue on the long scree-covered summit ridge round a final spectacular corrie to reach the summit at 06597 04294 (3hrs 35mins).

To descend, head southwest over schistose stones to find a faint path once the grass is reached. To avoid the deer-gathering grounds of Coire Mheil in the stalking season, leave the path below the loch and take to the rough grass moorland between the Allt a' Mheil and Loch

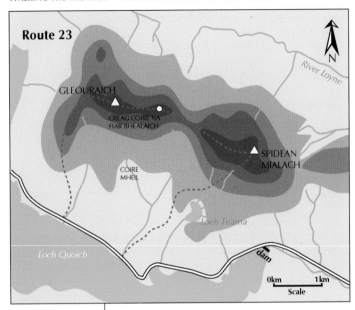

Spidean Mialach from Point 1006

Fearna, descending to the road, which is then followed back to your starting point.

ROUTE 24

Sgurr a' Mhaoraich (1027m)

Pronunciation: Skoor uh Vurr-eeth
Translation: Peak of the Shellfish

Distance:	10km
Ascent:	830m
Time:	3hrs 45mins
Maps:	OS sheet 33; Explorer map 414; Harvey's Superwalker map Kintail; Area Map 8
Parking:	roadside
Start:	follow footpath opposite parking area
Hostel:	YHA Loch Lochy
B&B/hotel:	Invergarry; Tomdoun
Camping:	Invergarry
Access:	tel: 01809 511220

This is a short and fairly easy climb that gains in character the higher you go. There is a notice board for walkers opposite a widening in the road where cars can be parked. As for other hills around Loch Quoich, the estate managers request that walkers keep to the ridges and avoid the corries, where deer gather and grouse breed.

From a parking place by Loch Quoich, nearly 1km beyond the bridge, a path leads up the long, gentle south ridge of Sgurr Coire nan Eiricheallach and progress can be made very quickly across the grassy slopes, which are interspersed occasionally with patches of stones. Once the top of Sgurr Coire nan Eiricheallach has been

113

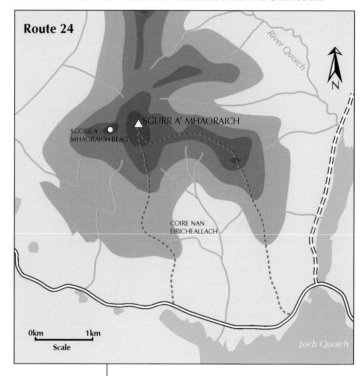

Route 24

SGURR A' MHAORAICH

SGORR A' MHAORAICH BEAG

COIRE NAN EIRICHEALLACH

River Quoich

N

Loch Quoich

0km   1km
Scale

reached, turn west along the ridge which dips and rises and becomes increasingly strewn with boulders and rocks. An old stone wall is crossed and re-crossed and, as height is gained towards **Sgurr a' Mhaoraich**, two or three large crags are turned before the summit cairn is reached at 98401 06538 (2hrs 30mins).

Return by the route of ascent, or, to make a circuit, descend via the south ridge of Sgurr a' Mhaoraich. This is a knobbly ridge, more rugged than the ascent, but all obstacles can be easily passed.

KNOYDART

ROUTE 25

Luinne Bheinn (939m);

Meall Buidhe (946m)

Pronunciation: *Loonya Vane; Miaowl Vooyuh*
Translation: *the Sea-swelling Mountain; Yellow Mountain*

Distance:	18km from Barrisdale
Ascent:	1590m (1790m if returning over Luinne Bheinn)
Time:	7hrs 30mins (from Barrisdale)
Maps:	OS sheet 33; Explorer maps 413 and 414; Area Map 8
Parking:	long-stay car park at Kinloch Hourn (small charge)
Start:	from Barrisdale take the track to Mam Barrisdale
Hostel:	At Inverie, but none on this side of the Mam Barrisdale. There is a bothy (small charge), a bunkhouse (for group bookings) and a small caravan for hire at Barrisdale. There is running water and a toilet in the bothy. (If you are thinking of leaving food in the bothy during the day, note that the building is home to an extended family of hungry mice.)
B&B/hotel:	Inverie
Camping:	Barrisdale
Access:	John Muir Trust, tel: 0131 5540114 and www.barrisdale.com

Cut off by mountains and sea from the rest of the mainland, the hills of Knoydart are harder to reach and their ascent requires rather more planning than other Munros. The area is known as the Rough Bounds of Knoydart, and not without reason.

It is possible to hire a boat from Arnisdale (the boatman is Murray Morrison, tel: 01599 522774), and on a fine

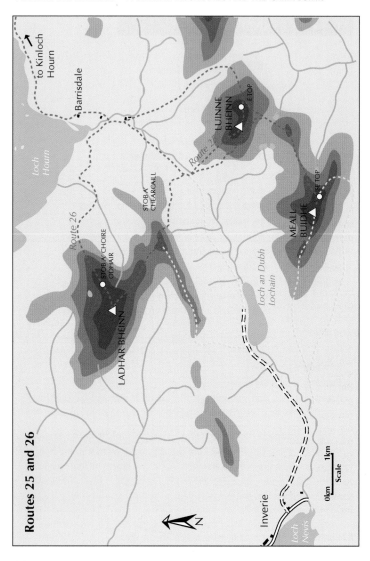

Routes 25 and 26

to Kinloch Hourn

Barrisdale

Loch Hourn

LUINNE BHEINN

E TOP

Route 26

STOB A' CHEARCAILL

Route 26

STOB A' CHOIRE ODHAIR

MEALL BUIDHE

SE TOP

Loch an Dubh Lochain

LADHAR BHEINN

N

Inverie

Loch Nevis

0km   1km

Scale

This is truly rugged country: rough, rocky, demanding and yet with a wild beauty that casts a special spell over walkers and climbers that draws them back time after time to experience its magical charms. Steep-sided hills and wild corries abound. The rock here is stripped naked from the hillsides and strewn around the landscape like a huge experiment gone wrong. The walking is hard and rough, but immensely rewarding, as it takes you through some of the most glorious scenery in Scotland.

day there can be no pleasanter way to arrive at Barrisdale, but the more usual ways of arriving are by ferry from Mallaig to Inverie or by walking in from Kinloch Hourn around the coast to Barrisdale. This coastal walk is about 10km long and, with a couple of steep little hills to climb en route, takes 2½–3hrs with a pack. It is also possible to reach Inverie via a very long walk from Glen Dessarry, perhaps with an overnight stay at Sourlies bothy.

From Barrisdale follow the track past the white bunkhouse and climb steadily up to the Mam Barrisdale. Most people climb the mountain by way of a muddy path that stays well below and to the west of the north-west ridge. However, a much better line can be found by following the ridge itself, as described here. At the very top of the pass take to the hill and climb steep grassy slopes up the Bachd Mhic an Tossaich and onto Luinne Bheinn's northwest ridge. There is a path, broken in places and very faint at first, that is perhaps more obvious in descent than ascent. Higher up the route becomes more stony, and towards the top of the ridge the path climbs to the far left, almost on the edge of the steep northern corrie, but the path on this side of the hill is less continuously rocky than the one on the southeast. At the top there are two cairns, quite close together: the second one marks **Luinne Bheinn**'s highest point at 86985 00728 (2hrs 50mins).

Enjoy the grandstand views over the magnificent Coire Odhair before continuing on to the East Top, which is just a couple of metres lower at 937m, then

Choire Odhair and Meall Buidhe from Luinne Bheinn

scramble down rocks to the southeast to reach a grassy apron. On a clear day there are wonderful views from here across to Sgurr na Ciche and further left along Loch Quoich to Sgurr Mor and the curving west ridge of Gairich. From the apron an easy spur extends to the southwest reaching a wide col at the head of Coire Odhair at 87150 00162. Unfortunately a couple of hundred metres have to be lost to reach this point.

The next little hill is climbed without difficulty and this leads on to Meal Coire na Gaoithe 'n Ear. Once again height has to be lost on the other side of this, although it is possible to bypass the very top by passing to its right (west). From the Bealach Ile Coire it is a straightforward climb to **Meall Buidhe**'s east top, although the ridge gets narrower and steeper towards the top. A short distance further on to the west-northwest the main top is reached at 84896 98976 via a broad, grassy saddle (4hrs 40mins).

There are various options for the return journey, but the safest ones involve getting back initially to the col at 87152 00128. It is possible to find a way back to the Mam Barrisdale from this point by dropping into the upper part of the corrie and then climbing high onto the shoulder of Luinne Bheinn's south-southwest ridge via a stony gully, then traversing round the southwest face of the mountain. A good descent path starts at 86289 00923 at a height of about 680m leading down to the north-northwest, but it is not cairned. Great care needs to be taken in reaching this point in poor visibility, however, as there is a great deal of dangerous ground hereabouts which is not fully represented on the 1:50,000 map. There have been fatalities among those trying to find a safe way off this side of the mountain.

One alternative is to return by the route of ascent, re-crossing Luinne Bheinn's summit. Another, rather easier, option is to return to the apron and then follow the mountain's east ridge from here, avoiding any craggy outcrops, to reach the Mam Unndalain, from where a good path leads down the glen directly back to Barrisdale.

ROUTE 26

Ladhar Bheinn (1020m)

Pronunciation: *Larrer Vane (usually referred to as Larven)*
Translation: *Hoof Mountain*

Distance:	14km
Ascent:	1200m
Time:	5hrs 45mins (from Barrisdale)
Difficulty:	some easy scrambling (barely grade 1) and a little exposure at times; whilst this is not really a technical route, the situations are serious
Maps:	OS sheet 33; Explorer maps 413 and 414; Area Map 8
Parking:	long-stay car park at Kinloch Hourn (small charge)
Start:	track to Mam Barrisdale from Barrisdale bothy
Hostel:	see previous route
B&B/hotel:	Inverie
Camping:	Barrisdale
Access:	John Muir Trust, tel: 0131 5540114 and www.barrisdale.com

The strong ridgelines and spectacular scenery around Ladhar Bheinn make for excellent walking. Whilst it is possible to make a fine circuit by starting up Creag Bheithe, crossing over Stob a' Chearcaill, then returning down the Druim a' Choire Odhair, this involves an awkward and sometimes unpleasant scramble up Stob a' Chearcaill's summit cone. The circuit described here misses out this minor top, but is still an excellent walk.

Ladhar Bheinn south-east ridge from Stob a' Choire Odhair – Meall Buidhe behind

Walk up the path to the Mam Barrisdale and head across grassy hills for 1½ km into Coire a' Phuill. Aim for the col to the left of Stob a' Chearcaill's conical summit. Do not be tempted to climb Stob a' Chearcaill direct from here unless you have a predilection for steep, greasy rock where the only holds are clumps of slimy moss and unstable tufts of grass. It can be done, but there have been accidents here. Well to the left of the stony cone of Stob a' Chearcaill is a grassy ramp that starts quite low down and is visible from afar. This is the key to gaining the ridge. Climb the ramp to the col and begin to admire the views of Ladhar Bheinn and its lovely ridges.

After a short climb to the southwest from the col, the main ridge to Ladhar Bheinn branches off to the right. The

ridge that continues to the southwest takes you down to Inverie. Continue along the rocky northwest ridge to **Ladhar Bheinn**. Quite a lot of height has to be lost – at one point fairly abruptly – followed by an easy scramble to regain height. A minor top is crossed before you drop again. Then comes the final climb to the summit, during which there are once again one or two easy scrambling moves. The summit is a long, narrow arête with three distinct peaks on it. A trig point sits on the northwest of these, but this is actually the lowest of the three. The middle top is the highest at 82405 03976 (3hrs 50mins).

Return to the southeast top (82565 03914), then drop sharply down to the northeast and continue over Stob a' Choire Odhair. There are wonderful views to the west, taking in one of Knoydart's many rocky corrie shows, and also to the south, looking back along the main ridge. Follow the route on along the Druim a' Choire Odhair, dropping steadily for almost 2½ km from Ladhar Bheinn's southeast top. There is a clear path along this section. Then head down grassy slopes to the southeast and cross the Allt Coire Dhorrcail to pick up a prominent path on its southeast bank. This path takes you right around the nose of Creag Bheithe above Barrisdale Bay and back to the bothy and campsite at Barrisdale.

Stob a' Chearcaill and Loch Hourn form Ladhar Bheinn's southeast ridge

121

HOURN

ROUTE 27

Beinn Sgritheall (974m)

Pronunciation: Bine Screehal
Translation: Mountain of Screes

Distance:	9km
Ascent:	1020m
Time:	3hrs 50mins
Maps:	OS sheet 33; Explorer map 413; Area Map 8
Parking:	in Arnisdale village
Start:	footpath signed to Beinn Sgritheall in middle of the village
Hostel:	YHA Ratagan
B&B/hotel:	Shiel Bridge
Camping:	Shiel Bridge
Access:	tel: 01599 522360

Beinn Sgritheall comes impressively into view as you drive across the headland from Ratagan and sits loftily above the little hamlet of Arnisdale. The traverse of this Munro is only a fairly short excursion, yet in clear weather the summit slopes command superb views across Loch Hourn to Knoydart and across the Sound of Sleat to Skye.

Start in Arnisdale along a path that follows a small burn, then cross to the east side of the burn and climb steeply up to the Bealach Arnasdail. From the top of the Bealach turn sharply uphill where a path climbs steeply towards the northern side of **Beinn Sgritheall**'s east top. There are bucket-sized steps higher up the slope and these lead eventually to a cairn on the east summit at 84538 12350. From here follow the ridge west to reach the summit

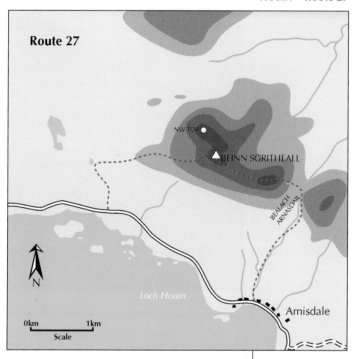

Route 27

NW TOP ○

△ BEINN SGRITHEALL

BEALACH ARNASDAIL

Loch Hourn

Arnisdale

N

0km   1km
Scale

Beinn Sgritheall from Luinne Bheinn

West ridge and descent of Beinn Sgritheall

slopes of the main top. The summit cairn is at 83591 12669 (2hrs 15mins).

To complete a pleasant circuit, once you have taken in the views, descend to the west down a shapely ridge, first dropping over a couple of rocky towers. The path is well defined. Once a small lochan is reached at 81675 12679 turn southeast and descend steeply to a stile and beyond it through a grove of fine oak and birch trees with an undergrowth of blaeberry and heather. This path, which can get quite muddy, and is unpleasant and awkward in slippery conditions, brings you back to the road a couple of kilometres northwest of your starting point.

If you decide to do the route in the opposite direction, bear in mind that there are no good parking spaces on this narrow road, so it would be better to leave your vehicle in Arnisdale. The start of the path through the wood may also be difficult to find if you go this way round. A very small cairn by the roadside at 81846 11923 marks the spot.

GLEN SHIEL

ROUTE 28

The Saddle (1010m), Sgurr na Sgine (946m)

Pronunciation: Skoor nuh Skeenya
Translation: Peak of the Knife

Distance:	12km
Ascent:	1270m
Time:	5hrs 50mins
Difficulty:	grade 2 scrambling with a couple of problems that are probably grade 3 (but most of the difficulties can be avoided at an easier grade on paths below the crest); some exposure
Maps:	OS sheet 33; Explorer map 414; Harvey's Superwalker map Kintail; Area Map 8
Parking:	roadside near start of path
Start:	footpath from A87 starting at 96846 14273
Hostel:	YHA Ratagan
B&B/hotel:	Shiel Bridge; Cluanie Inn
Camping:	Shiel Bridge
Access:	Dochfour Estate, tel: 01599 511282

Towards the bottom end of Glen Shiel, on the opposite side of the glen from the Five Sisters of Kintail, are two sharp ridges, rising up to high rocky summits. The climb up the Forcan Ridge to The Saddle, followed by an ascent of Sgurr na Sgine and a return down Faochag's northeast ridge, is one of the classic mountaineering circuits of the western Highlands, both in summer and winter.

Start a short distance below the Allt Coire Mhalagain, where a clear path leads onto the hill. Follow this over a small craggy knoll and around the northeastern flanks of

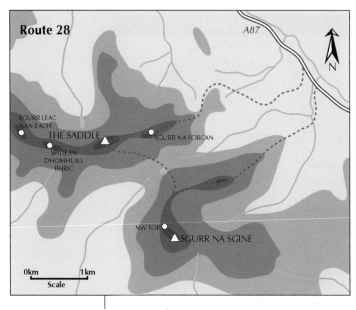

The Forcan Ridge is a hugely enjoyable scramble, albeit with one or two interesting problems along the way that may well tax the inexperienced. The return down Faochag looks steep and dramatic, but is grassy rather than rocky and offers no real difficulty to the walker in summer.

Meallan Odhar. When it reaches the crest of the ridge between Meallan Odhar and Biod an Fhithich the path cuts back across the northwestern flanks of Meallan Odhar to reach a col at the start of the Forcan Ridge. Fairly high up on this col the path divides. One branch leads up to the start of the ridge while the left-hand path avoids the ridge altogether, taking an easy route up to a small lochan on the Bealach Coire Mhalagain, between the Forcan Ridge and Sgurr na Sgine, from where an easy path leads up to the summit of **The Saddle**.

The start of the Forcan Ridge on The Saddle

To climb the Forcan Ridge, which most parties will want to do, continue uphill, staying close to the crest. The route is obvious because of the passage of many boots. At first there are only a few pieces of scrambling; higher up, however, there is more rock, and towards the top a large, awkward block has to be passed either to its left or its right, which is the first real tester. The top of the ridge is reached without further difficulty, after which there is a short descent before climbing the final slopes to The Saddle. The last 5m of this descent, however, pose the second problem, which is rather more demanding than the first. This section is quite steep and somewhat exposed. There are actually very good holds and it is not technically difficult, but walkers who have no

Faochag from Sgurr na Sgine

experience of scrambling or climbing may well feel intimidated here, especially if they don't have the security of a rope. A grassy gully bypasses this little wall, but to use it would really be missing the point of the route.

Once this pitch is negotiated there are no further major difficulties. Bear in mind, however, that the Mountain Rescue Team reports as many accidents on the next section leading up to the summit as it does on the 'bad step', perhaps because people relax a little too much too soon. Some interesting scrambling continues on a knife-edge towards the top, but again a well-used path below the crest avoids the remaining difficulties. Pass over the east top (Point 958) and continue to a little cairn on the summit at 93615 13112. There is a trig point a short distance beyond (3hrs 10mins).

Descend east from the trig point over scree and boulders, working your way across to the Bealach Coire Mhalagain. From this col there is a steep climb through more scree and stones to reach the western end of the long ridge between Faochach and Sgurr na Sgine. Follow the path south to reach **Sgurr na Sgine**'s northwest summit at 94393 11571, then cross the serrated summit ridge to reach the higher southeast summit a couple of hundred metres further on at 94628 11359 (4hrs 25mins).

To descend, retrace your steps to Faochach's east–west ridge and go along this to the stubby cone of Faochach's summit. From here the descent follows the impressive crest of the steep northeast ridge, which extends all the way down to the road. Perhaps surprisingly, this can be descended without difficulty. At the bottom the path crosses the Allt Mhalagain to reach the road just a short distance above the day's starting point.

THE SOUTH SHIEL RIDGE

ROUTE 29

Creag a' Mhaim (947m), Druim Shionnach (987m), Aonach air Chrith (1021m), Maol Chinn-dearg (981m), Sgurr an Doire Leathain (1010m), Sgurr an Lochain (1004m), Creag nan Damh (918m)

Pronunciation: *Krayk er Vime; Drime Hyunoch; Ernoch ur Chree; Merle Heen Jerrack; Skoor un Thurrer Leheen; Skoor un Lochan; Krayk nern Dav*
Translation: *Cairn of the Pass; Ridge of the Foxes; Ridge of Trembling; Bald Red Head; Peak of the Broad Oaks; Peak of the Small Loch; Crag of the Deer*

Distance:	24½km (from Cluanie Inn to lay-by at battle site)
Ascent:	1750m
Time:	8hrs 45mins (plus time to get back along the road)
Difficulty:	this is not a technical route, but it is quite committing; a long time is spent at high level with long gaps between escape routes
Maps:	OS sheet 33; Explorer map 414; Harvey's Superwalker map Kintail; Area Map 8
Parking:	lay-by on A87 at site of 1719 battl
Start:	from Cluanie Inn go east for 200m to start of private track
Hostel:	YHA Ratagan
B&B/hotel:	Shiel Bridge; Cluanie Inn
Camping:	Shiel Bridge
Access:	Dochfour Estate, tel: 01599 511282

The mountains on the southern side of Glen Shiel are linked by a single long, high-level ridge extending from Craig a' Mhaim in the east to Creag nan Damh in the west. The whole ridge as described here can be covered in a single memorable outing, but if it proves to be too much for one day it can conveniently be split into two by descending from Maol Chinn-dearg, about halfway along the chain.

The use of two cars makes the logistics of this walk much easier; however, there is also a daily bus service from Portree which comes up the pass, leaving Shiel Bridge at 9.35am. (Check the times, as these can change from year to year.) The bus will stop in the pass if requested (so long as it has room to pull in at a lay-by). This enables you to leave a car at the parking area at the site of the Battle of Glen Shiel to await your return, while you take the bus to Cluanie Inn at the top of the pass to the start of the walk.

A few metres east of Cluanie Inn a private road leads around the eastern flanks of Creag a' Mhaim. There are two or three possible lines of ascent. The quickest is to follow a path that leads off the track at 08196 11070, about 100m past a radio mast. It peters out higher up near the Loch a' Mhaoll Dhisnich, but the curving north rib of Druim Shionnach is climbed quite easily from here, past a crag at 825m (which can be turned on either side, or climbed direct to give some interesting scrambling) to the summit of Druim Shionnach. At the top, follow the main ridge back to take in **Creag a' Mhaim**. The more usual line of ascent involves more distance but is perhaps more obvious in mist and easier to follow. It follows the private road for 6½km until, a short distance before a substantial stone bridge, at GR 10122 07185, there is a clear path that leads off up the southeastern spur of the mountain. Follow this easily to the top. The summit cairn is at 08795 07763 (3hrs).

Continue easily along the ridge, which narrows at one point, to reach **Druim Shionnach**, less than 2km away (3hrs 30mins).

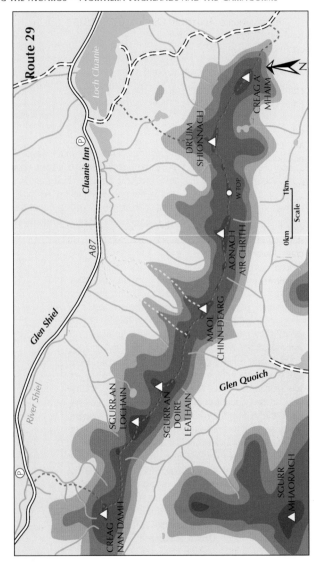

The next Munro, **Aonach air Chrith**, at 05108 08332 is about 2½km beyond Druim Shionnach. Don't be confused in poor visibility by the cairned minor top at 06295 08201, which is not a Munro (4hrs 20mins).

Continue west along the ridge, which is remarkably consistent in quality throughout its length, narrowing at times beyond Aonach air Chrith almost to an arête, and at other times being broader. There is a path along the ridge that is clear and easy to follow. Throughout there are schistose stones and occasional rocks, but these are not loose, numerous or steep enough to impede progress. The cairn of **Maol Chinn-dearg** is at 03224 08760, and here a decision has to be made whether to descend or complete the traverse (5hrs 5mins).

The line of descent is down the crest of the north-east ridge, the Druim Coire nan Eirecheanach, which starts quite steeply but continues easily, avoiding small crags lower down, to reach the road. An alternative descent starts 1km further along the ridge and follows a line down the northeast ridge of Sgurr Coire na Feinn –

Druim Shionnach – the South Shiel ridge

133

Sgurr an Lochain from Sgurr an Doire Leathain

the Druim Thollaidh. To continue the traverse, follow the main ridge down and across Sgurr Coire na Feinn, until it rises again quite sharply to reach **Sgurr an Doire Leathain**. The summit cairn lies a short distance to the northeast of the main line of the ridge at 01544 09913 and could possibly be missed in poor visibility (6hrs).

Now the ridge drops and rises sharply again over a rockier section. There is even a very short slab where a hand might be called into use – it can hardly be called scrambling – before the penultimate Munro is reached, **Sgurr an Lochain**. The summit cairn is at 00584 10413 (6hrs 35mins).

The final hill is now in sight, looming rather bulkily to the left of the minor top, Sgurr Beag. At the foot of Sgurr Beag the path divides. It is not difficult to cross this hill but, as it is not a Munro, many people evidently choose to bypass it, for the main path veers round to skirt its southwestern flanks. From the col to the west of Sgurr Beag, climb steadily up to reach the summit of **Creag nan Damh** at 98354 11192 (7hrs 35mins).

The quickest descent is via Creag nan Damh's northeast ridge (which is not to be confused with the ridge that goes over Sgurr a' Chuilinn). Go east-northeast from the summit for 200m, then head down to the northeast. From above, this 'ridge' hardly shows at all: it looks steep and most unpromising at first. Moreover the path is somewhat vague and seems to disappear halfway down. However, once you find the top, the route-finding is very straightforward and there are no difficulties in descent except for some long grass at the bottom. Once the ridge has been cleared, a stalker's path can clearly be seen leading out of Am Fraoch Choire and this is followed back to the road through a small, steep plantation (which offers more pause for thought than anything on the hill). Another longer descent continues west from Creag nan Damh to the Bealach Duibh Leac, and from here a path zigzags down into Coire Toiteil to rejoin the main road some 2km further west.

THE FIVE SISTERS OF KINTAIL

ROUTE 30

Sgurr na Ciste Duibhe (1027m),

Sgurr na Carnach (1002m),

Sgurr Fhuaran (1067m)

Pronunciation: *Skoor nuh Keeshta Two-yer; Skoor nuh Karnach; Skoor Ooweran*
Translation: *Peak of the Dark Chest; Rocky Peak; Wolf Peak*

Distance:	11½km
Ascent:	1380m
Time:	5hrs 15mins (plus time to get back along the road)
Maps:	OS sheet 33; Explorer map 414; Harvey's Superwalker map Kintail; Area Map 9
Parking:	lay-by on A87 beneath Bealach an Lapain at 00798 13622
Start:	footpath from road at 00798 13622
Hostel:	YHA Ratagan
B&B/hotel:	Shiel Bridge
Camping:	Shiel Bridge
Access:	National Trust for Scotland, tel: 01599 511231. Normally no restrictions on access

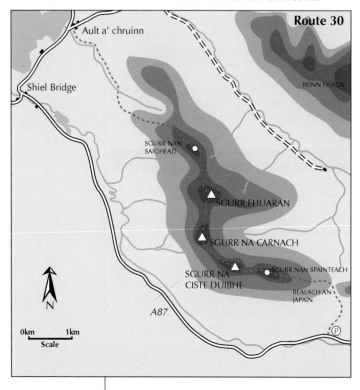

This justifiably popular route – the Five Sisters of Kintail – incorporates the three western Munros and two of their smaller sisters in the great chain of mountains on the north side of Glen Shiel. The character of the route is similar to the south Shiel ridge although the arêtes are generally sharper and in places rockier on this route, providing some excellent ridge walking in fine situations and, weather permitting, some wonderful views.

Start at the break between plantations below the Bealach an Lapain, where a muddy path climbs steeply up to the col which is the lowest point on the whole ridge. Head

Since the start and finish points of this walk are some 11km apart, the use of two cars (or a bike, or a non-walking co-operative driver) would obviate the need for a long walk back along the road. Alternatively, use may be made of the morning bus that comes up the pass from Shiel Bridge.

west from here and follow the obvious path as it climbs and falls over a number of mini-tops before reaching Sgurr nan Spainteach, 'Peak of the Spaniards', at 99146 15006. This is named after an advance force of 200 Spanish troops who joined the Jacobite rebellion in 1719. They were routed in battle in the glen and retreated to this hill, where they spent the night, before surrendering the next day to government troops. Beyond this peak the ridge narrows and becomes quite rocky. A steep pitch leads down to a cleft in the ridge. Either side will take you to the summit slopes of Sgurr na Ciste Duibhe, but the path (and the easiest route) goes to the right. Climb steeply up to the large summit cairn of **Sgurr na Ciste Duibhe** at 98406 14950 (2hrs 30mins).

Continue west then northwest along a well-defined path, dropping down to a stony col (97750 15490)

Sgurr na Carnach (right) and Sgurr Fhuaran from Shiel Bridge

Sgurr Fhuaran (Five Sisters of Kintail) from Ben Fhada

beneath **Sgurr na Carnach**. Here the direction veers more to the north. Climb quite steeply over scree to the summit cairn at 97718 15877 (3hrs 5mins).

The ridge continues to the north, dropping to another col before a stiff climb to **Sgurr Fhuaran**, whose summit cairn is at 97857 16674 (3hrs 45mins).

Descend northwest, then drop down to the north on a gracefully curving section of the ridge that leads to a dramatic-looking peak – Sgurr nan Saighead. This is crossed (although judging by the paths most people now chose to bypass it to the southwest), as is the next peak, Beinn Bhuidhe. There is a gradual descent from here down the broad northwest ridge to a wide col below Sgurr an t-Searraich. Before the col is quite reached, however, veer off to the north and drop down to cross the little burn, the Allt a' Chruinn. An obvious but rather muddy trail then leads down to the little settlement of Ault a' Chruinn. An alternative but less pleasant descent can be made from the wide col down a steep grassy bank to its southwest. This leads to a footbridge over the River Shiel just above Loch Shiel.

ROUTE 31

Ciste Dhubh (979m),

Aonach Meadhoin (1001m),

Sgurr a' Bhealaich Dheirg (1036m),

Saileag (956m)

Pronunciation: *Keeshtyer Ghoo; Ernoch Veeyann;*
Skoor uh Veeyallach Year-ick; Sarlak
Translation: *Black Chest; Middle Peak;*
Peak of the Red Pass; Little Heel

Distance:	22km
Ascent:	1510m
Time:	6hrs 15mins (plus time for travelling back along the road)
Maps:	OS sheet 33; Explorer map 414; Harvey's Superwalker map Kintail; Area Map 9
Parking:	parking area by Cluanie Inn
Start:	along private track opposite Cluanie Inn
Hostel:	YHA Ratagan
B&B/hotel:	Cluanie Inn/Shiel Bridge
Camping:	Shiel Bridge
Access:	Corrielair Estate, tel: 01738 828573 (for access to Ciste Dhubh); National Trust for Scotland, tel: 01599 511231. (For access to the rest – normally no restrictions)

Ciste Dhubh is a somewhat lonely hill, cast aside from the main ridge on the north side of Glen Shiel, but its steep sides and fine narrow ridge make it a very worthwhile objective. It is often climbed on its own, though this only makes for a short outing. For a fuller day it makes sense to link it to the three hills that form the eastern end of the great north Shiel ridge – a trio that is sometimes called the Three Brothers. Two cars or the use of a bike are a great help, but not essential, for the 8km journey back along the road at the end of the day.

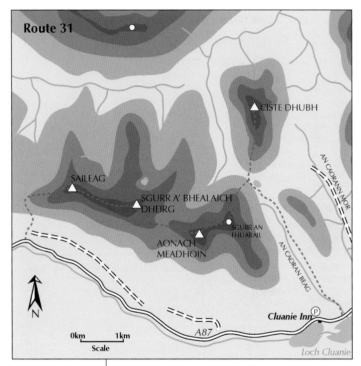

Route 31

CISTE DHUBH

AN CAORANN MOR

SAILEAG

SGURR A' BHEALAICH DHEIRG

SGURR AN FHUARAIL

AONACH MEADHOIN

AN CAORAN BEAG

N

0km 1km
Scale

Cluanie Inn Ⓟ

A87

Loch Cluanie

Start at the Cluanie Inn and follow a private track into An Caorann Beag. Continue on the path along the west side of the valley when the track runs out. An alternative path (which can get very muddy) starts from the A87 immediately to the east of where it crosses the Allt a' Chaorainn Bhig, then follows a line up the east side of the valley. Either way, reach the Bealach a' Choinich and cross this wet hinterland to the foot of Ciste Dhubh's southern nose. Climb steeply up this grassy slope to gain the ridge (the path here can get very wet and muddy in its lower section). Once on the narrow ridge climb over a sharp little minor top, or bypass it on the path that skirts its western flank, then continue pleasantly along the crest which rises and falls before the final climb to **Ciste Dhubh**'s small summit cairn at 06239 16611 (2hrs 30mins).

Return to the Bealach a' Choinich and from its southwestern side climb the steep grassy slopes of Sgurr an Fhuarail. Although the angle is quite steep the ground underfoot is good. Higher up a path appears and the slopes to the summit along the crest of the ridge are easier. There is a cairn at 05449 13965. Now you are on the main ridge and the next objective is Aonach Meadhoin to the west. The first section of this ridge is quite sharp and rocky but can be traversed on its crest without difficulty. Beyond this the ridge is broader and grassier, but still with some fine views down into Coire nan Eun. **Aonach Meadhoin**'s cairned summit is at 04891 13756 (4hrs 15mins).

Continue round the head of Coire nan Eun to the summit of **Sgurr a' Bhealaich Dheirg**. The summit cairn of this hill lies 100m northeast of the main ridge on a rocky spur, and it is an impressive sight perched up on a narrow spine of rock at 03521 14350 (5hrs).

Continue along the ridge to **Saileag**. This last hill of the day looks distinctly unimpressive from here, set

Ciste Dubh (right) and Sgurr nan Ceathreamhan from Sgurr an Fhuarail

Sgurr a' Bhealaich Dheirg's summit cairn

against the magnificent backdrop of the serrated Five Sisters ridge, but it is a pleasant walk along the crest of the ridge with a couple of sharp dips and rises before its summit cairn is reached at 01776 14830 (5hrs 35mins).

The easiest descent to the road is from the col – the Bealach an Lapain – just under 1km west of Saileag's summit. The descent path starts at 01028 14489 and heads off down the steep grassy slopes (can be very muddy) to emerge at a gap between plantations that leads back to the A87 at 00798 13622. Return along the road.

If Ciste Dhubh is to be climbed separately, the pleasantest way onto Aonach Meadhoin is up the grassy south ridge of Sgurr an Fhuaran, starting from the Cluanie Inn.

ROUTE 32

A' Chralaig (1120m),

Mullach Fraoch-choire (1102m)

Pronunciation: *Uh Chraalayk; Mooluch Fruackorrer*
Translation: *The Basket; Peak of the Heathery Corrie*

Distance:	15km
Ascent:	1110m
Time:	5hrs 25mins
Maps:	OS sheet 33; Explorer map 414; Harvey's Superwalker map Kintail; Area Map 9
Parking:	lay-by on A87 just west of Allt a' Chaorainn Mhoir
Start:	at signposted track to Gleann Gniomhaidh 200m east of Allt a' Chaorainn Mhoir
Hostel:	YHA Ratagan
B&B/hotel:	Cluanie Inn; Shiel Bridge
Camping:	Shiel Bridge
Access:	Corrielair Estate, tel: 01738 828573

Towards the western end of Loch Cluanie is a major break in the high mountains north of Glen Shiel – this is the pass of An Caorann Mor and it provides one of the easiest routes into the remote upper reaches of Glen Affric. To the right (east) of An Caorann Mor lie these two high but fairly straightforward Munros, connected by a fine, narrowing ridge. There are excellent views from both of them over the numerous surrounding Munros.

Start along the signposted track for just a few metres, then take to the steep grassy hillside, climbing northeast up a fairly relentless slope until the top of the ridge is reached and the angle eases. Continue for some 2km along this broad, easy ridge, climbing steadily until **A' Chralaig**'s

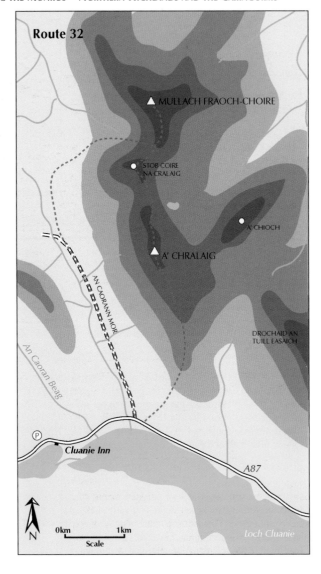

summit, topped by a well-constructed cairn, is reached at 09436 14794 (2hrs 20mins).

Glen Affric from A' Chralaig

Drop down over the twisting ridge until a short climb brings you to a minor top, Point 1008. From here the ridge drops to a col, narrowing considerably, then climbs in a curving line through a number of towers and pinnacles until **Mullach Fraoch-choire**'s summit is reached. Point 1008 gives a good view of this fine summit ridge. The path is never difficult as it winds in and out of the rocky towers on its way to the top at 09493 17142 (3hrs 25mins).

To descend, drop down into Coire Odhar from the col at 09342 16452. The path soon disappears, but continue down alongside one of the deeply etched little burns to wet ground at the bottom, where the path from Gleann Gniomhaidh is joined. After a couple of rather muddy kilometres this path turns into a track. Alternatively it is possible to descend via the Coire a' Ghlas-thuill to the south of Point 1008.

ROUTE 33

Carn Ghluasaid (957m),

Sgurr nan Conbhairean (1109m),

Sail Chaorainn (1002m)

Pronunciation: *Karn Gloorsage;*
Skoor nern Konnavathen; Sal Hooreen
Translation: *Hill of Movement; Peak of the*
Keeper of the Hounds; Heel of the Rowan Tree

Distance:	16km
Ascent:	1100m
Time:	5hrs 45mins
Maps:	OS sheet 34; Explorer map 414; Harvey's Superwalker map Kintail; Area Map 9
Parking:	off-road parking area at Lundie
Start:	along the Old Military Road, a short distance west of the parking area
Hostel:	YHA Ratagan
B&B/hotel:	Shiel Bridge; Cluanie Inn
Camping:	Shiel Bridge
Access:	Corrielair Estate, tel: 01738 828573

These three hills, lying at the eastern end of the long chain of Munros on the north side of Glen Shiel, are easily accessible from the A87 halfway along Loch Cluanie. Start at Lundie, where there is ample parking. All that remains of the former buildings here are their concrete bases.

Follow the Old Military Road for nearly 1km, then branch off to the right on a good path which gains height quickly to join the rocky southwest spur of **Carn Ghluasaid**. This ridge, which is quite sharp, gives way higher up to a gentle, rounded summit plateau comprising a number of

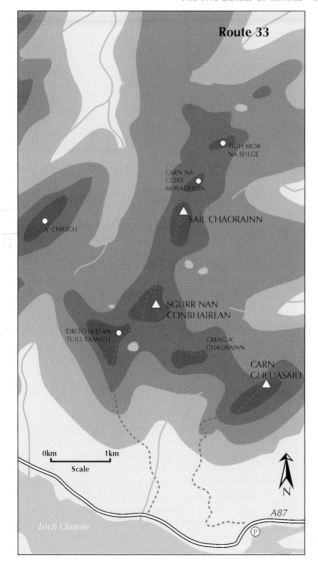

Route 33

TIGH MOR NA SEILGE

CARN NA COIRE MHEADHOIN

SAIL CHAORAINN

A' CHIOCH

SGURR NAN CONBHAIREAN

DROCHAID AN TUILL EASAICH

CREAG A' CHAORAINN

CARN GHLUASAID

0km   1km
Scale

N

A87

Loch Cluanie

P

Sgurr nan Conbhairean and Sail Chaorainn from Mullach Fraoch-choire

shallow mounds. Cross two of these mounds and continue to rise gently to reach the highest point, where there is a cairn close to the edge of the north face at 14559 12537 (2hrs 35mins).

On a clear day Sgurr nan Conbhairean stands out from here like a pointed tooth behind the smaller Point 998. Follow the impressive line of corries west then northwest. The path bypasses Point 998 to its south to arrive at the Glas Bhealach below **Sgurr nan Conbhairean**'s final slopes. Climb these to its large summit cairn at 12986 13885 (3hrs 15mins).

Sail Chaorainn sits in splendid isolation on a limb to the north, and the only easy way to reach it is to traverse the north ridge of Sgurr nan Conbhairean and then return the same way. This ridge is easy, and the path along it is clear, but a fair amount of height has to be lost in descent and regained on return. The summit cairn is at 13321 15452 (3hrs 55mins).

Retrace your steps to the lower flanks of Sgurr nan Conbhairean (you don't need to go right back up to the summit). A faint path weaves across the western slopes to reach the west-southwest ridge and thus over Drochaid an Tuill Easaich to a long ridge leading south over Meall Breac. There are crags along the east side of this ridge, but stay on its crest right down to the southern nose (there is a path but this becomes indistinct lower down). At 12114 11616 a small cairn marks the easiest point of descent and a path leads southeast from here over steep grassy slopes to the Allt Coire Lair by the Old

Military Road. Return along this, or along the main road, back to Lundie.

ROUTE 34

Beinn Fhada (or Ben Attow)

(1032m), A' Ghlas-bheinn (918m)

Pronunciation: *Bine Atter; Uh Glaz Vane*
Translation: *Long Mountain; the Grey-green Mountain*

Distance:	20km
Ascent:	1490m
Time:	7hrs 15mins
Maps:	OS sheet 33; Explorer map 414; Harvey's Superwalker map Kintail; Area Map 9
Parking:	Morvich – by mountain rescue post
Start:	along private road east of the mountain rescue post
Hostel:	YHA Ratagan
B&B/hotel:	Shiel Bridge
Camping:	Morvich
Access:	Beinn Fhada owned by the National Trust for Scotland, tel: 01599 511231 – normally no access restrictions; A' Ghlas-bheinn falls within the Inverinate Estate, tel: 01599 530055 or 01599 511250

These two muscular hills are guardians of the western end of Glen Affric and give a tough day's outing with fine views over the secretive hills of West Benula, as well as a less familiar perspective on the Five Sisters of Kintail and some of the other hills on the north Shiel ridge. Beinn Fhada is a huge, complex mountain with several rocky northern corries and a rather flat-topped summit. It can be climbed from Alltbeithe, but is more usually approached from Morvich, as described here. From this direction it combines conveniently with A' Ghlas-bheinn to make a good circuit.

149

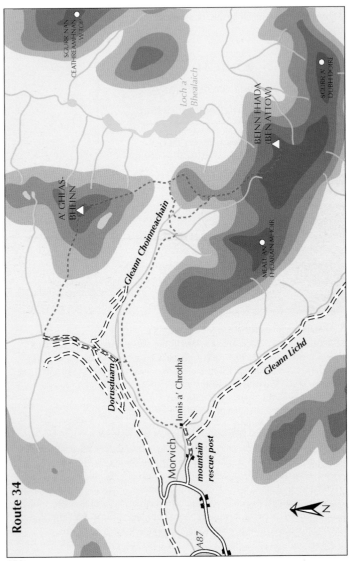

Route 34

SGURR NAN CEATHREAMHNAN W TOP

Loch a' Bhealaich

SGURR A' DUBH DOIRE

BEINN FHADA (BEN ATTOW)

A' GHAS-BHEINN

Gleann Choinneachain

MEALL AN FHUARAIN MHOIR

Gleann Lichd

Dorusduain

Innis a' Chrotha

Morvich

mountain rescue post

A87

N

Start at the parking area at Morvich and walk to the end of the private road, crossing a wooden bridge over the River Croe and passing to the left of Innis a' Chrotha. Just past the buildings a footpath leads off to the right, sign-posted to the Glomach Falls. Follow this into Strath Croe and, ignoring further signs to the falls, stay on the south side of the river as the path winds up into Gleann Choinneachain, heading towards the Bealach an Sgairne. The path crosses a burn coming down from one of Beinn Fhada's fine corries and climbs quite high onto the flanks of Meall a' Bhealaich before it branches at 00713 21364. The left branch continues to the bealach while the right branch doubles back across the face of Meall a' Bhealaich and climbs into the upper corrie before zigzagging up the easiest line onto **Beinn Fhada**'s north ridge. Climb this onto the ridge, which is reached at GR 01099 20736. From here the main path wanders

The western ridges of Beinn Fhada from near the summit

off round the head of the corrie; leave it to climb the ridge itself, staying just to the west of the stones and rocks on the edge, as these make for rather awkward progress. A large stone enclosure on the summit and a trig point are found at 01861 19243 (3hrs 30mins).

Retrace your steps down the ridge towards Meall a' Bhealaich. The northern face of this hill, directly above the col, is steep and dangerous, but a line can be found down grass to the northeast and an easy traverse then leads back to the col at 01498 21424. The path here is rather faint, however, and seems to be more visible from below; in bad weather it could be hard to locate the safest way down. An alternative is to follow the line of ascent right back to below the bealach and ascend from there on an obvious path, although this way is longer and also loses quite a lot of height. From the col climb steeply up the long, complex south ridge of **A' Ghlas-bheinn**, rising steadily over numerous rocky bluffs until the summit is reached at 00825 23095. There is a path all the way that never strays far from the eastern edge of the ridge (5hrs 30mins).

To descend, head west down the long broad ridge marked A' Mhuc on the OS map. If there is a path down this ridge it is more illusory than real. There are drawbacks to this, but look on the bright side: it gives you plenty of latitude to find a line of your own choosing. Head towards the corner of the trees where the Allt a' Leoid Ghaineamhaich is crossed by a small bridge. The slopes at the bottom are steep and grassy. A track is joined at this point and followed south alongside the burn, which is eventually crossed at a bridge. Continue on the track and take the first left turn, then follow a footpath past the ruined cottage at Dorusduain. A few hundred metres past the cottage another path leads off to the left to a footbridge over the river and rejoins the outward route.

GLEN AFFRIC

ROUTE 35

Mullach na Dheiragain (982m), Sgurr nan Ceathreamhnan (1151m), An Socach (921m)

Pronunciation: *Moonluch nuh Yerrigan;*
Skoor nern Kerravnun; Un Sorcoch
Translation: *Summit of the Kestrel;*
Peak of the Quarters (land shares); The Snout

Distance:	46km (20km from Alltbeithe plus 13km each way on the rough track to and from Alltbeithe)
Ascent:	1570m
Time:	7hrs from Alltbeithe; walking into Alltbeithe from Glen Affric car park takes about 3hrs (about 1hr 10mins by bike)
Difficulty:	this is a serious route with no easy lines of escape; a lot of height has to be regained to get back from the furthest Munro
Maps:	OS sheet 25; Explorer maps 414 and 415; Harvey's Superwalker map Kintail; Area Map 9
Parking:	cars can only be taken as far the car park at the west end of Loch Beinn a' Mheadhoin
Start:	track to Glen Affric YH; from there footpath behind the hostel
Hostel:	YHA Glen Affric and Cannich; independent Cannich. (If you are staying at Glen Affric hostel you will need to take a sheet sleeping bag and all your own food. Mattresses/blankets are provided. There is no phone but bookings can be made in advance through other hostels. A few beds are available for walkers who just turn up. There is a warden living in through the summer months. All rubbish must be carried out.)
B&B/hotel:	Cannich
Camping:	Cannich
Access:	National Trust for Scotland, tel: 01599 511231 (for Ceathreamhnan and An Socach); Inverinate Estate, tel: 01599 530055 or 01599 511250 (for Mullach na Dheiragain)

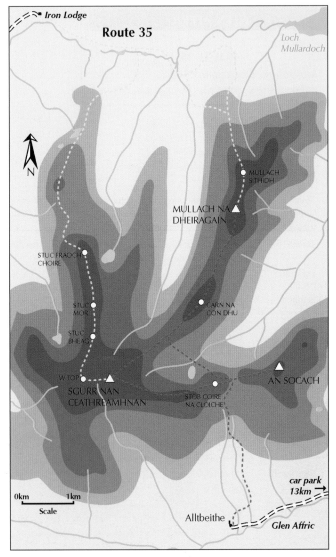

This group of hills is one of the most remote in Scotland. Although they can be accessed from a number of directions, the approaches are all long and most parties attempting them will spend at least one night camping at Iron Lodge in Strath Duilleach, or staying at Glen Affric Youth Hostel at Allltbeithe.

It is quite possible to cycle in from Cannich after breakfast, do this round of hills and be back in Cannich for an early tea (I have done it myself), but these are serious hills on account of their remoteness, the wildness of the terrain and also the fact that you have to climb out from the farthest Munro, regaining a lot of lost height. Some parties, perhaps less than fully fit, have been known to take 12hrs to complete the three hills from Alltbeithe.

The approach along Glen Affric is highly to be recommended as this is surely one of the loveliest of Scottish glens. A series of beautiful lochs fringed with an ancient Scots pine forest with some fine mountain scenery as a backdrop make this approach an absolute delight.

From the car park at the west end of Loch Beinn a' Mheadhoin the track to Alltbeithe can be cycled all the way, though it is very rough in places and occasionally

Sgurr nan Ceathreamhnan from An Socach

Sgurr nan Ceathreamhnan from summit of Beinn Fhada

quite steep. A path leads up behind the hostel and follows the Allt na Faing onto a rough col on the main ridge: the far side of the col is barred by steep cliffs, so head west uphill along the ridge for a short distance before plunging steeply to the northwest on a diagonal line down the hillside. If you have found the right line it is not too hard. Head across the rough, wild terrain of this very remote corrie towards the lowest point on the ridge between Sgurr nan Ceathreamhnan and its neighbour, unnamed on the 1:50,000 OS map, Point 967. Once this col has been reached the ridge offers easier progress for a while, but the summit of Point 967 is littered with large boulders and scree which require some careful footwork. Drop quite steeply down the far side of this top. From here the broad ridge continues more easily to the distant **Mullach na Dheiragain**. There is a superb panorama of mountain views from the modest cairn on the summit at 08044 25907 (3hrs 20mins).

The entire ridge now has to be traversed again in the reverse direction to reach **Sgurr nan Ceathreamhnan**. For the final rise to the summit it becomes quite narrow and rocky, but there are no difficult sections. There is a more substantial cairn here at 05704 22836 and the views are if anything even better than on Dheiragain (5hrs).

The ridge to the east snakes away from the highest point of Ceathreamhnan, rising and falling over two or three minor tops. The terrain is once again rough and wild, but the line is not hard to follow. Continue beyond the col you first crossed, then pass over another small top to reach the last climb of the day up **An Socach**'s western flanks. Many people seem to climb this hill on its own, but it is only 1km from the col and requires very little extra gain in height. The summit cairn is at 08819 22975 (6hrs 10mins).

Return to the col and follow the path back to Alltbeithe.

If An Socach is climbed as a separate excursion it can either be approached from the col as described here or, starting from above the ruin some 3km to the east of Alltbeithe, along its curving southeast ridge. From this same starting point a path leads up to a col to the northeast of the summit, and this can also be used as an ascent/descent route.

ROUTE 36

Mam Sodhail (1181m),

Carn Eige (1183m),

Beinn Fhionnlaidh (1005m)

Pronunciation: *Maam Sowell; Karn Ayr; Bine Ee-yoonly*
Translation: *Breast-shaped Hill of the Barn; File Cairn; Finlay's Mountain*

Distance:	27km
Ascent:	1940m
Time:	9hrs 35mins
Difficulty:	this is another serious route with no easy lines of escape; a lot of height has to be regained to get back from the furthest Munro
Maps:	OS sheet 25; Explorer maps 414 and 415; Area Map 9
Parking:	car park at the west end of Loch Beinn a' Mheadhoin
Start:	along private track to Affric Lodge
Hostel:	YHA Cannich; independent Cannich
B&B/hotel:	Cannich
Camping:	Cannich
Access:	Loch Affric Estate, tel: 01456 415350

Some hills yield with relative ease; others fight tooth and nail to resist the Munroist's advance. The three hills in this group lie deep in the mountain wilderness between Loch Mullardoch and Loch Affric, far from any roads, and are prized above many others on the Munro-bagger's list.

All three of these hills can be tackled from Iron Lodge to the west, but this approach is just as long and has little to commend it over the more usual approach described here from Glen Affric, which enables most of the route to be done in a circuit. Either way it is a good route to get under your belt. There are various permutations of the walk from Glen Affric, but whichever one you chose makes for a long and tough day out. Apart from the sheer distance involved, the ridge to Beinn Fhionnlaidh has to be reversed once you have climbed this distant hill and a lot of height has to be regained in doing so.

One approach to this walk follows a fairly clear stalker's path up the valley of the Allt Coire Leachavie. This starts some 4km past Affric Lodge and emerges on the col on the ridge to the southwest of Mam Sodhail's summit. A much finer line aesthetically, and with much more interest, climbs Sgurr na Lapaich and follows this long, steep-sided ridge directly to Mam Sodhail's top, as described here.

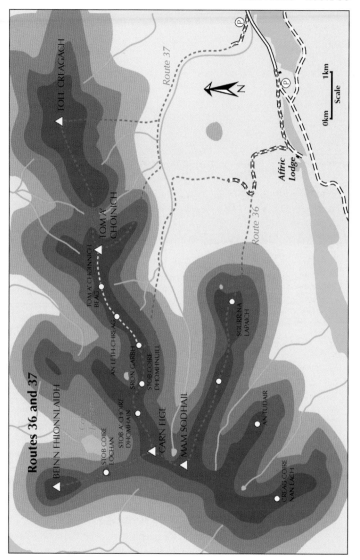

Routes 36 and 37

BEINN FHIONNLAIDH

TOLL CREAGACH

TOM A' CHOINICH

TOM A' CHOINICH BEAG

AN LETH-CHREAG

SRON GARBH

STOB COIRE DHOMHNUILL

STOB COIRE LOCHAN

STOB A' CHOIRE DHOMHAIN

CARN EIGE

MAM SODHAIL

SGURR NA LAPAICH

AN TUDAIR

CREAG COIRE NAN EACH

Affric Lodge

Route 37

Route 36

N

Scale

0km   1km

The east ridge of Carn Eige

From the car park, follow the private track to Affric Lodge and turn right onto a lesser-used track just before the buildings are reached. This track heads straight up the hillside for 1km then veers to the left (west) for another kilometre. At the point where it doubles back on itself, leave it for a faint path towards the east ridge of Sgurr na Lapaich. Cross some rather wet moorland until a grassy ramp leads up steeply to the upper part of the ridge. From here climb more easily up the crest of the ridge to the summit. Pass the first small cairn to reach a larger cairn marking the top. Both in terms of its height, its separation from other Munros and the grandeur of the surrounding scenery, it is hard to understand why this hill doesn't have Munro status. Continue across the stony summit onto the long, fine ridge leading to **Mam Sodhail**. A couple of minor tops are crossed before the final climb to the summit, and there are fine views on either side to the parallel ridges that lead to Ciste Dhubh and Carn Eige respectively. The summit cairn is a huge circular one at 11970 25338 (3hrs 50mins).

Descend quite steeply to a col on the north side of the hill, beneath Carn Eige, then climb up from the col to **Carn Eige**'s top (a little effort and time can be saved by traversing round to the left (west) of Carn Eige's summit from the col, as this hill has to be climbed again later). Drop quite steeply over scree and rocks down the north-northwest ridge of Carn Eige, passing the minor top, Point 917, and then climb more easily to **Beinn Fhionnlaidh**'s summit cairn at 11562 28267 (5hrs 20mins).

There is running water to the east of the Bealach Beag (the col at 832m), which may be appreciated in hot weather. Retrace your steps to the trig point and cairn on the summit of **Carn Eige** at 12356 26186 (6hrs 30mins).

By far the best descent from here is down Carn Eige's fine east ridge. Drop down to a col to the east of the summit, then climb the rounded shoulder of Point 1147. Just beyond this top go southeast around the head of Loch a' Choire Dhomhain. The ridge here is quite narrow and sharp at first and offers wonderful views over the loch and its superb northeastern corrie. A big pinnacle is passed on its right, and the path then weaves its way through more shattered pinnacles. Beyond Point 1131 the ridge continues, dropping sharply to a col before eventually leading on to Tom a' Choinnich. (This hill, along with Toll Creagach, could conceivably be included in your day's itinerary, but only if you are very fit.)

Just before Point 1131 is reached, descend a little spur to the southeast. When the nose of this is reached a path leads back northwest, dropping easily down the steep headwall of the corrie. Cross the floor of the corrie to the east and pick up the top of a stalker's path on its far side. Once again this leads steeply but easily down, this time to the Abhainn Gleann nam Fiadh, which is followed for over 1km to a crossing. The Landrover track crosses this river at a ford at 17286 25790, almost 1km to the west of the path marked on the OS map. This track can be followed on the south side of the river until it heads due south across the moorland, eventually passing the point where you started the morning's ascent. Continue along the track back to the car park.

ROUTE 37

Tom a' Choinich (1112m),

Toll Creagach (1053m)

Pronunciation: *Tom uh Hornich; Toll Kirrikuch*
Translation: *Hill of the Moss; Rocky Hollow*

Distance:	16km
Ascent:	1080m
Time:	5hrs 15mins
Maps:	OS sheet 25; Explorer map 415; Area Map 9
Parking:	roadside parking area just before the bridge over the Abhainn Gleann nam Fiadh
Start:	along private track that starts opposite parking area
Hostel:	YHA Cannich; independent Cannich
B&B/hotel:	Cannich
Camping:	Cannich
Access:	Corrielair Estate, tel: 01738 828573

These two hills lie at the eastern end of the huge chain of mighty hills that stretch along the north side of Glen Affric. They are the most easily accessed of the Munros hereabouts and are also the most easily climbed.

Whilst these hills could be tagged on to the end of a very long excursion over Mam Sodhail, Beinn Fhionnlaidh and Carn Eige, most mortals will prefer to climb them on their own. They are contrasting hills – the round, bald dome of Toll Creagach having little in common with Tom a' Choinich's sharp rocky ridges – but they make a good circuit together, and offer a gentler day out than some of their more challenging neighbours.

From the parking area, follow a track which stays close to the Abhainn Gleann nam Fiadh. After 3½km the track

dwindles to a path, but continues alongside the river deep into the Gleann nam Fiadh. Follow this as far as the Allt Toll Easa, the small burn coming off Tom a' Choinich's east face, and just beyond the burn take to the hillside up a path that heads directly up the curving southeast ridge of **Tom a' Choinich**. The summit cairn is at 16407 27324 (2hrs 55mins).

Descend to the east down a steep little ridge to the Bealach Toll Easa at 872m. From here the character of the terrain changes as you cross the minor top, Point 951, and continue in an east-northeasterly direction. The walking now is over gentle grassy slopes sprinkled with quartzite scree up the rounded dome of **Toll Creagach**. There are two cairns and a trig point on top, 19425 28263 (4hrs).

From the summit drop due south over a series of long stony terraces. Descend through long grass lower down, avoiding the small crags of Beinn Eun by staying to their west. This brings you back to the footpath which is followed down to the road.

Tom a' Choinich across the Abhainn Gleann nam Fiadh

STRATHFARRAR/MULLARDOCH

ROUTE 38

An Socach (Glen Elchaig) (1069m)

Pronunciation: *Un Sorcoch*
Translation: *the Pig's Snout*

Distance:	43km (of which 25km can be cycled)
Ascent:	1090m
Time:	7hrs 25mins if using a bike to Iron Lodge – add about 4hrs if walking all the way
Maps:	OS sheet 25; Explorer maps 429 and 414; Area Map 10
Parking:	parking area just west of Killilan
Start:	along estate road through Killilan
Hostel:	YHA Ratagan
B&B/hotel:	A87 Kyle to Inverinate
Camping:	Morvich in Strath Croe
Access:	Inverinate Estate, tel: 01599 530055 or 01599 511250

Of the three Munros called An Socach this is certainly the most difficult to access. In fact it is one of the most remote Munros in Scotland. It forms part of the huge chain of high peaks between Glen Strathfarrar and Glen Cannich and can be reached from either of these glens, but with no less difficulty than the route described here.

The approach to An Socach along Glen Elchaig makes use of the long estate track from Killilan to Iron Lodge. Cars cannot be taken along this track, but it can be cycled for some 13km. For the most part it is a good track, tarmacked for the first few kilometres and quite easy going for the rest. Bikes should be left just above Iron Lodge. From

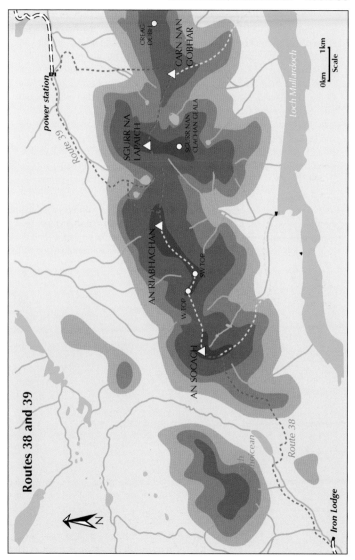

Routes 38 and 39

A fit party might wish to include An Socach with An Riabhachan and Sgurr na Lapaich as described in Route 39, but it would add a lot of time to an already long day, and the time limits imposed by the estate in Glen Strathfarrar may make this quite impossible. One pleasant approach might be to take a boat from the eastern end of Loch Mullardoch to the outflow of the Allt Coire a' Mhaim, then to climb the southern ridge of the mountain, to the west of Coire Mhaim, and continue around the circuit of other hills to finish on Creag Dubh, before returning to the road-end by the Mullardoch Hotel. One problem with this, however, is the availability of a boat. At present there is one boat operating a service on Loch Mullardoch, but it may not be available when you want it.

Coire Mhaim from the summit of An Socach (Glen Elchaig)

here continue on the path to Loch Mhoicean, climbing quite steeply at first up a deeply cut valley. Just before the loch is reached, cut across a wet meadow and cross the little burn, the Doire Gairbhe. Continue round the

edge of the loch for a short distance, then climb up towards the col between Cairn na Breabaig and Meall Shuas. It is best to cross the small burn that flows down from this col before you get too high, otherwise you have to cross peat hags at the top. Continue uphill through quite deep grass to the top of the ridge just north of Meall Shuas. There are a few more peaty runnels and bluffs higher up, but these are easy to avoid.

The going is easier once the stony ridge is gained. Follow it round to the foot of **An Socach**. Then climb quite steeply straight up the grassy slope to the summit ridge. Follow the ridge round to the prominent trig point at 10052 33271, where there are good views of An Riabhachan to the northeast and also to the southeast looking out over the dramatic lochan-strewn bowl of Coire Mhaim (4hrs 55mins using a bike to Iron Lodge; add about 2hrs if walking all the way).

Return by the route of ascent. Those who cycled to Iron Lodge will find the return cycle ride particularly enjoyable.

ROUTE 39

An Riabhachan (1129m),

Sgurr na Lapaich (1150m),

Carn nan Gobhar (992m)

Pronunciation: *Un Reeavochan;*
Skoor na Lapeech; Karn nern Go-er
Translation: *the Grey (or Speckled) One;*
Peak of the Bog; Hill of Goats

There is a notable absence of roads in the 1600km² covered by Sheet 25 of the OS Landranger series. This trio of giants sits squarely in the centre of this remote mountain stronghold and makes an excellent outing for the fit hillwalker.

Distance:	17km
Ascent:	1510m
Time:	6hrs 40mins
Maps:	OS sheet 25; Explorer map 430; Area Map 10
Parking:	by power station at the far end of public road in Glen Strathfarrar GR: 18339 38104
Start:	follow the track that starts above the power station into Gleann Innis an Loichel
Hostel:	YHA Cannich; independent Cannich
B&B/hotel:	Cannich; Struy
Camping:	Cannich
Access:	see box

These big, remote hills lie to the north of Loch Mullardoch and require rather more careful planning than most. They can be approached via a long walk along the northern banks of Loch Mullardoch or, if a boatman can be found, by taking a boat to the mouth of the Allt Socrach and walking from there, perhaps taking in also the western Munro of this complex group – An Socach (see Route 38). A slightly shorter outing can be had from Glen Strathfarrar, as described here, but this involves a time restriction, with the need to get back to the far end of the glen before the gate is locked at 6.00pm. In fact there should be plenty of time to do this unless you are very slow, in which case this group of hills may have to be tackled in two outings.

An Riabhachan from the summit of An Socach

Access

Access to Glen Strathfarrar by car is restricted to certain hours. From the end of March to the end of October access is allowed between the hours of 9.00am and 6.00pm on Mondays, Wednesdays, Thursdays, Fridays and Saturdays. On Sundays access is allowed between 1.00pm and 6.00pm. The gate is kept locked on Sunday mornings and all day on Tuesdays. For access simply ring the doorbell at the gatekeeper's cottage, but do not expect to be allowed in or out if you turn up outside the designated times. If you are on foot or bike there are no restrictions on access to the glen at any time, although you should check for restrictions to the hills during the stalking season as this is a key area for stalking. Braulen Estate, tel: 01463 761235; Gatekeeper, tel: 01463 761260

Drive to the very far end of the glen, crossing over both dams at the eastern end of Loch Monar. Vehicles should be left at the small power station where this road ends. From here, walk along the track that continues on the north side of Gleann Innis an Loichel. Pass a small dam and continue along the track for nearly 2km before crossing the river. Follow the obvious all-terrain-vehicle track that zigzags up a bulge in the hillside to the west of the Allt an Eas Bhain Mhoir. Once in the corrie there is a choice of routes. The quickest is to cross the little burn that flows from Loch Beag and climb steeply onto the northern ridge of An Riabhachan – Meall Garbh – avoiding rocks where possible, then continue up the ridge to the east top. The alternative is to go deep into the corrie between the two lochs, passing quite high above the southern end of Loch Mor through a boulder field to reach a steep ramp at the head of the corrie. Climb this ramp to the col, then follow the ridge above the Creagan Toll an Lochain. Once the top is reached, the summit ridge is broad and grassy. Pass the cairn at the eastern top – GR 13825 34750 – to reach **An Riabhachan**'s main summit cairn at 13367 34473 (3hrs 20mins).

Retrace your steps and drop down to the col at 15255 34475, then climb quite steeply up the southwest

Loch Mullardoch in distance from the summit of Sgurr na Lapaich

ridge of **Sgurr na Lapaich**, which becomes increasingly stony, to the trig point and stone enclosure at 16092 35115 (4hrs 50mins).

At this point the scenery changes, for the east ridge of Sgurr na Lapaich is rocky and littered with boulders. A rib of inclined rock drops steeply to the east. A fairly obvious path drops through the boulders to the south of this rib, however, providing a steep but easy descent to the col below Carn nan Gobhar. This path goes to the right (south) of a steep little valley to reach the col at 17135 34695. Continue more easily up to the summit cairn of **Carn nan Gobhar** at 18193 34350 (5hrs 40mins). The smaller cairn reached first is fractionally higher than the larger one a few hundred metres further on.

To descend, begin by heading northeast to avoid the steepest ground, then work back towards the north, dropping into the very rough terrain of the open corrie. Cross the Allt Garbh-choire without difficulty and pass either side of Point 438. If you pass to the left of this point, you are now faced by a large section of deer fencing enclosing a wooded part of the hillside; the fence is there to encourage regeneration of the trees. Skirt around this to the right to find an easier way back down to the power station.

ROUTE 40

Sgurr na Ruaidhe (993m),

Carn nan Gobhar (992m),

Sgurr a' Choire Ghlais (1083m),

Sgurr Fhuar-thuill (1049m)

Pronunciation: *Skoor na Roy-yer; Karn nern Go-er;
Skoor uh Hother Glash; Skoor Ooer Hillyer*
Translation: *Red Peak; Hill of Goats;
Peak of the Grey-green Corrie; Peak of the Cold Hollow*

Distance:	24km (6km of which can be cycled)
Ascent:	1550m
Time:	6hrs 30mins (plus time for walking/cycling back along the road)
Maps:	OS sheet 25; Explorer map 430; Area Map 10
Parking:	roadside at junction of track near the Allt Coire Mhuillidh
Start:	follow the rough track uphill
Hostel:	YHA Cannich; independent, Cannich
B&B/hotel:	Cannich; Struy
Camping:	Cannich
Access:	see Route 39 for access restrictions to Glen Strathfarrar. Scottish Natural Heritage, tel: 01463 723132 or 01463 761235; Gatekeeper, tel: 01463 761260

Glen Strathfarrar is surely one of Scotland's most enchanting glens, and these four hills on its northern side offer an excellent circuit over mixed but fairly easy terrain in a wonderful setting. Although the group forms a natural circuit, the start and finish points are several kilometres apart; if a bike can be left near the road where the walk ends, this will enable you to avoid a long road walk at the end of the day.

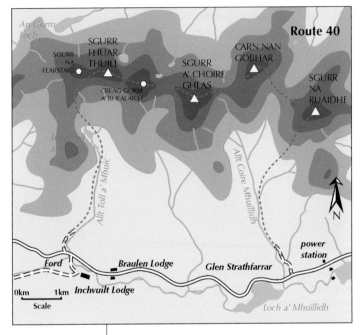

Start where a track joins the road between Loch Beannacharan and Loch a' Mhuillidh and follow this uphill until it turns into a footpath. The path follows the Allt Coire Mhuillidh for a couple of kilometres until it crosses a burn coming off the south of **Sgurr na Ruaidhe**, then it turns right and climbs the grassy southwest ridge of the hill in a direct line up to the summit. Just before the top there is a very slight dip before the cairned summit is reached at 28900 42602 (2hrs 40mins).

Descend west-northwest down a broad grassy ridge to a col, then climb the ridge on the other side almost due north to a plateau at its top, then curve around the top of **Carn nan Gobhar**'s southeastern corrie before the short climb to its summit. The top of this hill is covered in mossy boulders. The summit cairn is to the right of the summit ridge at 27311 43880 (3hrs 25mins).

From the southern end of the bouldery summit ridge, head southwest down a wide mossy ridge, then veer to the west when the ridge begins to narrow, until you reach another col. Climb the ridge on its far side, which is narrower and steeper than before, until the stony summit of **Sgurr a' Choire Ghlais** is reached. There are two cairns and a trig point on top: the cairn to the right (north) is the higher at 25843 43048 (4hrs 15mins).

Drop down over the jumble of boulders to the northwest, where the ridge narrows and easier ground is reached. Follow it for just over 1km to the foot of Creag Ghorm a' Bhealaich, then climb the sharp ridge quite steeply to a small cairn perched on its summit crest overlooking Coire na Sguille at 24477 43497. From here there is a gentle descent to the west before the final easy climb up **Sgurr Fhuar-thuill** to a prominent cairn at 23581 43750 (5hrs 10mins).

The descent follows a good stalker's path which starts just to the west of the next col at 23025 43684. A small cairn marks the start of the path which clings to the side of Sgurr na Fearstaig's south ridge, then passes to the east of the dark waters of Loch Toll a' Mhuic. From the loch the path follows the Allt Toll a' Mhuic and in 3km brings you back to the road a short distance above the stalker's cottage at Inchvuilt.

Loch Toll a' Mhuic from Sgurr Fhuar-thuill

MONAR

ROUTE 41

Bidein a' Choire
Sheasgaich (945m), Lurg Mhor (986m)

Pronunciation: Beedyan uh Korrer Heskeech; Loorug Voar
Translation: Peak of the Corrie of the Farrow Cattle; Big Shin

Distance:	30km (of which 10km could be cycled)
Ascent:	1800m (or 1982m returning by the outward route)
Time:	9hrs 55mins (about 1hr less if using a bike on estate track)
Difficulty:	this is a long, serious route with no easy lines of escape; height has to be regained to get back from the furthest Munro
Maps:	OS sheet 25; Explorer map 429; Area Map 10
Parking:	Forest Enterprise car park in Craig, almost opposite start
Start:	follow the private track across railway line (see 'Access' below)
Hostel:	independent Craig
B&B/hotel:	Lochcarron; Strathcarron; Achnasheen
Camping:	Lochcarron
Access:	West Monar, tel: 01463 761267. Walkers should satisfy themselves that they have the necessary permission from Network Rail to use the railway crossing.

The huge tract of uninhabited wilderness between Glen Carron and Glen Shiel contains some of the most remote and wild Munros in Scotland. Whilst some hills on the fringes of this great mountain massif can be accessed fairly easily, others like Bidean a' Choire Sheasgaich and Lurg Mhor really have to be worked for. In view of their distance from the road and the rough nature of the terrain to be covered, as well as the superb mountain scenery they lie in, it is well worth waiting for a good day before you tackle this pair.

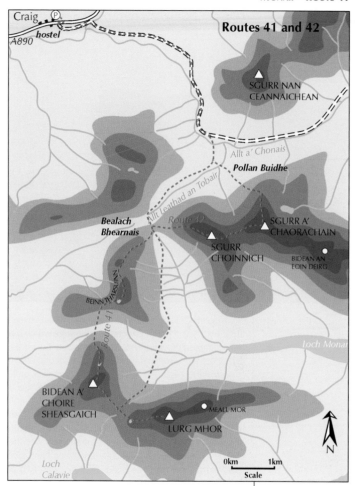

Routes 41 and 42

Cross the railway line at the crossing in Craig and follow this track in a huge arc as it runs alongside the Allt a' Chonais. Ignore a couple of turnings to your right and continue climbing into the upper valley. There used to be three crossings of the river. Two of these consist of a pair

Bidein a' Choire Sheasgaich from Beinn Tharsuinn

of wires stretched between posts; the other one, between these two, was a perilous wooden footbridge which has now collapsed (hopefully not with anyone on it). Pass the first of the wire crossings and cross at the second one. It is possible to cycle this far, although the track is quite steep in places and one of the gates on the track seems to have been designed to exclude bikes.

Once you are across the river, a stalker's path leads up for nearly 3km to the Bealach Bhearnais. The north-east nose of Beinn Tharsuinn now confronts you, and this can be climbed without difficulty on its left-hand side (northeast), away from the rocks. Continue past two or three minor tops to the stony summit at 05522 43338, where a small cairn marks the top. Descend south to reach a lochan, then pass this and drop for a short distance steeply down over rocks to the west to reach a grassy col. A diagonal traverse down from this col to the southwest leads to another col, which lies beneath the steep north face of Bidean a' Choire Sheasgaich. Follow the line of an old stone wall across this col and continue on the same line on the other side.

The route up the steep rocky face that now confronts you is not obvious from below, but there is a faint path leading up through the crags, and if you find and follow this path all obstacles are easily turned. It would be prudent to keep to this path as there is a lot of dangerous ground on this side of the mountain. About halfway up on the left, the path finds a grassy ramp up a rift in the face that is visible from afar. Once you reach this ramp the route is straightforward and the path is clear. The ramp emerges at a dark lochan. If you are returning this way look out for the small cairn that marks the start of the descent. Continue climbing the ridge over a series of stony in-cut shelves formed by inclined strata. Pass another lochan before the final ridge, sharper and steeper than before, rises to **Bidean a' Choire Sheasgaich**'s modest summit cairn at 04911 41255 (5hrs).

Descend easily to the southeast, cross a broad col and climb to the remote summit of **Lurg Mhor** at 06478 40439 (5hrs 55mins).

Stalking in these hills seems to take place during a shorter period than in many other areas, but during this time it would be advisable to return by the outward route, taking great care on the north face of Sheasgaich. Although this way back involves more vertical ascent it is much drier than the alternative, which is to descend steeply from the col between Sheasgaich and Lurg Mhor and then head across rough peat moorland around the end of the south east ridge of Beinn Tharsuinn. A long haul up the head of this desolate corrie brings you back to the Bealach Bhearnais. Return from here via the outward route.

ROUTE 42

Sgurr Choinnich (999m),

Sgurr a' Chaorachain (1053m)

Pronunciation: *Skoor Chorneech; Skoor uh Hoo-a-rahen*
Translation: *Mossy Peak; Peak of the Rowan Berries*

Distance:	22km (of which 10km could be cycled)
Ascent:	1180m
Time:	6hrs 30mins (about 1hr less if a bike is used)
Maps:	OS sheet 25; Explorer map 429; Area Map 10
Parking:	Forest Enterprise car park at Craig
Start:	cross railway line opposite car park (see 'Access' below) and follow estate track
Hostel:	independent Craig
B&B/hotel:	Lochcarron; Strathcarron; Achnasheen
Camping:	Lochcarron
Access:	Achnashellach Estate, tel: 01520 766266. Walkers should satisfy themselves that they have the necessary permission from Network Rail to use the railway crossing.

The River Meig and the upper reaches of the Allt a' Chonais share a long, deeply incised, rather secretive high valley that gives access to a number of Munros. The two hills at the southwestern end of this valley give a pleasant circular walk.

From the car park at Craig, go up to Pollan Buidhe as for the previous route. Cross the second of the two-wire bridges over the Allt a' Chonais and follow the path up to the Bealach Bhearnais. The west ridge of **Sgurr Choinnich** starts here. Climb up through several tiers of rocks, staying on the crest of the ridge. There is a path that winds up through the rocks and it is nowhere difficult. After a few

false summits the hard work is done and the ridge becomes narrow, almost sharp, and levels off. Continue to the very small summit cairn at 07629 44616 (3hrs 45mins; about 25mins less if using a bike to Pollan Buidhe).

To reach Sgurr a' Chaorachain, continue along the ridge, which stays fairly level for a couple of hundred metres, then at 07837 44469 the direction changes to west-northwest and a gravelly descent path takes you down to a col. This path avoids the fairly steep, jumbled rocks above the northern crags, staying well to the south of them, then returns to the edge at the col. It is possible to make a descent to the valley from this col, staying to

Sgurr a' Chaorachain from Sgurr Choinnich

the right of the burn, but I would not recommend it unless you have a pressing reason to abandon the route. The descent from here is very steep at times and the best line down is not always obvious from above, especially in poor visibility. Instead, continue the short distance up to the summit of **Sgurr a' Chaorachain**, which boasts a very substantial cairn (GR 08755 44727) compared to that of its neighbour – such is the equity of life (4hrs 25mins).

The descent from here is quite straightforward. Head north along the rounded, mossy north ridge of Sgurr a' Chaorachain, dropping down until it briefly levels off. At about 08699 45370 turn northwest and drop steeply down the grassy flanks of the ridge to easier ground below. Cross the Allt Leathad an Tobair (you may need to follow this downstream for some way to find a crossing – not because of the size of the burn but because access to it is made difficult by a very steep bank on its southern side). Once across, the path is rejoined a short distance above the two-wire bridge. From here, return by the outward route. A continuation to Maoile Lundaith is quite possible from Sgurr a' Chaorachain by passing to the north of the Lochan Gaineamhach to reach the Drochaid Mhuilich, but this would make for a very long day indeed.

Sgurr a' Chaorachain from Moruisg

ROUTE 43

Maoile Lunndaidh (1007m)

Pronunciation: *Merle Lon-dye*
Translation: *Bald Hill of the Wet Place*

Distance:	28km (of which 17km can be cycled)
Ascent:	1000m
Time:	8hrs (2hrs less if a bike is used on the estate track)
Maps:	OS sheet 25; Explorer maps 429 and 430; Area Map 10
Parking:	Forest Enterprise car park at Craig, opposite railway crossing
Start:	follow estate track across railway line (see 'Access' below)
Hostel:	independent Craig
B&B/hotel:	Lochcarron; Strathcarron; Achnasheen
Camping:	Lochcarron
Access:	Glencarron and Glenuig, tel: 01520 766275. Walkers should satisfy themselves that they have the necessary permission from Network Rail to use the railway crossing.

There is a good view of Maoile Lunndaidh from Sgurr nan Ceannaichean. It stands like a great lump at the head of the valley, split in the centre by a deep fissure – the Fuar-tholl Mor. Although the hill is a long way from the road, access to it is fairly straightforward via the Landrover track to Glenuaig Lodge at the foot of the hill.

Walk or cycle as for the previous two routes up the estate track to Pollan Buidhe and continue on this track to Glenuaig Lodge. After heavy rainfall the crossing of the infant River Meig might be easier a little further back, before you reach the lodge. Head southeast over peaty ground to the foot of the north ridge of Carn nam Fiaclan and climb the heathery slope steeply, passing through a steep boulder field higher up, which is interspersed with blaeberry and heather. The slope is fairly relentless, but

181

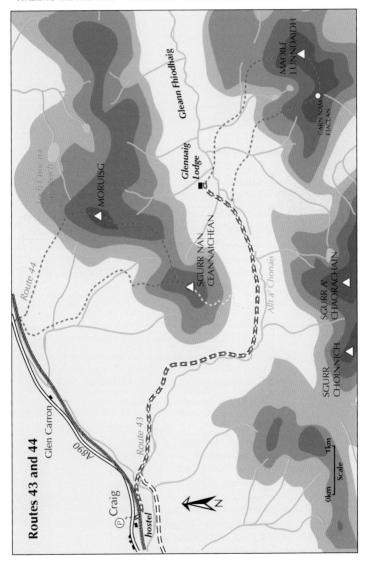

Routes 43 and 44

MAOILE LUNNDAIDH

CARN NAM FIACLAN

Gleann Fhiodhaig

Glenuaig Lodge

MORUISG

Loch Cnoc na Feannaiche

Route 44

SGURR NAN CLANNAICHEAN

Allt a' Chonais

SGURR A' CHAORACHAIN

SGURR CHOINNICH

Route 43

Glen Carron

A890

Route 43

Craig

P

hostel

N

1km

Scale

0km

some interest is provided by glimpses into the rocky corrie – Fuar-tholl Mor – to the left. Pass the summit cairn of Carn nam Fiaclan and go round the head of the corrie to a small cairn that sits on a little rounded lump between the two corries (one to the northwest and one to the southeast). The view across the magnificent U-shaped corrie of Toll a' Choin to Loch Monar is the redeeming feature of what is otherwise a rather uninspiring Munro. The summit cairn of **Maoile Lunndaidh** is clearly visible about ¾km further on, sitting atop another (rather larger) rounded lump at GR 13522 45855. In poor visibility it could make a difficult target on this featureless plateau (4hrs 45mins; less if a bike is used on the estate track).

To descend, complete the circuit by dropping north over stony ground towards the broad col between Maoile Lunndaidh and Creag Dhubh Mhor. As you approach the col, veer left down a valley, cross the burn and head back across the wet, peaty ground of the valley floor to Glenuaig Lodge and the track.

Maoile Lunndaidh from Sgurr nan Ceannaichean

183

ROUTE 44

Moruisg (928m),

Sgurr nan Ceannaichean (915m)

Pronunciation: *Moorishk; Skoor nern Kyanichan*
Translation: *Big Water; Peak of the Merchants*

Distance:	11km
Ascent:	960m
Time:	5hrs 15mins
Maps:	OS sheet 25; Explorer map 429; Area Map 10
Parking:	lay-by on A890 1½km west of Loch Sgamhain
Start:	from lay-by follow path across river and under railway, then onto open hillside
Hostel:	independent Craig
B&B/hotel:	Lochcarron; Strathcarron; Achnasheen
Camping:	Lochcarron
Access:	Glencarron and Glenuig, tel: 01520 766275

Between Glen Carron and Gleann Fhiodhaig a line of hills sit shoulder to shoulder, forming a continuous broad ridgeline above the 750m contour for 9 or 10km. This line reaches its highest eminence at its western end, where Moruisg and Sgurr nan Ceannaichean rise above the rest of the group. These hills can be climbed by way of a stalker's path from the south. The more usual approach – and perhaps the better route as it forms a circuit – is from Glen Carron, as described here, starting from the A890 about 1½km west of Loch Sgamhain.

From the lay-by follow the path across the river and under the railway line. From here, head southeast across wet ground, rising straight up the grassy hillside. The middle section is steep, but without any real difficulty. Towards the top the angle is easier and for the last few metres the grass gives way to stones. There are two cairns

Sgurr na Ceannaichean from Moruisg

on **Moruisg**'s roughly level summit ridge: the larger one, reached first at 10293 50191, is in fact a little lower than the second one, about 200m to the southwest at 10117 49931. In clear weather there are good views of Torridon, Fisherfield and the fairytale hills of Damph and the Coulin Forest (2hrs 25mins).

Drop down pleasant mossy slopes around the head of Coire Toll nam Bian, past Point 854. The descent then passes through some slabby rocks to a col beneath Ceannaichean. From the col climb sharply up to the west to join **Ceannaichean**'s north ridge and then continue on to its summit dome. This top also has fine views, particularly of the Monar Forest hills. The cairn is at 08683 48133 (3hrs 40mins).

The descent follows the north ridge straight down – with a little turn to the left at 08847 48529 to avoid tumbling down a gully into the corrie and another small detour at 08697 49307 to avoid a little rash of crags, which can be turned on the left. Below the crags head northeast to cross the Alltan na Feola, then join the stalker's path on its north side just before this reaches a gate. Stay on the path alongside this pretty tree-lined burn and then go across some wet grassland to arrive back at the rail and river crossing.

COULIN

ROUTE 45

Maol Chean-dearg (933m)

Pronunciation: *Merle Hyaan Jerrack*
Translation: *the Bald Red Head*

Start at Coulags and follow a well-constructed path along the Fionn-abhainn, crossing over to its west bank after 2km. About 1km beyond the bridge pass by a substantial and well-maintained bothy, then after

Distance:	16km
Ascent:	900m
Time:	5hrs 30mins
Maps:	OS sheet 25; Explorer map 429; Area Map 10
Parking:	lay-by close to start of path where the A890 crosses the Fionn Abhainn at Coulags
Start:	through gate just east of river to start of footpath
Hostel:	independent Craig
B&B/hotel:	Lochcarron; Strathcarron
Camping:	Lochcarron
Access:	Ben Damph Estate, tel: 01445 791252

The hills to the north of the River Carron make a fine prospect from distant vantage points and they lose none of their appeal when viewed from closer quarters. Maol Chean-dearg is a fairly easy peak to 'bag', but gives excellent views over the surrounding tops.

Beinn na h-eaglaise from summit of Maol Chean-dearg

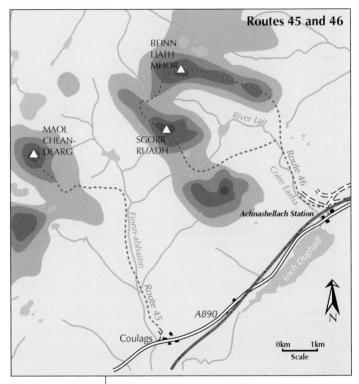

another ½km pass a strange little upright rock – the Clach nan Con-fionn. There are many landscape features in the Highlands associated with folk tales and this rock is the place where the mythical Celtic folk hero Fionn MacCumhail, the father of Ossian, was supposed to have tethered his hunting dogs.

Half a kilometre further on, the path divides. Turn left here and climb steadily up to the Bealach a' Choire Garbh, still on a substantial path, where you are greeted by the splendid rocky spectacle of An Rùadh Stac. After a pause to admire the architecture of this wonderful structure, turn uphill again and climb steeply up the nose of **Maol Chean-dearg**'s southeastern ridge. At the top of this nose the ridge levels out. Continue over shattered quartzite rocks to a rise, then a slight dip before the foot of the final dome. This is contrastingly composed of sandstone. Climb steeply up awkward blocks of this stone to the large summit cairn at 92409 49897. You are rewarded by more fine views over the strange rock landscape of Damph and Coulin. The little Beinn na-h-Eaglaise to the northwest is a particularly interesting structure (3hrs 30mins).

Return by the route of ascent.

ROUTE 46

Beinn Liath Mhor (926m),

Sgorr Ruadh (962m)

Pronunciation: *Bine Leeya Voar; Skoor Roy-yer*
Translation: *Big Grey Mountain; Red Peak*

Distance:	17km
Ascent:	1320m
Time:	6hrs 55mins
Maps:	OS sheet 25; Explorer map 429; Area Map 10
Parking:	roadside lay-by at Achnashellach on A890 in Glen Carron
Start:	follow private track that starts by a phone box and cross railway line (see 'Access' below)
Hostel:	independent Craig
B&B/hotel:	Lochcarron; Strathcarron
Camping:	Lochcarron
Access:	Achnashellach Estate, tel: 01520 766266. Walkers should satisfy themselves that they have the necessary permission from Network Rail to use the railway crossing.

Cross the railway line and follow the track through the gate to the right. The track soon meets a forestry road at

This circuit offers one of the finest walks in this part of Scotland. It is full of interest, continually throwing up little problems, and offers a succession of glorious views, particularly across the Coire Lair and northwards to the dramatic Torridon hills.

Beinn Liath Mhor from the east ridge

a sharp bend. Ignore the forestry road and turn sharp left on another track that leads out towards the open hill. After less than 1km turn left again onto a footpath which initially doubles back on the track. This footpath is amusingly signposted 'footpath'. Follow this alongside the river and climb steadily uphill to more open country. After about 2km a cairn marks a division in the path. The path to the left leads across the River Lair after a few metres. This is your return route at the end of the walk. Just a few metres beyond this cairn, another cairn marks another junction of paths. This time the path to the left leads up the valley floor to the col between Liath Mhor and Sgorr Ruadh – a useful escape route if required later in the day. Once again take the path to the right, which leads beneath the nose of Beinn Liath Mhor's east ridge and continues on to Loch Coulin. After ½km, a third cairn at the highpoint of the path marks the start of the steep climb onto the ridge. Go straight uphill until the angle eases and quartzite screes take over from grass and heather. The first top – Beinn Liath Mhor's east top – has a large cairn and offers the first of the day's fine views of Torridon and other hills. Continue along the undulating ridge, mostly on shattered quartzite stones, until you arrive at the main summit cairn of **Beinn Liath Mhor** at 96409 51968 (3hrs 40mins).

Continue westwards over extensive scree, then veer southwest until the rock changes abruptly to an impressive, dipping sandstone pavement. After a short distance this ends in a steep crag at its southwestern end above a small lochan. The easiest way down this crag may not be easy to find in poor visibility. It starts at a very small cairn at 95933 51645 and leads straight down to the lochan without difficulty. (Alternatively, an escape route passes to the east of the crag and leads down to the valley floor.) Pass round the east end of the lochan. The hill now in front of you, which rises to Point 769, now has to be crossed. It is best not to go straight over the top as this leads to crags and difficult ground on the other side. Instead, a faint path leads round to the left, which eventually drops quite steeply down to the next col, beneath

Sgorr Ruadh's northwest ridge and just east of another small loch. Climb from the loch up a grassy ramp to the west to gain the ridge and then follow a path along the ridge, rising quite steeply at times but without further difficulty, through more quartzite scree to the summit cairn at 95918 50508 (5hrs 10mins).

After admiring more fine views from the summit, head east down easy slopes at first, then veer southeast and drop more steeply over awkward boulders and grass, picking the easiest line around small crags until more level ground is reached on the very rough col between Sgorr Ruadh and Fuar Tholl. This huge col is littered with boulders, hillocks, rocks, bogs and lochans. The descent path, which is quite distinct once you find it, leads down from the far side of this col, passing quite close to the impressive north buttress of Fuar Tholl. This path is followed back to the River Lair, which is crossed just before rejoining the outward route. There is not normally a problem crossing the river at this point unless it is in spate. If there is a danger of this, the river can be inspected on the outward route and an alternative descent should then be followed from Loch a' Bhealaich Mhoir, passing close up against the steep flanks of Sgurr Ruadh's southeast nose, then passing to the left (west) of Loch Coire Lair, where an easier crossing may be found.

THE ISLE OF SKYE

THE ISLE OF SKYE: INTRODUCTION

For their sustained grandeur, ruggedness and complexity the Cuillin hills on Skye (Routes 47–54) are quite unlike anything else on the Munroist's round. They are widely regarded as the finest mountains in Britain. Their scale is alpine, and for many people the quality of the mountaineering experience that can be had in this range matches almost anything else in the world. The hillwalker should be aware, however, that the Munros here require a different approach from other Munros in several important respects.

Perhaps the most obvious feature of these hills, which sets them apart from most of the others, is the sheer quantity of exposed rock. Once height is gained in the Cuillins you can search in vain for mossy slopes, grassy cols or almost any sign of vegetation other than the odd patch of lichen. Most of the rock in the Cuillin hills is gabbro, which is a great attraction to climbers on account of the excellent friction it offers. But there are many parts of the ridge where it is dangerously loose and friable, and in places it is cut through by basalt dykes, which can be slippery when wet.

Route-finding on rock is quite a different skill from doing so on grassy hills, and the consequences of being off route can be much more serious. In addition to these qualities the Cuillin hills are made up of steep-sided peaks, narrow and often difficult ridges that require climbing or scrambling skills, and highly complex corries. In poor visibility finding safe routes onto the summits and then off them again can be a tricky business even for experienced climbers. When the weather turns bad things can quickly become serious.

To make matters worse the navigator cannot rely on the usual tools of his trade. The rock here is highly magnetic in many places, which renders compass readings unreliable, and maps are difficult to interpret in this sort of landscape. The 1:50,000 maps lack sufficient detail and the 1:25,000 maps have so many close contours that they can be very hard to read. The only map I would recommend is the Harvey's Superwalker, which includes a detailed map of the whole ridge at a scale of 1:12,500.

These remarks are not intended to put you off, but simply to introduce a note of caution. If you are not comfortable with scrambling and route-finding on rock, go with someone experienced who can offer a rope if it is needed. If you are new to these hills it would make sense to reserve at least your first few outings for days when the clouds are above the tops and the ridge is mist-free. Never be afraid to turn back if conditions deteriorate or if you feel unsure of your ability.

ROUTE 47

Sgurr nan Gillean (964m)

Pronunciation: Skoor nern Gillian
Translation: (probably) Peak of the Gullies,
but usually taken to mean Peak of the Young Men

Distance:	11km
Ascent:	1010m
Time:	4hrs 50mins
Difficulty:	scrambling grade 2; see Skye introduction above
Maps:	OS sheet 32; Explorer map 411; Harvey's Superwalker map Skye The Cuillin; Area Map 9
Parking:	roadside close to the Sligachan Hotel
Start:	footpath from the A863, about 100m west of the hotel
Hostel:	YHA Glen Brittle
B&B/hotel:	Sligachan Hotel
Camping:	Sligachan
Access:	Macleod Estate, tel: 01470 521206. Normally no restrictions on access at any time of year.

At the northwest end of the Cuillin chain stands one of its toughest, most interesting peaks – Sgurr nan Gillean. Although it is one of the most visible and also one of the best-known mountain outlines when viewed from Sligachan, the easiest route to its summit is hidden from view and demands quite a long and complex approach across rough ground. The approach has been made very much easier of late by the upgrading of the path.

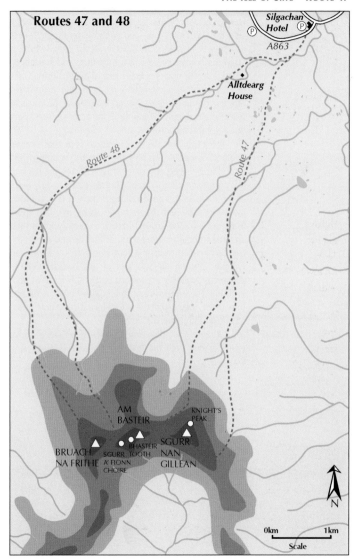

Routes 47 and 48

Silgachan Hotel

Ⓟ   Ⓟ

A863

◆ *Alltdearg House*

Route 48

Route 47

KNIGHT'S PEAK

AM BASTEIR

BRUACH NA FRITHE   SGURR A' FIONN CHOIRE   BHASTEIR TOOTH   SGURR NAN GILLEAN

N

0km   1km
Scale

From Sligachan follow the path across a wooden bridge over the Allt Dearg Mor and continue on the path over rough, wet moorland to the Allt Dearg Beag, which is also crossed by a bridge. Leave the burn and make for a sharp little rise that is actually one of the enclosing walls of the Coire Riabhach. Follow the path, then drop down into this corrie and pass around the back of the corrie to exit it quite steeply by climbing the scree-covered path on its southern enclosing wall.

At the top, skirt the steep crags on your right to enter another corrie – this one much more bouldery and closed in by steep and difficult rock. Go to the back of this corrie and climb a scree-covered path to a low point in the rocks of the headwall. From here it is possible to make an easy exit through the rocks into an upper boulder field. The ground here is extremely rough and covered in boulders and scree. Climb up and across the boulder field to reach the southeast ridge of **Sgurr nan Gillean**. Finding the way out of this boulder field in descent is probably the trickest part of this route in poor visibility. There are several small cairns, but it is easy to miss them amongst all the scree. Take a good note of the layout on the upward journey.

Sgurr nan Gillean from Coire Riabhach

Once on the ridge, stay on its crest to the top. Move easily at first until the first real obstacle is reached: a

*Southeast ridge of
Sgurr nan Gillean*

steep little crag blocking the way. To the right of the crag is an obvious crack line; this gives very good holds and is surprisingly easy both in ascent and descent. Stay on the crest of the ridge above this crag until another crag blocks the way. There are two obvious breaks in this crag – one a crack line on the left, the other a small blocked chimney on the right. The chimney is the easiest line, providing good positive holds which again make movement easy both in ascent and descent. It is tempting at first glance to look for easier options on the left at various points in the ascent, but staying on the crest is safer and easier despite first appearances, though it perhaps requires a bolder approach. Continue delicately over blocks where the ridge narrows, then cross a delightful smooth, red, sloping slab, which gives excellent friction, and eventually reach the final section where the ridge becomes very narrow, but is not difficult. The summit cairn is a wonderful viewpoint at 47151 25297 (3hrs).

Return by the route of ascent.

ROUTE 48

Am Basteir (934m),

Bruach na Frithe (958m)

Pronunciation: Am Bashtyer; Broo-uch na Freeyer
Translation: The Baptizer (but often translated as the
Executioner); Slope of the Deer Forest

Distance:	14km
Ascent:	1090m
Time:	5hrs 25mins
Difficulty:	scrambling grade 2; see Skye introduction above
Maps:	OS sheet 32; Explorer map 411; Harvey's Superwalker map Skye The Cuillin; Area Map 9
Parking:	Sligachan
Start:	footpath from A863, about 100m west of the hotel
Hostel:	YHA Glen Brittle
B&B/hotel:	Sligachan Hotel
Camping:	Sligachan
Access:	Macleod Estate, tel: 01470 521206. Normally no restrictions on access to the Cuillin hills at any time of year.

From Sgurr nan Gillean to Bruach na Frithe, the main Cuillin ridge is quite as dramatic as any stretch of rock in Britain. Whilst the west ridges of both Gillean and Am Basteir demand difficult scrambling or rock climbing, and the Bhasteir Tooth is off-limits altogether unless you are a competent climber, it is possible to get from Am Basteir to Bruach na Frithe by way of an easy traverse across scree on the north side of the main ridge, as described here. The two Munros can thus be climbed in a single outing that gives a good taste of this popular part of the Cuillins.

Start from Sligachan on the path that crosses the Allt Dearg Mor and the Allt Dearg Beag, as you would if you

Am Basteir and Bruach na Frithe from Sgurr nan Gillean

Looking south through the Bealach nan Lice

were heading for Sgurr nan Gillean. At 47630 26989, however, just before you descend into the Coire Riabhach, a cairn marks the start of a path on the right that leads up along the easy lower section of the Pinnacle Ridge, passing above (to the east of) the Bhasteir gorge. Follow this path, faint in places, across easy slabs to just below the start of the climbing on Pinnacle Ridge. At this point leave the ridge and, still on a faint path, cross the scree to your right, without gaining height on it. From here the path continues towards the middle of the corrie, skirting rocks on the left. Eventually it climbs a scree path directly up towards Am Basteir and then cuts steeply back beneath Am Basteir's east ridge to reach the Bealach a' Bhasteir.

From the bealach climb easily up the first section of ridge. There is a difficult vertical drop about two-thirds of the way up which calls for a short abseil. If you chose to abseil then make sure you leave the rope in place to help you back up on your return. Most people avoid this problem pitch, however, by finding a way down onto ledges on the left – these enable you to get back to the crest of the ridge at the col just beyond the abseil pitch. The difficulty is getting onto the ledges. They dip rather alarmingly down to the southeast below the bealach and no easy way down to them is immediately obvious, especially in thick weather. From the Bealach a' Bhasteir, climb the ridge to a prominent knob of rock before working your way down to the left. As you drop down, a traverse line appears; it is like a little shelf leading gently back onto the ledge. If you can't see which ledge you should be heading for, continue easily along the ridge to the abseil point where all becomes clear, then return to find your way down. Once the bad step has been passed there are no further difficulties. There is a small cairn on the summit of **Am Basteir** at 46570 25289 (2hrs 50mins).

Enjoy the views then return the same way back to the bealach. For those who relish a little climbing there is a quick way back onto the ridge starting just a short distance along the ledge below the abseil pitch. It is a short, steep climb but on excellent holds. (It would be very committing and also fairly elusive to find this in the other direction.) From the bealach, drop down the way you came, then climb up on a path that traverses beneath the north face of Am Basteir, staying close to the rocks, until the Bealach nan Lice is reached. There is a good view across Lota Corrie through the gap to the south. Pass around Sgurr a' Fionn Choire and climb the easy east ridge of **Bruach na Frithe** to the trig point at 46092 25189 (3hrs 50mins).

There are three options for the descent. Either return by the outward route or, if you are a confident scrambler, descend by the northwest ridge (scrambling grade 2 in ascent), staying close to the crest for most of the way to eventually join the path along the Allt Dearg Mor back to Sligachan. This is not the easiest of scrambles, and in poor weather route-finding can be difficult. Most people will probably opt for the third way: going back down the east ridge of Bruach na Frithe, then following a well-worn path through boulders into the Fionn Choire. There are cairns lower down leading you across fairly feature-less ground to the Allt Dearg Mor, where a good path leads back to Sligachan.

ROUTE 49

Sgurr a' Mhadaidh (918m),

Sgurr a' Ghreadaidh (973m)

Pronunciation: *Skoor uh Vathee; Skoor uh Ghredee*
Translation: *Peak of the Fox; Peak of Thrashing*

Distance:	10km
Ascent:	1060m
Time:	4hrs 40mins
Difficulty:	scrambling grade 1, with a short section of grade 3 on either side of An Dorus; see Skye introduction above
Maps:	OS sheet 32; Explorer map 411; Harvey's Superwalker map Skye The Cuillin; Area Map 9
Parking:	roadside at hostel
Start:	footpath alongside the Allt a' Choire Ghreadaidh – starts opposite the hostel
Hostel:	YHA Glen Brittle
B&B/hotel:	Sligachan Hotel
Camping:	Glen Brittle
Access:	Macleod Estate, tel: 01470 521206. Normally no restrictions on access to the Cuillin hills at any time of year.

Nestling in the middle of the ridge on either side of the An Dorus gap – and less well-known than many of the Cuillin hills – this interesting pair put up a strong defence and the would-be Munroist must make some tricky moves on rock to reach their summits.

From the youth hostel follow the path alongside the Allt a' Choire Ghreadaidh, crossing over to its north bank after a couple of kilometres. The upper corrie is a vast but fairly uncomplicated amphitheatre split into two by the protruding rocky spur of Sgurr Eadar da Choire. The

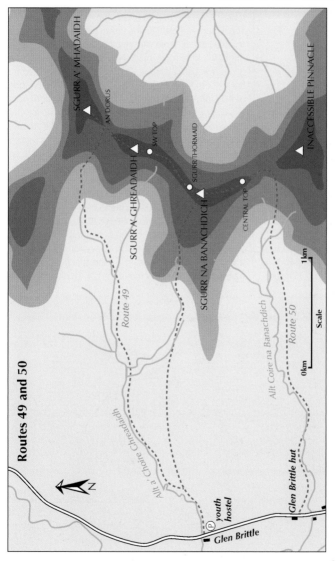

Routes 49 and 50

N

SGURR A' MHADAIDH

AN DORUS

SW TOP

SGURR THORMAID

INACCESSIBLE PINNACLE

SGURR A' GHREADAIDH

SGURR NA BANACHDICH

CENTRAL TOP

Route 49

Route 50

Allt a' Choire Ghreadaidh

Allt Coire na Banachdich

Scale

0km   1km

Glen Brittle hut

youth hostel

Glen Brittle

easiest access to both of these Munros is via An Dorus – The Door – a cleft in the ridge with a trail of scree leading down from it. Head straight towards this, through a little rocky defile beneath the northern flanks of Sgurr Eadar da Choire. The scree slope is hard work, but it doesn't last long. The first few moves on either side of An Dorus form the hardest part of the ascent of both peaks, but there is really nothing to fear from either. To ascend **Sgurr a' Mhadaidh** the first move off the ground, stepping up to the right, is a little awkward, although there are good positive holds. Beyond this there are no real difficulties, although there is some loose rock and scree to contend with higher up. Check that the rock is sound before trusting your full weight on it. Climb straight up to the summit via the shattered rock to the left of the ridge. The cairn is at 44707 23501 (2hrs 40mins).

Return to An Dorus by the same route and next turn your attention to the short, steep section that leads up from the col towards Sgurr a' Ghreadaidh. The easiest line starts from the very top of the col. Don't be tempted

Sgurr a' Mhadaidh (right) and Bruach na Frithe (left)

by a line that starts a couple of metres down to the east. It is much harder. Once again there are numerous good positive holds, and the difficulties are all behind you after a few metres. If you are planning to return by the same route it is a good idea to rehearse the downward moves while you are on them. Follow the ridge up, staying close to the crest or just to its right (west). There is at least one false trail that leads to greasy and more difficult slabs on the east side of the ridge. Soon another little gap is reached – the Eag Dubh (or Black Notch) – and this is passed to its left without difficulty. The next apparent obstacle is a tower that blocks the way – The Wart. This is turned to its right, again without difficulty, and a short way beyond it the summit cairn of **Sgurr a' Ghreadaidh** is reached at 44533 23119 (3hrs 10mins).

Return by the route of ascent, unless of course you prefer to make a longer day of it by continuing along the ridge to Sgurr na Banachdich. If you chose to continue, bear in mind that there are no lines of descent until the west ridge of Sgurr na Banachdich is reached, and although this offers an easy way off, it involves some tricky navigation if the visibility is poor. There is no great technical difficulty in the next section of the ridge (although it is usually given a grade 3), but it requires great care as it narrows to a genuine knife-edge arête with a delicious degree of exposure on both sides. This can feel intimidating. Many parties will find it extremely exhilarating, but those who don't have a head for heights will probably not. Beyond Sgurr a' Ghreadaidh's south top the ridge becomes broader again, although there is again some loose rock to contend with. Continue up to Sgurr Thormaid, where the ridge provides more scrambling; there are three towers of increasing difficulty before the top is reached – the Three Teeth – but these can be bypassed by a path on the right. The descent down the southwest ridge of Sgurr Thormaid involves some more scrambling, with the main difficulties being passed on the right (west) side. The easiest descent from Sgurr na Banachdich goes down its western shoulder into Coire an Eich as described in Route 50.

ROUTE 50

Sgurr na Banachdich (965m)

Pronunciation: *Skoor na Bannach-hich*
Translation: *(probably) Milkmaid's Peak,*
but usually translated as Smallpox Peak

Distance:	10km
Ascent:	980m
Time:	4hrs 25mins
Difficulty:	scrambling grade 2; quite tricky route-finding; see Skye introduction above
Maps:	OS sheet 32; Explorer map 411; Harvey's Superwalker map Skye The Cuillin; Area Map 9
Parking:	lay-by opposite the Glen Brittle Memorial Hut
Start:	footpath from back of lay-by
Hostel:	YHA Glen Brittle
B&B/hotel:	Sligachan Hotel
Camping:	Glen Brittle
Access:	Macleod Estate, tel: 01470 521206

The simplest way of 'bagging' Sgurr na Banachdich is to climb it via Coir'an Eich and return the same way. A rather tedious path climbs steeply up through scree towards the Diallaid ridge, then wanders over rough bouldery ground up to the summit. It is much more interesting, however, to approach the peak via the main ridge, either by including it in with Route 49 or by starting from Coire nan Banachdich and scrambling along the south ridge to the summit. This latter option is described here.

Start from the Glen Brittle Memorial Hut and follow the path up alongside the Allt Coire na Banachdich to the spectacular waterfall of Eas Mor. Leave the main track to Coire Lagan here and take a left branch, staying alongside the burn. The path enters Coire na Banachdich at its

southern end, passing over the bottom rocks of Window Buttress. Once you are in the corrie, stay well to its south, just to the left of the southernmost burn. A path of sorts climbs up quite close to this burn, passing to the right of the rocks that now loom up in front of you. There are occasional cairns but these can be hard to spot amidst all the scree.

Continue with a little scrambling up a scree-covered ramp that leads round above the rocks. These rocks incidentally provide some pleasant and quite easy scrambling so long as you pick your route and don't stray too far to the north. Eventually a steep scree slope is reached leading straight up to the Sgurr Dearg ridge. Climb this until a path leads off northeast to the Bealach Coire na Banachdich. If using this as a descent route, it is important to ensure that you traverse a sufficient distance to the southwest to clear the main buttress before dropping down into the corrie. It can be a difficult line to locate in poor visibility.

The route continues from the left (west) side of the bealach, crossing a little tower and continuing along the crest of the ridge. There is a broken path some way below

Sgurr a' Ghreadaidh from Sgurr na Banachdich

Bealach Coire na Banachdich looking towards Coruisk

the crest on the Glen Brittle side that avoids any difficulties if desired, although care needs to be taken over some occasional suspect rock. The ridge over the South Top becomes quite narrow. Cross the gap and either continue scrambling over the Centre Top or follow a series of broken ledges on its west flank. Although these ledges avoid most of the scrambling difficulties there are still a

couple of awkward moves. Finally climb more easily to the main summit of **Sgurr na Banachdich** which offers excellent views in virtually all directions.

To descend, follow the gravelly path through boulders and scree to the west-northwest to reach the junction of the An Diallaid and Sgurr nan Gobhar ridges. A pleasant way back from here is to go along the easy ridge of Sgurr nan Gohbar, then drop quite sharply down a scree slope at its southwestern tip. The more usual route is to skirt briefly along the edge of the An Diallaid ridge, then drop down the scree-covered slopes of the southwestern flanks of that ridge into Coir' an Eich. There is a well-worn path here. At the bottom, cross meadows to rejoin the Coire a' Ghreadhaidh path to the youth hostel, then walk back along the road. Descending this way, or indeed by the route of ascent into Coire na Banachdich, requires careful navigation in poor visibility, particularly if you haven't done them before.

ROUTE 51

Sgurr Dearg

(the Inaccessible Pinnacle) (986m),

Sgurr Mhic Choinnich (948m)

Pronunciation: *Skoor Jerrack; Skoor Vee Chonneech*
Translation: *Red Peak; MacKenzie's Peak*
(named after John MacKenzie, an early Cuillin guide
and one of the first ascensionists)

There are two little words that can make the average walker break out into a cold sweat and etch fear onto their faces; those words are the 'In Pin'. It is the hardest Munro summit to reach, involving rock climbing, abseiling and a good deal of exposure on the way. Many a would-be Munroist has had sleepless nights in anticipation of an ascent; no doubt some have been put off altogether by troubling thoughts of that famous knife-blade ridge.

Distance:	14km
Ascent:	1130m
Time:	6hrs (queues on the 'In Pin', which are not uncommon, can add substantially to this – avoid peak periods if you can)
Difficulty:	scrambling grade 2 for parts of the route, but the 'In Pin' demands moderate rock climbing in an exposed position and an abseil from its summit; see Skye introduction above
Maps:	OS sheet 32; Explorer map 411; Harvey's Superwalker map Skye The Cuillin; Area Map 9
Parking:	Glen Brittle campsite or roadside at the memorial hut, depending on the approach selected
Start:	footpath (as for Route 50)
Hostel:	YHA Glen Brittle
B&B/hotel:	Sligachan Hotel
Camping:	Glen Brittle campsite
Access:	Macleod Estate, tel: 01470 521276. Normally no restrictions on access at any time of year.

There is no doubt that this route does need to be prepared for in a different way from other Munros. Although only a short abseil is involved, this is no place to be abseiling for the very first time. Inexperienced parties should practise the techniques involved before they set out. The route should not be attempted by novices unless at least one person in the party has previous experience of rock climbing and rope management. Having said all this, however, there is really nothing for the novice to fear. Bear in mind that thousands of others have gone before you and lived to tell the tale (again and again and again in most cases). The occasional timid soul might be rather unnerved by the ordeal, but really very few will be mentally scarred for life!

There are three 'easy' routes to Sgurr Dearg. One follows the path into Coire Lagan and ascends the An Stac Screes – not an undertaking for the faint-hearted. This approach then follows the trail to the foot of the 'In Pin' by passing to the left of the huge towers of An Stac on the crest of the ridge. Another route climbs Sgurr Dearg's west ridge either from the memorial hut or the camp site. This route climbs through scree and boulders to reach Sgurr Dearg Beag before the ridge narrows and offers some short sections of scrambling (most of which can be bypassed if desired). The third option is to follow the route described above (see Route 50) via Coire na Banachdich. Before the bealach is reached, however, climb up rocks on the right to gain the crest of the main ridge and follow this without difficulty to a long scree slope that leads to **Sgurr Dearg**'s summit.

Enjoy a sedentary view of the 'In Pin' from here before you drop down a well-trodden trail to the foot of its east rib and prepare to do battle. Roped parties split the ascent into two pitches. The crux of the route (its hardest moves) probably comes just at the start of the second pitch, but there are adequate holds all the way and the rock gives excellent friction. From a technical point of view the climb hardly rates as a proper rock climb – honestly – but this extraordinary blade of rock is so narrow that there is considerable exposure on both sides and this can undermine the confidence of the inexperienced. It is not a route you would choose to do in a strong wind. When the top is reached at 44406 21595,

The 'In Pin' and main ridge from the summit of Sgurr Mhic Choinnich

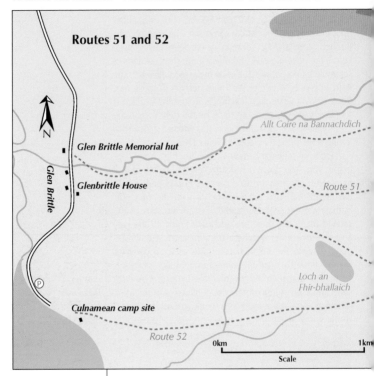

and you clamber onto the summit block to 'top out' (3hrs 40mins), you will surely feel it was well worth the effort.

There is a wire thread belay *in situ* at the base of the Boulder Stone at the top of the steep west ridge, from which you can abseil. Abseiling is fun to do, but on a real rockface on a single rope there are risks involved. Make especially sure that loose clothing and hair cannot get tangled in your abseil device. It would be prudent to safeguard your descent with a prusik knot unless you are using a safety rope. Novices will find it much easier if they have left their sacs at the foot of the climb.

Follow the eroded path down around the southern flanks of An Stac, bearing left over a shoulder. This little

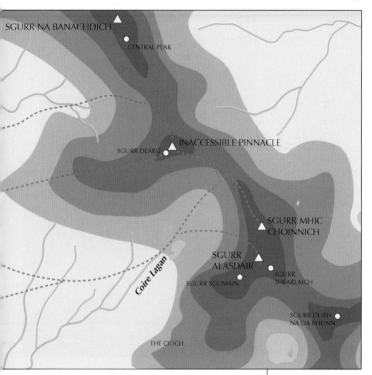

left turn is easily missed, and missing it would take you rapidly down onto dangerous ground. Staying close to the foot of the face, continue down to the An Stac screes, which can be used as an escape route if required, then climb a short distance up to the Bealach Coire Lagan to rejoin the crest of the main ridge. At first the ridge is broad and level until an eruption of rocks is reached. Here the scrambling begins and the route goes round to the right (southwest) on a rising line that involves some interesting moves. These never become really difficult, however, and they are generally lacking in exposure. Once the crest of the ridge is regained, stay on it. There is a big drop into Coire Lagan and quite steeply sloping slabs on the Coruisk

*Abseiling down the
west side of the
Inaccessible Pinnacle*

side. Gradually the ridge gets narrower and the exposure increases. The final tower is climbed on its right (south-west) side to reach the summit of **Sgurr Mhic Choinnich**. There are exceptional views from the top in good weather. The cairn and a rather tawdry plaque are at 45027 21038 (4hrs 50mins).

Peer over the edge if you dare, to see if you can locate the onward route to Sgurr Thearlaich – not everyone's cup of tea. The King's Chimney climbs up to your left and Collie's ledge passes beneath the summit to the right on the Coire Lagan side.

To descend, return to the An Stac screes and slither down them into Coire Lagan to join the obvious path back to the campsite.

ROUTE 52

Sgurr Alasdair (992m)

Pronunciation: *Skoor Alasdair*
Translation: *Alasdair's Peak (named after the first recorded
ascensionist: Alasdair Nicolson)*

Distance:	9km
Ascent:	990m
Time:	4hrs
Difficulty:	scrambling grade 1; see Skye introduction above
Maps:	OS sheet 32; Explorer map 411; Harvey's Superwalker map Skye The Cuillin; Area Map 9
Parking:	outside Glen Brittle campsite
Start:	footpath from back of campsite (past toilet block)
Hostel:	YHA Glen Brittle
B&B/hotel:	Sligachan Hotel
Camping:	Glen Brittle
Access:	Macleod Estate, tel: 01470 521206. Normally no restrictions on access to the Cuillin hills at any time of year

Sgurr Alasdair is the highest peak in the Cuillin and is situated at an inter-esting part of the ridge between Coire a' Ghrundda and Coire Lagan. For the average walker, however, it is rather cut off from neighbouring peaks by difficult ground, leaving the tedious screes of the Great Stone Chute as the only means of both ascent and descent. From a route-finding point of view it is one of the easiest of all Munros, but this certainly cannot be said of the effort required to reach its summit.

Follow the prominent path from the campsite's toilet block into Coire Lagan, staying to the left when the path branches after just over ½km. This path rises steadily into the corrie, taking the rounded, glacially eroded slabs on the lower corrie floor direct. The upper corrie contains a

The An Stac screes from the summit of Sgurr Alasdair

beautiful clear blue loch encircled by some of the Cuillin's best-known peaks. Cross the valley floor to the start of the Great Stone Chute on the right and prepare to do battle. On a good day, if you are lucky, it's a case of two steps up and one back. Some parties try to climb to the right of the main fan, then cut back at the top beneath the rocks. Many people have commented on the depletion of stones in the Chute in recent years. They may be right about this, but I can't personally detect too much difference now from when I first came here over 30 years ago. One thing is certain, however; there are still enough stones to make movement in a downward direction more likely than up.

From the little col at the top, assuming you do manage to reach it, you can turn your attention to **Sgurr Alasdair**'s southeast ridge. Traverse left for a couple of metres at the start of the rocks, then climb easily up the ridge to the narrow summit – a wonderful place for views. There is some loose rock and much scattered scree on this ridge, and it cannot be overemphasised how important it is to ensure that none of this goes over the edge. A little carelessness here would put people in the Stone Chute at great risk of injury. If you have a climber's helmet the Stone Chute is one place where you definitely should be wearing it. The tiny summit cairn is at 44999 20754 (2hrs 45mins).

In descent, return the same way to the col. Sgurr Mhic Choinnich and the 'In Pin' can be reached along the ridge from here via Collie's ledge, but only if you are very confident of your climbing ability. Careful route-finding is required, and parts of the traverse involve some awkward down-climbing and are harder than anything else described in these volumes. Non-climbers should return back down the Stone Chute to the corrie. If you have enough energy left to face another scree slope, the An Stac screes can be climbed to give access to these other Munros, as described in Route 51.

ROUTE 53

Sgurr Dubh Mor (944m),

Sgurr nan Eag (924m)

Pronunciation: *Skoor Doo More; Skoor nern Yek*
Translation: *Big Black Peak; Peak of the Notches*

Distance:	14km
Ascent:	1170m
Time:	6hrs 45mins
Difficulty:	scrambling grade 2 if the easiest options are found on Sgurr Dubh Mor; see Skye introduction above
Maps:	OS sheet 32; Explorer map 411; Harvey's Superwalker map Skye The Cuillin; Area Map 9
Parking:	in, or just outside, Glen Brittle campsite (there is a charge if you park inside)
Start:	footpath behind campsite (starts behind toilet block)
Hostel:	YHA Glen Brittle
B&B/hotel:	Sligachan Hotel
Camping:	Glen Brittle
Access:	Macleod Estate, tel: 01470 521206. Normally no restrictions on access to the Cuillin hills at any time of year

Coir' a' Ghrunnda, from which these southernmost Cuillin Munros are climbed, is one of the most magnificent corries in Scotland. It is a complex place with boilerplate slabs, waterfalls, huge crags and a beautiful loch – and that's just on the corrie floor. Above it tower great gabbro spires and sheer faces of rock in a truly awesome *tour de force* of natural architecture. This corrie often seems to be the first to mist up in the prevailing south-westerly winds and also the last to clear.

Follow the footpath from the campsite, crossing over a farm track and heading up towards Coire Lagan. In less than 1km the path divides. The left branch leads up to

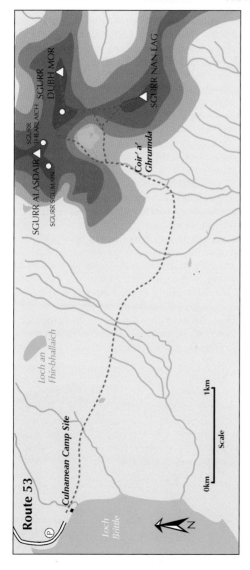

Route 53

SGURR ALASDAIR
SGURR SGUMAIN
SGURR THEARLAICH
SGURR DUBH MOR
SGURR NAN EAG
Coir' a' Ghrunnda
Loch an Fhir-bhallaich
Culnamean Camp Site
Loch Brittle

1km
Scale
0km

N

P

Coire Lagan; the right branch heads round the southern nose of Sron na Ciche into Coir' a' Ghrunnda. Take the right-hand branch across a burn, and 1km further on cross the Allt Coire Lagan. The path fragments beyond this. Keep to the left (upper) route wherever there is an option and pass close beneath the rocks of Sron na Ciche.

From here on the complex grandeur of Coir' a' Ghrunnda begins to reveal itself. The key to gaining access to the upper part of the corrie is to stay well to the left, close up to the rocks. The first major obstacle – a large crag blocking the left side of the corrie – can in fact be passed either to its right (staying tight up against its black, wet walls) or by taking a higher line round to its left. Eventually the loch is reached, nestling in its magnificent setting in the upper corrie.

The way to the main ridge from here is not immediately obvious. To gain it you need to head north for a short distance until you come almost beneath the Thearlaich Dubh gap (one of the biggest problems on the main ridge traverse). You get a good view of it from here and you might well be thankful that you don't have to cross it. At this point suddenly the way onto the ridge becomes obvious. By heading back to the northeast the Bealach Coir' an Lochain is easily reached. Scramble easily up to the southeast from the bealach to reach the

Sgurr nan Eag (right) Sgurr Dubh na Da Bheinn (left) from the top of the Great Stone Chute

summit of Sgurr Dubh na Da Bheinn. There is a sharp drop to reach the col below Sgurr Dubh Mor from here. Scramble down steeply, but without difficulty, and follow a gravelly path to the left of the connecting ridge. From the col the path crosses over to the south side of this ridge, then comes back up via an easy staircase to the start of the scrambling.

The face to be climbed is steep, but does not feel particularly exposed, perhaps because it is broken by numerous grass and gravel ledges into a number of short pitches. There are many options to choose from. If one line feels too hard, try a different one; but remember the way you have come because you'll shortly have to climb back down the same way. The easiest options are really not difficult at all; though it should perhaps be said that walkers whose nightmares inhabit such places may appreciate the security of a rope, and an experienced climber to hold it, especially in descent. The little cairn on top of **Sgurr Dubh Mor** may not be placed on the highest point (which appears to be a few metres to the east), but perhaps this is just an illusion, 45723 20540 (3hrs 35mins).

Enjoy the wonderful views from this point, then return with care to the summit of Sgurr Dubh na Da Bheinn and drop down quite steeply but without difficulty to a col to its south. The vertical walls of the Caisteal a' Garbh Choire block the way here, but follow a path round to its left (east) and continue up the ridge to **Sgurr nan Eag**. Stay close to the crest or just to its right to find a fairly easy line to the top. Once the climbing is done, continue across the rough, broad, fairly level ridge to reach a rather impressive cairn at 45717 19531 (4hrs 35mins).

Descend the same way back down the ridge until part-way down a faint path leads off to the left and drops quite steeply in places over scree to reach the southern end of Loch Coir' a' Ghrunnda. If you find yourself on difficult rock you have gone astray. A less pleasant alternative is to return to the col in front of the Caisteal a' Garbh Choire and descend steeply over scree and rough boulders from here. From the loch, return by the outward route.

ROUTE 54

Bla Bheinn (928m)

Pronunciation: Bla Vine
Translation: Blue Mountain

Distance:	8km
Ascent:	930m
Time:	4hrs
Difficulty:	scrambling grade 1; see Skye introduction above
Maps:	OS sheet 32; Explorer map 411; Harvey's Superwalker map Skye The Cuillin; Area Map 9
Parking:	car park by B8083 just south of the Allt na Dunaiche
Start:	back along road to footpath on north side of the Allt na Dunaiche
Hostel:	YHA Broadford; independent Kyleakin
B&B/hotel:	Broadford
Access:	John Muir Trust, tel: 0131 5540114. Normally no restrictions on access at any time of year

Bla Bheinn is an isolated mountain with a distinctive outline and some excellent scrambling, particularly on its northeastern ridge over Clach Glas. The usual route up Bla Bheinn from Loch Slapin (described here) may not be the most interesting outing in Skye, but on a clear day the view from the top is arguably the best.

Take the Elgol road from Broadford and park on the west side of Loch Slapin just south of the Allt na Dunaiche at the foot of the mountain. From the car park, walk back a short distance along the road and start up the footpath on the north bank of the river. The path rises pleasantly, crossing the river after 1½km and then crosses a tributary burn shortly afterwards. At this point it climbs more steeply into the Coire Uaigneich. As you enter the corrie

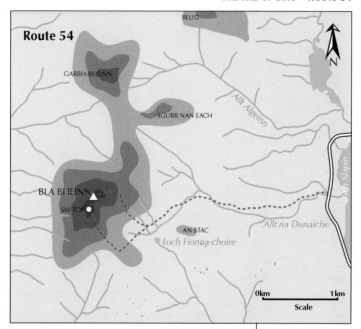

leave the main path and strike uphill to your right. A clear footpath zigzags up the steep flank of **Bla Bheinn**'s east ridge. This soon becomes scree covered. Continue upwards towards the rocks; when these are reached a couple of easy scrambling moves lead to the final summit climb. The summit views over the hills of the Red Cuillin and the whole panorama of the Black Cuillin across the Strath na Creitheach are quite exceptional. The cairn is at 52996 21726 (2hrs 40mins).

It is well worth going a few hundred metres further to the southwest top. Cross a narrow bridge between the two peaks and enjoy a little scramble to the summit on the far side, just four metres lower than the main top, at 52872 21497. The views from here are just as fine.

The best descent is by the route of ascent, although it is also possible to continue from the southwest top by

The Red Cuillin from Bla Bheinn's east ridge

going southeast down to the col between Points 583 and 624 on the Harvey's map. From here you can drop very steeply down into the corrie below and rejoin the outward route.

TORRIDON

ROUTE 55

BEINN ALLIGIN

Tom na Gruagaich (922m),

Sgurr Mhor (986m)

Pronunciation: *Bine Ahleegin;*
Tom na Grooyageech; Skoor Voar
Translation: *Jewelled Mountain; Hill of the Damsel; Big Hill*

Distance:	11km
Ascent:	1290m
Time:	4hrs 55mins
Difficulty:	scrambling grade 1; some exposed sections
Maps:	OS sheets 19 and 24; Explorer map 433; Harvey's Superwalker map Torridon; Area Map 10
Parking:	car park by bridge over the Abhainn Coire Mhic Nobuil
Start:	path on the left (west) side of the bridge
Hostel:	YHA Torridon
B&B/hotel:	Torridon
Camping:	Torridon
Access:	National Trust for Scotland, tel: 01445 791221. Normally no restrictions on access at any time of year.

Torridon holds a special place in the hearts of those who love mountains. It is unlike anywhere else. The mountains here rise straight up from sea level in a succession of towering and awe-inspiring sandstone buttresses that seem to throw scorn on the very idea of human ascent.

Of these three peaks, **Beinn Alligin** is perhaps the least threatening in appearance and also the easiest to climb.

225

The big three – Liathach, Beinn Alligin and Beinn Eighe – all recline quite close to the roadside like brooding monsters, completely indifferent to the puny aims of man. The tops of these red sandstone giants offer nothing to dispel this sense of awe. Having succeeded in finding a way up them, the mountaineer is confined to an extraordinary aerial world of narrow, often castellated, ridges that run for miles above the plunging cliffs without any possibility of retreat.

From the west side of the bridge over the Coire Mhic Nobuil a well-trodden stony path leads onto the hillside and climbs quite rapidly to the north-northwest. It soon passes over a stile and continues over occasional rocks and sections of peat around the nose of Beinn Alligin's

Sgurr Mhor (Beinn Alligin) from Tom na Gruagaich

steep southern buttress. Once around this nose, climb steadily up into the huge gully of the Coire nan Laogh. Towards the top of this is an impressive asymmetrical amphitheatre laced with tiered bands of rock in its upper

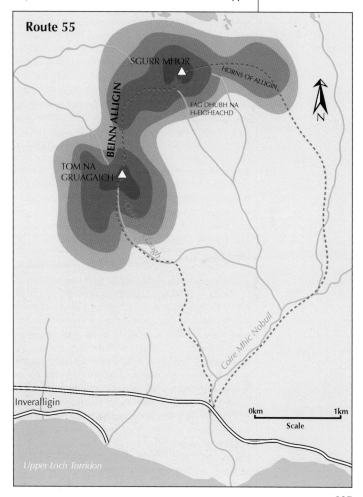

Route 55

SGURR MHOR

HORNS OF ALLIGIN

BEINN ALLIGIN

EAG DHUBH NA H-EIGHEACHD

N

TOM NA GRUAGAICH

Coire nan Laogh

Coire Mhic Nobuil

Inveralligin

0km   1km

Scale

Upper Loch Torridon

reaches. The path leads through this amphitheatre, bearing right as it rises. There is a small cairn on the exit slopes and from here it is just a short climb to the summit of **Tom na Gruagaich** at 85963 60140 (2hrs 15mins).

From the summit cairn, follow the ridge to the north, staying close to its crest. Descend for 150m over boulders and a series of rocky steps. There is a little easy scrambling in places but without any difficulty or exposure. The path is eroded and easy to follow, with a number of alternatives at every obstacle. From a col at 766m the ridge rises over a minor top which has its own small cairn, then falls again before rising quite steeply to the summit of **Sgurr Mhor**. Just below this summit there is an impressive gash in the mountain, slicing down its southeast side from top to bottom. This is the Eag Dhubh na h-Eigheachd (the Deep Gash of the Wailing). According to local legend shepherds used to hear wailing coming from the gash, but when one of them climbed down to investigate he never returned – hardly surprising when you take a look down. The path passes round the edge of this gash and gives good views into the Stygian depths below. The summit cairn is a little further on at 86552 61275 (3hrs 10mins).

Those who fainted when they looked down into the plummeting depths of the wailing gash had better return by the route of ascent. Those who gazed into the abyss with mild amusement can continue over the Horns of Alligin, the three prominent pinnacles that now confront you. There is some scrambling of an easy nature and some exposure on a couple of fairly steep sections, but this is not the territory of the rock climber and most hillwalkers will feel it is easily within their grasp. The correct line is fairly obvious and tackles each obstacle head on. Finish by descending quite steeply over the southern spur of this curving ridge, dodging little crags, and join up with a stalker's path that leads back to the car park. It is possible to avoid the steepest part of the descent by veering to the south-southwest off the final spur and then working your way back to the path.

ROUTE 56

LIATHACH

Spidean a' Choire Leith (1055m),
Mullach an Rathain (1023m)

Pronunciation: Lee-aghuch;
Speedyan a Horrer Lay; Mooluch un Rahen
Translation: the Grey One;
Peak of the Grey Corrie; Height of the Pulleys

Distance:	10km
Ascent:	1190m
Time:	5hrs 45mins
Difficulty:	exposed scrambling grade 1.5; whilst much of this is avoidable, the alternative path below the crest is also exposed
Maps:	OS sheet 25; Explorer map 433; Harvey's Superwalker map Torridon; Area Map 10
Parking:	lay-by on A896 ½km east of Glen Cottage and just west of the start
Start:	footpath starts by a passing-place in the road at 93615 56660 and runs alongside the Allt an Doire Ghairbh
Hostel:	YHA Torridon
B&B/hotel:	Torridon; Kinlochewe
Camping:	Torridon
Access:	National Trust for Scotland, tel: 01445 791221. Normally no restrictions on access at any time of year.

Liathach, the Grey One; its very name brings a shudder to the spine. Its huge unwelcoming buttresses tower up from Glen Torridon to make one of the most imposing mountain vistas in Britain. It is a fortress, well defended against assault from almost every angle of approach. And those who do find a way to the top discover that its two Munros are separated by a narrow castellated ridge that hangs over 3000ft of space on either side.

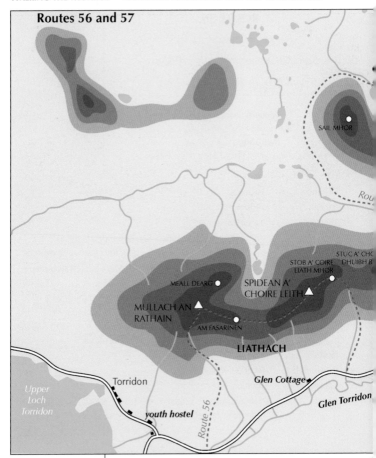

Routes 56 and 57

SAIL MHOR

Rou

STUC A' CHO
STOB A' COIRE   DHUIBH B
LIATH MHOR
MEALL DEARG   SPIDEAN A'
CHOIRE LEITH
MULLACH AN
RATHAIN
AM FASARINEN
LIATHACH

Torridon   **Glen Cottage**
Upper
Loch
Torridon   **Glen Torridon**
youth hostel   Route 56

Follow the well-trodden path alongside the Allt an Doire
Ghairbh over steep and sometimes rocky ground until the
angle eases in the upper corrie. High up in this corrie the
path is blocked by a steep gully and does an abrupt turn
to the right, rising to a col on the main ridge at 833m.
Turn left (west) onto the ridge and climb over blocks and
scree past a cairned top at 93473 58188, and then go

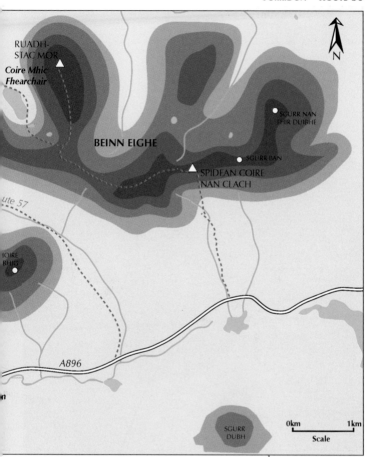

over another minor top before a short, steep drop in the ridge brings you to the foot of **Spidean a Choire Leith**'s summit screes. Climb scree and big quartzite blocks to the large summit cairn at 92932 57955 (3hrs).

At this point some parties take one look at the ridge ahead and go straight back down the way they came. But in truth there is no need to be deterred by the awful

Fasarinen pinnacles – Liathach

prospect of the Fasarinen pinnacles now confronting you. The true line over the crest of the pinnacles involves interesting and occasionally steep scrambling with some moves in very exposed positions. A wrong move here would land you nearly 3000ft down in Coire na Caime. Fortunately those who are not willing to risk such an inconvenience can still complete the traverse by following an exposed walker's path on the south side of the ridge.

From the summit of Spidean, drop steeply to the southwest over boulders and eroded scree to a narrow col, where it is immediately apparent that the time has come to pin your colours to the mast. Hard men and women (and some soft ones who have left their glasses in the car) can be seen heading uphill here with nonchalant smiles. The rest cling timorously to the muddy path that creeps around the heights of Liathach's southern cliffs. This path too is fairly exposed and is crumbling awkwardly in one or two places. What else would you expect on such a mountain? But with care there is nothing here in summer that the average hillwalker could not cope with. In winter, of course, it is a very different story. Once the cairn of Am Fasarinen is reached at 92177 57372 all difficulties are over and it is a straight-forward grind up to the jagged top of **Mullach an Rathain** at 91189 57677 (4hrs).

To descend, head west for 30m, where a small cairn marks the start of the steep dust trail that passes for a path. The erosion here is very great and care is required for a few hundred metres. The top section of this path can be missed out by continuing for a short distance beyond the cairn down the southwest ridge of Mullach before dropping into the gully. Eventually the path becomes more friendly as it winds down the Toll Ban, passing a couple of excellent springs on the way. Lower down it abandons the river to find an intricate route through the sandstone crags and emerges at the road at 91398 55391. Although a small cairn marks this point, the lower section of this path might be quite hard to find and follow in the opposite direction.

ROUTE 57

BEINN EIGHE

Ruadh Stac Mor (1010m),
Spidean Coire nan Clach (993m)

Pronunciation: Bine Ehyer; Roower Stack More;
Speedyan Korrer nern Klach
Translation: File Mountain; Big Red Steep Hill;
Peak of the Stony Corrie

Distance:	17km
Ascent:	1180m
Time:	6hrs
Difficulty:	no specific technical difficulty, but this is a big, serious mountain with very few escape lines
Maps:	OS sheets 19 and 25 (Beinn Eighe falls awkwardly between the two maps. The OS 1:25000 Explorer map 433 avoids this awkward split); Harvey's Superwalker map Torridon; Area Map 10
Parking:	car park beside the road (A896) where it passes over the Allt a' Choire Dhuibh Mhoir
Start:	footpath from the road at east end of car park
Hostel:	YHA Torridon; independent Kinlochewe
B&B/hotel:	Torridon; Kinlochewe
Camping:	Torridon
Access:	Scottish Natural Heritage, tel: 01445 760254. Normally no restrictions on access at any time of year.

Beinn Eighe is the third of the great Torridonian giants. Like the others it is composed of huge beds of red Torridonian sandstone, but it is capped by a grey-white quartzite which gives it a strange snowy-white appearance from below, as if it was covered in ash or snow.

Beinn Eighe is a remarkable structure both scenically and geologically. Some of the oldest known living creatures are fossilised in its rocks. Quartzite pipe-rock, which contains the fossil remains of early animals, can frequently be seen along the summit ridge – the 'pipes' are the casts of worm burrows. In common with its near neighbours it has very few points of access to its upper reaches and its summits are highly prized by hillwalkers.

From the road a good path leads northeast then north, parallel to the Allt a' Choire Dhuibh Mhoir, gaining height steadily as it rounds the eastern end of Liathach and enters the Coire Dubh Mor – a wild pass that separates the two giants of Liathach and Beinn Eighe. Continue to the top of this pass. At GR 93660 59329 a less obvious path leads off unobtrusively to the northwest skirting around the great prow of Sail Mhor. This path has become very easy to walk since a lot of time and expense went into upgrading it all the way up to Loch Coire Mhic Fhearchair. The landscape to the north is wild, wet and desolate: an untouched remnant of the Ice Age, with huge buttressed hills towering up here and there from the wet plateau.

Coire Mhic Fhearchair itself is an impressive place with its massive rock architecture enclosing a large and rather beautiful loch. Cross the burn below the loch and follow the path around the loch and past another two pools that nestle beneath the massive Triple Buttress of Coinneach Mhor. There are actually two paths, one on

Looking down into Coire Ruadh Staca, Beinn Eighe

235

Coire Mhic Fhearchair from the upper col, Ben Eighe

either side of the corrie, which both circumvent the large, slabby rock steps that cut across the upper part of the corrie. Head for the southeast end of the corrie, where the col above is at its lowest, and climb up (or alongside) the obvious brown eroded scree slope. Higher up there is a natural staircase of rock steps to the immediate left of the scree, which makes progress very easy. From the col, a narrow ridge leads off to the northeast, then broadens and veers to the north to reach the summit cairn of **Ruadh Stac Mor** at 95145 61137 (3hrs 35mins).

Retrace your steps to the col, then continue up a rocky edge to the east peak of Coinneach Mhor, where there is a cairn at 95027 60088. From here, head southeast along a broad shoulder where the path is not obvious for a while. Soon the ridge narrows, however, and the path is once again clear. The route from here to Spidean is a wonderful airy traverse along a narrow ridge with huge drops on either side and spectacular views. The walking is not difficult; nor is it intimidating. But in a very strong wind it is probably not a place you'd want to be. Pass a small cairn as you cross a minor top at 96106 59483 and then climb to another top at 96515 59634, where there is a trig point encircled by a cairn. In thick weather it would be easy to mistake this for the summit of **Spidean**, but this lies a little further on at 96621 59765 (4hrs 45mins).

The easiest descent to the road goes down through the Coire an Laogh. There are a couple of paths into the corrie. One starts at a small cairn a short distance to the southeast of the summit. Another leads off the south-southeast ridge. From here it is easy going alongside the upper reaches of the Allt Coire an Laoigh. Once again, major works have been done on the footpath here and walkers are strongly requested to keep faithfully to it to avoid further erosion. The path takes you easily back to the road a couple of kilometres up from the car park.

It is possible to traverse the entire ridge by starting from Kinlochewe and then, once Spidean is reached, reversing the route described here. This makes a very fine expedition indeed, but it does require the use of more than one vehicle.

KINLOCHEWE

ROUTE 58

Slioch (980m)

Pronunciation: *Shlierch*
Translation: *(possibly) The Spear*

Distance:	20km
Ascent:	990m
Time:	6hrs 30mins
Maps:	OS sheet 19; Explorer map 433; Area Map 10
Parking:	car park at road-end in Incheril
Start:	follow footpath to northwest from back of car park
Hostel:	YHA Torridon; bunkhouse Kinlochewe
B&B/hotel:	Kinlochewe
Camping:	Kinlochewe
Access:	Letterewe Estate, tel: 01445 760302

At the southeastern end of Loch Maree lies Slioch, its distinctive craggy form guarding the southern edge of the great wilderness of Letterewe and Fisherfield. The only straightforward ascent of this hill is from the east, which is just as well since this is the only direction from which it can easily be approached.

From the car park at Incheril, follow the footpath along the Kinlochewe river, taking an indistinct right fork at a small cairn at 02078 64247 to avoid getting caught up in the swamps of the river delta. After nearly 5km, cross the Abhainn an Fhasaigh at a little wooden bridge and then immediately bear right, climbing up alongside the river. After about ½km a small cairn marks the start of the path that leads up between Meall Each and Sgur Dubh into the

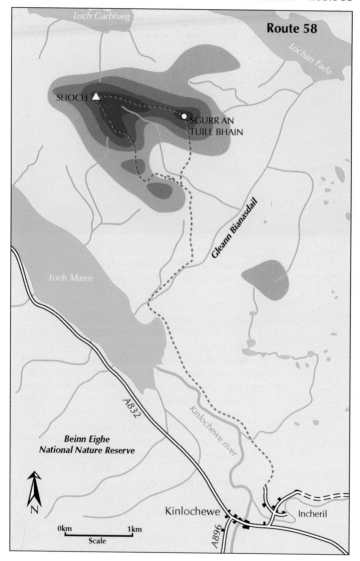

Loch Maree from the summit of Slioch

high corrie to the southeast of Slioch. Wind around beneath Sgurr Dhbh and then, aiming for the lowest point on the skyline, climb the steep, heathery hillside to emerge at a col just northwest of Sgurr Dubh.

Cross the small hill to the northwest of the col and drop down to a loch (not named on the 1:50,000 map). There are actually two lochs here but the western one does not come into view until you get higher up. Pass to the east of the loch and climb steeply up an eroded sandy path that takes you to a minor cairned top at 00747 68501. The hard work is now done and the trig point is visible less than ½km on, across a small dip, at 00501 68865. A couple of hundred metres beyond the trig point is another cairn which is usually taken to be **Slioch**'s true summit, although the OS map gives both points as having the same height. From here there are excellent views across the many little islands of Loch Maree and also to surrounding peaks, GR 00474 69065 (4hrs).

To descend, either return by the upward route or continue round the head of the corrie to Sgurr an Tuill Bhain. Cross this top and descend its southeastern ridge for just over ½km, then come back to the southwest and cross the corrie floor to rejoin the outward route.

THE FANNAICHS

ROUTE 59

A' Chailleach (997m), Sgurr Breac (999m), Sgurr nan Each (923m), Sgurr nan Clach Geala (1093m), Meall a' Chrasgaidh (934m)

Pronunciation: *Uh Chalyok; Skoor Vrack; Skoor nern yak; Skoor nern Klach Gee-aller; Miaowl uh Chrasgee*
Translation: *Old Lady; Dappled Hill; Hill of the Horse; Hill of the White Stones; Hill of the Crossing*
The meaning of Fannaich is obscure, it but possibly derives from the Gaelic for 'gentle slope'

Distance:	22km
Ascent:	1740m
Time:	8hrs
Maps:	OS sheets 19 and 20; Explorer maps 436 and 435; Area Map 10
Parking:	lay-by a few metres west of the track
Start:	follow private track to loch from road at 16235 76060
Hostel:	YHA Ullapool; Dundonnell; Aultguish bunkhouse on A835
B&B/hotel:	Aultguish Inn; Ullapool
Camping:	Dundonnell; Ullapool
Access:	West Fannich, tel: 01445 720223

In the heart of Wester Ross lies a wild and rugged tract of land of over 1000km² in which there are no metalled roads; only a small handful of estate tracks make inroads into this area, and these are mostly in the fringe of forest to the east. This is mountain country. To the west lie the great forge of An Teallach and the wild, remote hills of the Letterewe Forest; to the east the Fannaichs. The A832 describes a huge arc around the whole area as if fearing to enter this hostile mountain kingdom.

The Fannaichs are a robust group of hills lying to the north of Loch Fannich (with the exception of Fionn Bheinn, which is usually counted as one of the group). They demand a bold and energetic approach, yet a reasonably fit party can nevertheless climb the five western Fannaichs described here in a single day. Alternatively, if the idea of doing these five in one outing seems a little daunting, they could easily be split into two by using the stalker's path along the Allt Breabaig as an ascent/descent path.

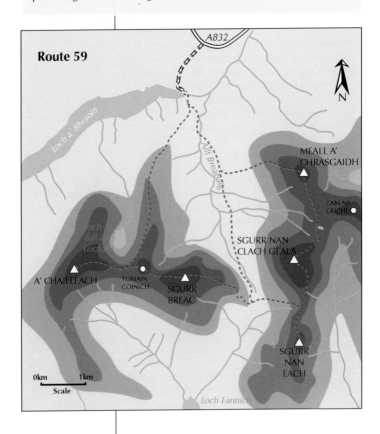

Start from the bend in the A832 near the eastern end of Loch a' Bhraoin. Follow a track that leads from the road past a ruined croft and over a footbridge at the end of the loch. About 100m beyond the bridge a fainter path leads off to the right. This path heads boldly up the steep prow of the Leitir Fhearna, winding its way through the upper crags until it reaches flat ground. (If using this route as a means of descent in poor weather, the start of the path down can be an elusive target. Fortunately there is a small cairn at 15421 73924 – the descent path begins a few metres to its northeast.) Once you have reached the cairn, head across the wild peat moorland to the main spine of the Druim Reidh ridge. There is a faint path which takes an indirect line, heading to the southwest before it then turns south, seeking out the highest ground.

Towards the top of the Druim Reidh veer right, avoiding the summit of Tomain Coinich, and cross a small boulder field to its west to reach the col below A' Chailleach. Climb easy slopes to the summit of **A' Chailleach** at 13621 71405 (2hrs 40mins).

Return to the col and cross the next hill, Tomain Coinich (this can be bypassed by going around the steepish slopes to its south, but little is gained by doing so). Next, climb east up the steep little ridge to **Sgurr**

A force 10 gale whips the water up from the surface of Loch Toll an Lochain below A' Chailleach

The Fannaichs from Sail Liath

Breac. There are two tops on Sgurr Breac, each with a small cairn, and in poor weather it is unclear which of the two is the higher. The summit is in fact the second cairn at 15818 71105 (3hrs 30mins).

Continue east and then southeast to descend by the southeast ridge. A path winds around minor obstacles, quite steeply near the bottom, to bring you to the wide col separating the north and south river systems. If you've had enough for the day you can follow a good stalker's path from here back to your starting point. If you're still feeling strong, continue due east up a steep grassy slope to the col between Sgurr nan Clach Geala and Sgurr nan Each, avoiding a band of greasy rocks halfway up. From the top of the col climb up through boulders and scree to the summit of **Sgurr nan Each** at 18466 69751 (4hrs 45mins).

Retrace your steps to below the boulders and then climb the south ridge of **Sgurr nan Clach Geala**. The path, which is faint at times, keeps close to the edge above Coire Mor, veering left (northwest) after 1km to reach the summit at 18432 71460 (5hrs 40mins).

From here the ridge narrows and there are dramatic drops to the east into Coire Mor. Drop down the rocky ridge to the northeast and come off it at the bottom to arrive at a little lochan nestling in the col. Head north for 300m over wet ground and then strike up the final slope of the day, which is fairly gentle and grassy, to reach the summit cairn of **Meall a' Chrasgaidh** at 18479 73328 (6hrs 10mins).

The descent from Meall a' Chrasgaidh is mercifully pleasant after quite a tough day. Go west down soft blaeberry and heather slopes, which steepen considerably towards the bottom, then rejoin the stalker's path along the Allt Breabaig. This path crosses the Allt Breabaig at a ford a little lower down. Although it is not deep, the river may be awkward to cross at this point when in spate, but there are other potential crossing places further downstream which may prove easier.

ROUTE 60

Beinn Liath Mhor Fannaich (954m), Sgurr Mor (1110m), Meall Gorm (949m),

An Coileachan (923m)

Pronunciation: *Bine Leea Voar Fannich; Skoor More; Miaowl Gorm; Un Colocan*
Translation: *Big Grey Hill of the Gentle Slope; Big Mountain; Blue-green Hill; the Little Cock*

Distance:	24km
Ascent:	1310m
Time:	8hrs
Maps:	OS sheet 20; Explorer map 436; Area Map 10
Parking:	Roadside on A835 where road crosses the Abhainn an Torrain Duibh
Start:	footpath leads alongside river past a small weather station
Hostel:	YHA Ullapool
B&B/hotel:	Ullapool; Altguish Inn
Camping:	Ullapool; Dundonnell
Access:	Lochluichart, tel: 01463 235353 or 01997 414224. If approaching from Fannich Lodge, tel: 01997 414318

The eastern Fannaichs are big rounded, grassy hills with a series of steep broken northeast faces, most notably that of Sgurr Mor, where wet crags tumble steeply into deep corries. They are protected to the north by some wild moorland. This tough, long walk enjoys all the virtues and vices of this remote and windswept landscape.

Although these hills can most easily be approached from Fannich Lodge, the ascent of all four from this side involves doubling up over much of the ground. The ascent from the A835 in the north, described here, is more varied and satisfying scenically and also provides a more interesting circular walk.

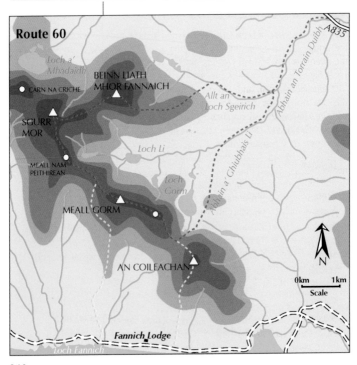

Route 60

Sgurr Mor from Beinn Liath Mhor Fannaich

Start from the west of Loch Glascarnoch and just west of the bridge over the Abhainn an Torrain Duibh. Follow the riverbank past a small weather station to the Allt an Loch Sgeirich. (Incidentally, the weather station has a Met Office web cam, and you can view the weather at this site online any time you like at the Met Office website.) Follow the Allt an Loch Sgeirich for about 1km to Point 25302 72204, where you cross it. Climb the broad moss and heather ridge of Creag Dhubh Fannaich to its top at 23580 71889. The walking becomes easier nearer the top, where the grass has been clipped short by the wind. From here, move down to a small col and then climb easily up to **Beinn Liath Mhor Fannaich** over easy stone blocks near the top. The cairn is at 21960 72394 (3hrs 5mins).

From the summit cairn descend steeply over awkward blocks to the col below Sgurr Mor, making sure that you avoid the steep-sided corrie to the northwest. There is a substantial stalker's path part-way along the rim of this corrie that goes past a small stone-built shelter. The path continues onto the main ridge to the south of Sgurr Mor, so it must be left behind for the steep grassy slopes of **Sgurr Mor**'s summit. These are climbed to a prominent, neatly constructed stone cairn at 20326 71801 (4hrs).

From Sgurr Mor, head south down a series of grassy steps formed by the erosion of the rock strata to a broad, stony ridge which leads to a small cairn on the next top, Meall nam Peithirean at 20738 70884. Continue on the crest of the ridge to Meall Gorm. Don't be seduced by the main stalker's path that disappears off to the right; in fact this leads down to Fannich Lodge before Meall Gorm is reached. Instead keep to the high ground and climb easily over a pavement of broken, flat slabs to the summit cairn of **Meall Gorm** at 22196 69568 (5hrs 10mins).

Continue east, then southeast, past the remains of another more extensive stone shelter, to a small cairn at 23207 69168 on an unnamed minor top. At this point you descend over rough, awkward stones and blocks southeast to the Bealach Ban at 775m. Cross the col and climb the grassy slopes of **An Coileachan** through a couple of bands of boulders to the reach the final summit of the day, where another neatly constructed cairn sits atop a small crag at 24184 68007 (6hrs 10mins).

To descend, return to the Bealach Ban. It is possible to descend from the lowest point of this col into the corrie above Loch Gorm, but the steep grass here can be uncomfortably wet and slippery. A better line may be found 100m or so further east, where the terrain may be a bit more bouldery but is not so steep or slippery. In thick weather it may be hard to find the best line. Aim not for the loch itself but for the col below the Meallan Bhuidhe at 24275 69200. From here work around the hill and cross rough ground where there are extensive peat hags and pools until the Abhainn a' Ghiuthais is reached.

Continue downstream on either side of the Abhainn a' Ghiuthais, which can easily be crossed whenever you choose. There is even the convenience of a footbridge at 25238 71263 (such little treats may be welcome at the end of a hard day). Once on the northwest side of the burn there is an intermittent path through rough, wet heath before the Allt an Loch Sgeirich is reached. Cross this last burn without difficulty to rejoin the path you started on and follow this easily back to the road.

ROUTE 61

Fionn Bheinn (933m)

Pronunciation: Feeown Vane
Translation: Light-coloured Hill

Distance:	12km (returning via Sail an Tuim Bhain)
Ascent:	790m
Time:	4hrs
Maps:	OS sheets 20 and 25; Explorer map 435; Area Map 10
Parking:	parking area by A832 in centre of village
Start:	farm track from A832 east of car park
Hostel:	YHA Torridon; independent Craig, Kinlochewe
B&B/hotel:	Achnasheen; Kinlochewe
Camping:	Kinlochewe
Access:	tel: 01445 720223

Fionn Bheinn is the most southerly of the Fannaichs and it is also probably the easiest. It rises gently above the little village of Achnasheen on the A832. Some people might hold this one back for one of those rare poor-weather days occasionally experienced in the northern Highlands.

From the phone box in the centre of the village, go 100m east along the A832 to a track that leads through gates to the east bank of the Allt Achadh na Sine. The track starts before you reach a row of houses fronted by a lay-by (parking by visitors is discouraged here). Follow the track through gates to the river, passing a small water treatment plant. From here a path follows the burn pleasantly uphill. Eventually when the contours begin to run out, veer round to the north-northeast and cross the peat moorland, skirting the west flank of Creagan nan Laogh. Aim for a small crag just to the left of the shallow col, though the exact line really does not matter. Once on the

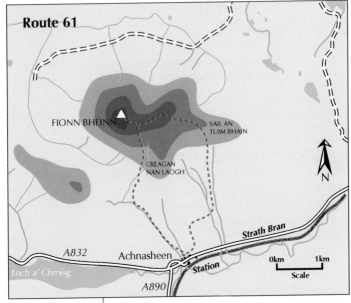

Route 61

FIONN BHEINN

SAIL AN TUIM BHAIN

CREAGAN NAN LAOGH

N

Strath Bran

A832

Achnasheen

Station

Loch a' Chroisg

A890

0km   1km
Scale

col, which forms the head of the craggy northern corrie – Toll Mor – turn left and skirt around the head of the corrie to reach the pointed summit of **Fionn Bheinn**, where there is a trig point but no cairn at 14771 62137 (2hrs 20mins).

Descent can be made by the same route or, to add a little variety, by going on to the east top at 15575 62056,

A wide-angle shot of the northeast corrie of Fionn Bheinn

where there is a small cairn, and then following either the broad south ridge of Creagan nan Laogh or the east ridge of Sail an Tuim Bhain. To do the latter, continue east until you reach a beautifully constructed stone dyke and follow this for a short distance before turning south down a soft grass and moss slope. You can follow one of the many little burns that drain this hillside until an enclosure of forest is reached. This can be skirted on its west side along a fenced corridor to return to your starting point.

STRATHVAICH

ROUTE 62

Am Faochagach (954m)

Pronunciation: Am Fookagach
Translation: the Heathery Place

Distance:	13km
Ascent:	760m
Time:	4hrs
Difficulty:	the river crossing on this route can be impassable when the river is in spate
Maps:	OS sheet 20; Explorer map 436; Area Map 11
Parking:	roadside parking area on A835 just west of bridge over the Abhainn an Torrain Duibh
Start:	from the road cross a small stile to a path
Hostel:	YHA Ullapool; independent bunkhouse Aultguish Inn
B&B/hotel:	Aultguish Inn on A835; Ullapool
Camping:	Ullapool
Access:	Strathvaich Estate, tel: 01997 455226

Park just west of Loch Glascarnoch on the A835 (at the same starting point as for the eastern Fannaichs). Across

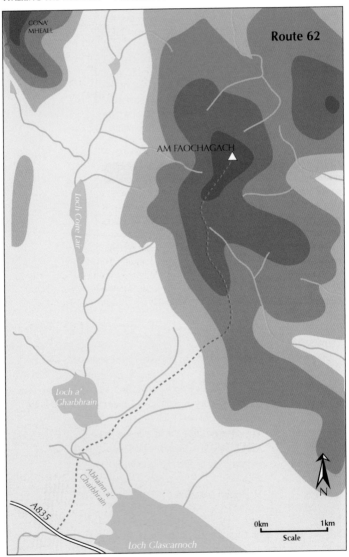

This route has acquired a reputation for being extremely wet, and the crossing of the Abhainn a' Gharbhrain is sometimes held to be well nigh impossible for much of the year. In truth it is probably no worse on either count than many of the other river crossings described in these volumes. In times of spate expect difficulties, but after a few dry days the numerous large stepping-stones across the river provide a fairly easy passage.

the road a small stile leads onto the peat moorland, and a path leads across this to a point where the Abhainn a' Gharbhrain has split into two channels. It is quite possible to cross the river here, though in my view an easier crossing may be had a few hundred metres upstream, before the river divides. If the crossing proves really problematic you could always take off your boots and paddle through.

Once across, pass over or round a couple of large mounds of glacial moraine and head uphill alongside the Allt na h-Uidhe. A path follows this pretty little burn on its southeast side for 1½km. Higher up, head for the centre of the shallow col at GR 30320 76899.

Looking northwest from the summit of Faochagach

There is easy walking along the rounded stony ridge, passing first over a minor top with a small cairn at 30226 77640 (which is not actually its highest point). Continue northwards, dropping down into a broad col before turning northeast up the flanks of **Am Faochagach**. There is actually a short drop, not clear on older OS 1:50,000 maps, before the rounded summit dome is reached. The summit cairn is at 30366 79362 (2hrs 30mins). Accurate navigating in poor visibility could be problematic on these broad, featureless ridges, but apart from the eastern cliffs most of the slopes around here are crag-free and fairly benign.

Return by the same route.

WYVIS

ROUTE 63

BEN WYVIS

Glas Leathad Mor (1046m)

Pronunciation: Glaz Leeyad Voar
Translation: Big Grey-green Hill

Distance:	14km
Ascent:	1020m
Time:	4hrs 50mins
Maps:	OS sheet 20; Explorer map 437; Area Map 11
Parking:	parking area just off road a few metres south of the bridge over the Allt a' Bhealaich Mhor
Start:	footpath from A835 on north side of Allt a' Bhealaich Mhor
Hostel:	independent Aultguish Inn bunkhouse; YHA Ullapool or Inverness
B&B/hotel:	Gorstan; Aultguish Inn
Camping:	Urray on A832 north of Muir of Ord; Dingwall
Access:	Forest Enterprise, tel: 01463 791575 and 01349 830405

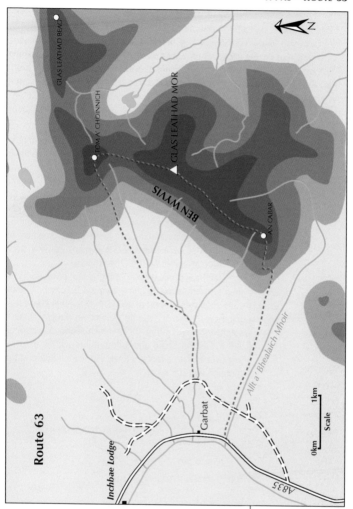

Route 63

From the road take the footpath that starts at the north side of the bridge. It is discreetly signposted. The path, which has been extensively repaired and upgraded

This isolated humpback of a hill looks innocuous enough from the A835, and its long windswept summit ridge has a character that is different from anything else on the Munro round; it is more reminiscent perhaps of the Brecon Beacons in Wales than a Highland mountain. But avalanches are not unknown here in winter and the rounded form of the hill seems to be a magnet to powerful winds.

recently, winds pleasantly alongside the burn heading for the southwest ridge of An Cabar, Ben Wyvis's southern outpost. Climb the ridge mostly on its south side to two prominent cairns near the top. Once the main summit ridge has been gained it is an easy 2km walk along the clipped, mossy grass to reach **Glas Leathad Mor**, the highest point on this broad, undulating top. Look out for the Golden Plover and the rare Dotterel that breed on the summit ridge here. There is a trig point inside a stone enclosure at 46299 68366 (2hrs 45mins).

Continue northeast, dropping gently down to a col, then turn northwest to climb Tom a' Choinnich. A small cairn marks its summit at 46352 70009 (3hrs 20mins).

From here it is a gentle walk down the grassy west-southwest ridge of Tom a' Choinnich. Come down to the Allt a' Gharbh Bhaid and follow it through the trees for just over 1km to a forestry track that leads south past the footpath you started on.

ROUTE 64

Ruadh Stac Mor (918m), A' Mhaighdean
(967m), Beinn Tarsuinn (937m),
Mullach Coire Mhic Fhearchair
(1019m), Sgurr Ban (989m),
Beinn a' Chlaidheimh (916m)

Pronunciation: *Rooa Stack More; Uh Vaygian; Bine Tarshin;*
Mooluch Korrer Veek Errorcur; Skoor Ban; Bine uh Chly-ev
Translation: *Big Red Hill; The Maiden;*
Transverse Mountain; Hill of the Corrie of
Farquhar's Son; White Hill; Mountain of the Sword

Distance:	43km (35km from Shenavall)
Ascent:	2940m (2580m from Shenavall)
Time:	16hrs 30mins (14hrs from Shenavall)
Difficulty:	an exceptionally long, tough walk with a lot of vertical ascent and two river crossings, both of which may be impossible when river is in spate; bivouac gear should be carried
Maps:	OS sheet 19; Explorer map 435; Area Map 10
Parking:	lay-by at Corrie Hallie on A832 south of Dundonnell
Start:	track leads off from road quite close to lay-by
Hostel:	YHA Ullapool
B&B/hotel:	Dundonnell
Camping:	Dundonnell
Access:	Fisherfield/Letterewe Estate, tel: 01445 760302 and Gruinard Estate, tel: 01445 731240

Follow a track from Corrie Hallie along the Gleann
Chaorachain and after about 4km turn off to the right on

These hills, far from any road, are often referred to collectively as the Fisherfield Six, or sometimes just the Big Six. They are certainly the most remote of all the Munros: in poor weather they are largely inaccessible, and in the stalking season hillwalkers are discouraged from entering the area at all. Climbing all these hills in a single outing is a big undertaking; in fact, however they are climbed, they pose a real test for the would-be Munroist.

The pioneering 16th-century traveller and mapmaker Timothy Pont covered his map of this area with the words 'Extreme Wilderness'. Little has changed in the intervening years that would alter this description, and the area is still known as the Great Wilderness.

The bothy at Shenavall, which is under the auspices of the Mountain Bothies Association, is an excellent base for doing these hills, but even starting from here it is a very long and arduous journey to complete all six Munros and return to Corrie Hallie in a single day. It would be wise to take the wherewithal for a bivouac. The hills can be split into smaller groups and approached from Poolewe, Kinlochewe or from the road to the east of Loch a' Bhraoin; however, all these approaches are very long and bivouacs may still be required (the return journey from Poolewe, for example, just to tackle Ruadh Stac Mor and A' Mhaighdean, is over 40km).

The circuit described below is certainly tough, particularly in terms of the amount of vertical ascent involved, but it is a wonderful expedition, the memory of which will not easily fade. It should be saved for a fine spell of weather for reasons that are explained below.

a footpath marked by a cairn (at 10083 82321). This is the same start as for the route on An Teallach described below. Follow this down over rough, rocky and sometimes wet ground, dropping down a sharp little valley alongside a burn to reach the bothy at Shenavall (8km; 2hrs 30mins).

Turn right out of Shenavall and go straight down to the Abhainn Strath na Sealga. A few stones have been placed to try and improve the river crossing, but unless you are very lucky you are likely to get wet feet. If the river is in spate it will not be possible to cross it, nor

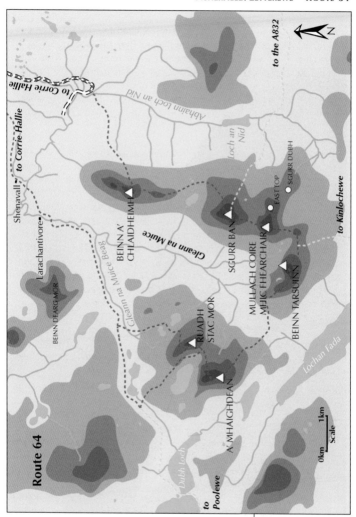

should you try. There are two other river crossings, one
at the end of the day, either of which could prove

259

The summit rocks of A' Mhaighdean

impossible in such conditions. For this reason it would not be wise to attempt this route if rain or poor weather is forecast. You could be stranded when the rivers rise,

and evacuation by a rescue team in the event of any accident could be virtually impossible for many days.

Head across marshy ground towards Larachantivore and walk upstream from here looking for the best crossing of the Abhainn Gleann na Muice. Once across, follow the stalker's path into Gleann na Muice Beag. The path climbs up at the head of this valley and heads over towards Dubh Loch, eventually finding a tortuous route to Poolewe. You should abandon the path, however, about ½km beyond the steep climb. Head south across rough ground, crossing the little burn that flows down from the Lochan a' Bhraghad, and then follow this burn up to a high plateau below the northeastern slopes of **Ruadh Stac Mor**. Anyone who has seen these slopes lit up by the first rays of the morning sun will fully appreciate the mountain's name. Pass between the two lochs and head southeast until you clear the rocks that are at the northern end of the hill, then strike uphill, fairly steeply, on grass at first, staying well to the right of the summit. Once the ridge has been gained, continue up to the stony summit. The cairn is at 01855 75651 (4hrs from Shenavall).

To proceed to A' Mhaighdean, go southeast for just a few metres, then head southwest down a clear path that leads through the steep upper crags of the mountain. This path vanishes amongst boulders lower down. Cross the boulders and head directly for the col below. Another line of steep crags seems to bar access to the col, but there is a break in these crags where the path becomes clear again. It is important to find the right line here as there is only one safe route through these crags. A short scree slope leads down to the col. Cross rough, rocky ground onto A' Mhaighdean's northeastern slopes, then climb the grassy bank to the summit ridge. Go south to the top. There are fine views of **A' Maighdean**'s summit as you approach it along the ridge. The cairn is set amongst rocks at 00781 74907 (5hrs from Shenavall).

The easiest way back to Shenavall from here is to descend from the col between A' Mhaighdean and Ruadh Stac Mor, passing to the east of Fuar Loch Mor and to the northwest of Lochan Feith Mhic'-illean to regain the

Mullach Coire Mhic Fhearchair summit with Sgurr Ban behind

stalker's path. To continue with the circuit, however, go down easy grassy slopes to the southeast of A' Mhaighdean. Head for a rocky pavement to the right of crags. An easy line leads down from the middle of this pavement to the wide, peaty col (02125 73560) below Beinn Tarsuinn, your next objective. Cross the col and climb steep grassy slopes to reach the northwest ridge of Beinn Tarsuinn. Aim for the lower part of the ridge to your left, then climb (still quite steeply but rather more easily) up the ridge. There are good views of the rest of the route from here. Higher up there is a dramatic change in scenery as the ridge narrows and becomes rocky and crenellated with a number of sandstone towers and pinnacles. A little easy scrambling is even called for before the final climb curves round to **Beinn Tarsuinn**'s summit at 03957 72781 (7hrs from Shenavall).

Drop down from the summit to the east-southeast over grassy slopes, interspersed lower down with numerous rocky steps. The next obstacle – Meall Garbh – can be bypassed on the left by an obvious path that leads around its northwestern flanks. From the col beyond Meall Garbh, climb quite steeply up **Mullach Coire Mhic Fhearchair**'s south ridge through a band of sandstone to reach the mountain's capping of white quartzite blocks bedded in a fine silver sand. The summit cairn is at 05209 73497 (8hrs 15mins from Shenavall).

Drop down over more quartzite blocks along a clearly defined edge to the north. The path then veers off this edge to the right to find the easiest route through the lower band of rocks. Although it is quite steep, the path is fairly obvious here and the only real difficulty in this section is the slipperiness of the ground on account of the sand. Cross the col to Sgurr Ban and make for the left-hand side of its south ridge. Another path starts part-way up to the left of the rocky crest of the ridge. The upper slopes of **Sgurr Ban** are covered by a huge expanse of quartzite blocks and stones. Cross a large plateau of these blocks at the top to reach the substantial summit cairn at 05584 74548 (9hrs 5mins from Shenavall).

The descent of Sgurr Ban is quite wearisome for about 2km across more of these awkward stones and blocks. It is a testing section towards the end of a long day. Drop carefully to the northeast for about 2km, passing a small shelter constructed out of the stones, to reach two small lochs on the col. Next, climb the long south ridge of **Beinn a' Chlaidheimh**, passing over a minor top to reach a broad col at the foot of the final climb. The summit is at 06121 77576 (10hrs 50mins from Shenavall).

There are various options for the descent from Beinn a' Chlaidheimh. You could continue to the northern end of the summit ridge then drop very steeply down to the north-northwest to return to Shenavall. If you are heading back to Corrie Hallie, perhaps the easiest descent is to start just south of the summit on a little spur that curves round to the east, then pass round the northern end of this to avoid crags. There is a steep descent from here initially with a few small intermittent crags to avoid. Head northeast over rough ground to reach the Abhainn Loch an Nid at the point where it starts to bend round to the northwest. There are many good stepping-stones by a little island in the river. Cross wet ground on the other side to reach the estate track and follow this, uphill initially, for some 8km back to Corrie Hallie.

AN TEALLACH

ROUTE 65

Sgurr Fiona (1060m),

Bidein a' Ghlas Thuill (1062m)

Pronunciation: *Skoor Fiona; Beedyan uh Glaz Hail*
Translation: *Mountain of Wine (or White Mountain);*
Peak of the Grey-green Hollow

Distance:	15km
Ascent:	1320m
Time:	6hrs 10mins
Difficulty:	scrambling grade 3 if the main ridge is followed direct; difficulties can be bypassed on paths to the west
Maps:	OS sheet 19; Explorer map 435; Area Map 10
Parking:	lay-by on A832 at Corrie Hallie
Start:	along private track which is close to lay-by
Hostel:	YHA Ullapool; independent Dundonnell
B&B/hotel:	Dundonnell
Camping:	Dundonnell
Access:	tel: 01854 655252

The massive drop to the east of An Teallach and the wonderful sight of the castellated tops of red Torridonian sandstone from both north and south offer some of the most dramatic and memorable scenes to be found in British mountains.

From Corrie Hallie follow the track up Gleann Chaorachain until at 10083 82321 a footpath to Shenavall leads off to the right. This is followed for a further 1½km almost to the foot of Sail Liath's southeast

Between Little Loch Broom and the Great Wilderness of Fisherfield and Letterewe rises one of Scotland's most impressive mountain ranges: An Teallach (The Forge). The traverse of An Teallach's castellated ridge from Sail Liath to Bidein a' Ghlas Thuill is rightly regarded as one of Scotland's classic routes. It does involve some serious scrambling across a series of rock pinnacles; however, the non-scrambler can still enjoy this route by following easier paths to the southwest that circumvent the difficult section. Whether the scramble is included or not, this route is finer than the easy path up from Dundonnell.

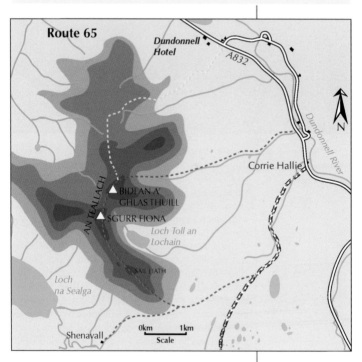

ridge. Cross heather to reach the ridge, which is climbed direct to the top. There are two or three little trails that wind their way up here, but none is necessary – the going

The An Teallach traverse from Bidein a' Ghlas Thuill

is quite straightforward over heathery ledges and bouldery scree towards the top. It is worth stopping for a rest on this ridge just to look back at the wonderful remote wilderness of Fisherfield. If you haven't yet climbed the Fisherfield Six, this will give you a good perspective on what you have in store. If you have climbed them, you can look back and gloat.

Pass the summit cairn of Sail Liath at 07169 82476 and descend quite steeply to the west. From the col, climb the fine little peak of Cadha Gobhlach then descend again quite steeply to the north, then northwest, to another col. From this col there is a stiff climb to reach the foot of the Corrag Bhuidhe buttress. When you are quite high above the col you are faced with a choice. Ahead of you lie the pinnacles of Corrag Bhuidhe, which offer quite a hard and sometimes exposed scrambling challenge. For the average hill walker without scrambling or climbing experience they would be a daunting prospect – and it is worth remembering that there have been fatalities here. However, they do offer a fine mountaineering route across the hill with some spectacular rock scenery and some very airy situations.

Walkers who are not tempted by such delights can veer off on a path to the left which bypasses the most difficult scrambling section and emerges on the west ridge of **Sgurr Fiona**. From here it is an easy climb up to the summit.

If you accept the challenge of the pinnacles, however, you must next climb the two short, steep pitches up the southeast tower of Corrag Bhuidhe on rounded but firm sandstone holds. There is an escape route to the left after the first pitch, which bypasses the most difficult section, but even this has its own 'bad step' and requires some care. From the top continue over or round the other pinnacles, which offer a variety of scrambling options culminating in the shapely spire of Lord Berkeley's Seat. The direct route up the crest of the middle pinnacle is very exposed, but a line from lower down to its left offers a much easier passage. The drop into the corrie to the east from Lord Berkeley's Seat is one of the biggest and most impressive in Britain. Beyond Lord Berkeley's Seat scramble down over sandstone ledges and continue to the summit of **Sgurr Fiona**. The summit cairn is reached at 06408 83665 (4hrs 5mins).

Descend the sandy ledges of Sgurr Fiona's north ridge and climb easily up to **Bidein a' Ghlas Thuill**'s trig point at 06904 84359, which has good views of the ridge you have just traversed (4hrs 40mins).

Continue north, dropping steeply down to the col between Bidein and Glas Mheall Mor. A small cairn marks the start of a steep, sandy descent into the shadowy corrie below, which is fringed with the towering cliffs of Bidein's east ridge. Follow a faint path east, staying close to the burn. Eventually this passes a waterfall and crosses an inclined sandstone pavement before tunnelling through a thicket of rhododendron bushes to emerge at the road. It is not recommended to do this route in the reverse direction unless you are very confident of your climbing ability.

CONIVAL (FREEVATER)

ROUTE 66

Eididh nan Clach Geala (928m), Meall nan Ceapraichean (977m), Cona' Mheall (980m), Beinn Dearg (1084m)

Pronunciation: *Eye-tee nern Klach Geeyaller; Miaowl nern Kee-aprikan; Kon-eye-val; Bine Jerrack*
Translation: *Nest of the White Stones; Hill of the Lumpy Hillocks; Joined Hill; Red Mountain*

Distance:	26km (6km of which can be cycled)
Ascent:	1390m
Time:	7hrs 50mins (about 1hr can be saved cycling through the trees)
Maps:	OS sheet 20; Explorer map 436; Area Map 11
Parking:	off-road ¾km south of Inverlael Farm, at start of private track
Start:	follow the private track from the road
Hostel:	YHA Ullapool; independent Ullapool
B&B/hotel:	Ullapool
Camping:	Ullapool
Access:	Foich Estate, tel: 01854 655274

The four hills collectively known as the Deargs are all accessible in a single day from the A835 at the southern end of Loch Broom, as described here. They sit quite tightly together amid some rugged and beautiful countryside and make a fairly long but very enjoyable outing. Cona' Mheall and Beinn Dearg are also sometimes climbed from the south, and the southern aspect of these hills has much to commend it too.

Proceed from the A835 along the private track, passing a turning on the left and another one on the right about

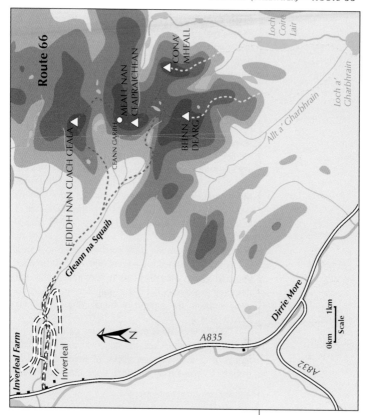

1km further on. Shortly beyond this the track swings left across the burn and then climbs on the north side of the burn to the edge of the forest. It is possible to cycle to this point. Continue on the constructed footpath on the north side of the River Lael for nearly 3km, passing a couple of waterfalls in the sharply incised valley until at GR 23398 83453 a small cairn marks the start of a path on the left which is followed up towards the Lochan a' Chnapaich. About ½km before this lochan is reached turn off over heathery ground towards the west ridge of **Eididh nan**

Clach Geala. Traverse this ridge on a slanting line to make a fairly gentle gradient, which brings you to the foot of the final grassy summit slope. Climb grass and boulders, some of which are definitely 'geala' (white), to the summit cairn at 25715 84320 (3hrs 30mins).

From the stony summit there is a good view down to the fishing port of Ullapool and also across to An Teallach, the Fisherfield hills, the Torridon hills and the Fannaichs. Descend southeast to a wild, rocky col with several lochans in it. From this side it is easy to pick out the line of ascent on the other side of the col; it follows a grassy ramp through a profusion of small crags. This line may not be so easy to find if doing the route in reverse. **Meall nan Ceapraichean** has two rounded stony summits – the 'lumpy hillocks' of its name – the south hillock being just the highest by 10m at 25728 82534 (4hrs 15mins).

Continue down the stony southeast ridge to a wide col. A small unnamed hill – Point 886 – stands between you and Cona' Mheall. Cross or circumvent this hill, dropping to a further col before climbing straight up the stony slope to the summit of **Cona' Mheall** at 27516 81618 (5hrs).

Retrace your steps to the col and pass to the left (south) of Point 886. Cross the stone wall and then climb alongside it to the upper slopes of **Beinn Dearg**. Be thankful as you toil up the steep slope that you weren't

Looking north from Eididh nan Clach Geala

*Beinn Dearg
from the col*

the one who had the job of coming up here every day to build this wall. It extends along the whole length of Beinn Dearg's west ridge. Cross over the wall where it changes direction and climb the last short leg to the summit at 25943 81176 (5hrs 55mins).

Return to the col and follow a path alongside the infant River Lael past a small lochan, rejoining your outward route lower down the valley.

ROUTE 67

Seana Bhraigh (927m)

Pronunciation: *Shenner Vrye*
Translation: *Old Upland*

Distance:	22km (16km of which can be covered by bike on a private track)
Ascent:	780m
Time:	5hrs (if using a bike along Strath Mulzie); about 2hrs more if walking
Difficulty:	the full circuit via Creag an Duine involves scrambling grade 1 and a short exposed section of scrambling grade 2; this is avoided altogether by the route described here.
Maps:	OS sheet 20; Explorer maps 436 and 440
Parking:	there is a parking area for walkers' cars before Corriemulzie Lodge, just beyond a wooden cottage – about 2½km past Duag Bridge
Start:	continue on the private track along Strath Mulzie
Hostel:	YHA Ullapool; independent Inchnadamph and Ullapool
B&B/hotel:	Oykel Bridge; Lairg
Camping:	Lairg
Access:	Corriemulzie Estate, tel: 01863 766683

Seana Bhraigh is a lovely hill, rich in wild flowers, and the circuit of its two ridges starting up the steep rocky northeast ridge to Creag an Duine, passing round the head of the corrie and descending the grassy northwest ridge, makes an excellent outing. This does involve some scrambling, however, including a couple of short though steep and exposed sections, which may not be to everyone's liking. However, these difficulties can be avoided by both ascending and returning via the northwest ridge as described here.

The track to the hill along Strath Mulzie crosses the Corriemulzie river at a ford, but there are huge boulders

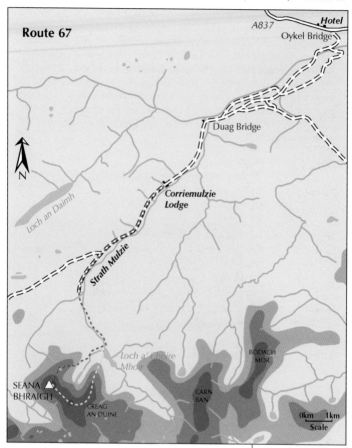

by the side of the crossing which make this a fairly easy task. More problematic is crossing back over the river below the Loch a' Choire Mhoir when you leave the track behind. There are few obvious places. Perhaps the easiest option is to cross just beyond the outflow of the loch, where the river is quite wide but shallow. Be prepared to get wet feet or take off your boots. Once across, follow

Seana Bhraigh has the reputation of being the most remote Munro because its summit is some 20km from the nearest tarmac road. This is perhaps a little unjustified since cars can now be left some 2½km beyond Duag Bridge and a good private track can be used for the rest of the distance (about 8km) right up to the base of the hill. Many parties elect to take bikes to eat up these long miles, and this brings Seana Bhraigh into the category of a fairly easy day out. The hill can also be climbed from the west from Inverlael, however this lacks some of the scenic and logistical advantages of the northern approach.

The Luchd Choire from Seana Bhraigh

the burn that comes down from Loch Luchd Choire and climb up into the corrie. When you are just beyond the lip of the corrie, climb the grassy slopes on your right onto the northwest ridge and follow this over the little top at 760m to a small lochan. From here it is a steady climb up the final slope which is covered with blaeberry and heather and peppered with rocks. There is a stone enclosure at the summit of **Seana Bhraigh** 28181 87860 (3hrs 5mins if using a bike along Strath Mulzie).

Return by the same route. You may be tempted to descend by the boulder slopes below the small lochan, but this is not recommended: they are mossy, slippery and loose – the perfect recipe for a lower-limb injury.

INCHNADAMPH

ROUTE 68

Conival (987m),

Ben More Assynt (998m)

Pronunciation: *Kon-eye-val; Ben More Assynt*
Translation: *Shoulder of the Big Hill; Big Hill of Assynt*

Distance:	18km
Ascent:	1200m
Time:	6hrs 20mins
Maps:	OS sheet 15; Explorer map 442; Area Map 11
Parking:	car park just off A837 by hotel entrance at Inchnadamph
Start:	along private road just north of River Traligill
Hostel:	YHA Ullapool
B&B/hotel:	Inchnadamph, Ullapool
Camping:	Ullapool; Ardmair (5km north of Ullapool)
Access:	Assynt Estate office, tel: 01571 844203

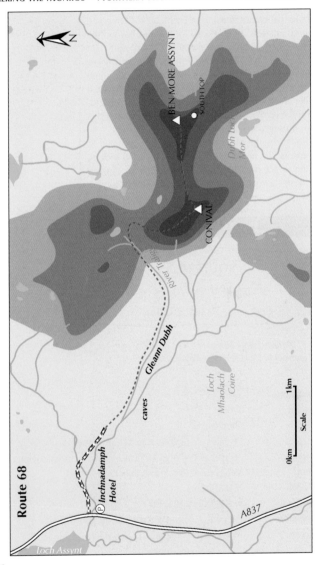

The landscape of the far northwest of Scotland – the old counties of Ross-shire and Sutherland – is like an illustration from a children's fairytale. Its wild mountain moorland is studded with a myriad lochs and pools and punctuated by extraordinarily shaped hills that rise up in improbable arcs out of the ground. Ben More Assynt and Conival are the two highest hills in this rough and rugged stretch of the northern Highlands. They give wonderful views across this strange expanse of land.

Starting from Inchnadamph, where there is a car park by the hotel entrance, walk 100m up the main road and, just beyond the bridge over the River Traligill, go up the private roadway past a number of cottages to Glenbain. About 1km beyond Glenbain at GR 27011 21081 the path divides, with the right-hand branch crossing the burn and

Conival from Gleann Dubh

Ben More Assynt from Conival

heading up to caves. Take the left-hand branch; this keeps close to the north bank of the River Traligill and heads up Gleann Dubh, with the huge silver-grey bulk of Conival rearing up ahead. The path crosses grassy meadows and peat and stays close to the burn all the way. Head for the col between Beinn an Fhurain and Conival. At the top of the steep section you emerge into a high, shallow corrie fringed with rocks. Head for the lowest point of the col, where the rocks are at their lowest and a short, easy scramble brings you onto the col. From here climb the broad quartzite ridge until the summit of **Conival** is reached. The summit cairn, a stone enclosure, is at the southeast end of the ridge at 30357 19939 (3hrs 30mins).

The ridge from Conival to Ben More Assynt is a wonderful airy traverse to a high, remote hill. At times it narrows a little, but never deliciously so. Start by descending big blocks to the east until a path on the ridge is reached. In thick weather it can be difficult to work out exactly where you are on this ridge, for it switchbacks over a number of little tops and dips, and the rough stony path is a real ankle-twister, making it hard to count paces. When you think you must have come to **Ben More**'s summit and a small cairn greets you, there is still a little way to go.

Drop down 20m over boulders and then climb steeply up to reach the true summit. Two small cairns a few feet apart mark the highest point at 31839 20147 (4hrs 15mins).

There is a descent further along Ben More's south ridge, dropping very steeply around crags to boggy ground, then coming back through the col between Conival and Breabag Tarsuinn. The easier and perhaps pleasanter way back is to return by the route of ascent.

STRATH VAGASTIE

ROUTE 69

BEN KLIBRECK

Meall nan Con (961m)

Pronunciation: Ben Klee-breck
Translation: Hill of the Cliff Slope

Distance:	11km
Ascent:	830m
Time:	4hrs 5mins
Maps:	OS sheet 16; Explorer map 443; Area Map 11
Parking:	roadside by A836 at 54575 30880
Start:	cross the River Vagastie just below the car park
Hostel:	YHA Carbisdale Castle
B&B/hotel:	Crask Inn on A836; Lairg
Camping:	Lairg
Access:	Clebrig Estate, tel: 01549 411245, and (if approached from further south at Crask) Altnaharra Estate, tel: 01549 411220

Once across the burn, pass round some deer fencing and climb over a small subsidiary ridge to reach the southern end of Loch na Glas-choille. From here another ridge is

Ben Klibreck can be done in the same day as Ben Hope, but when it is approached from due west, as described here, it is a tougher climb than Ben Hope and should not be underestimated. There is a small pull-in off the A836 at GR 54575 30880 where there is enough room for several cars to be parked, and from here the River Vagastie can usually be crossed quite easily except after heavy rainfall.

crossed to reach the northern end of Loch nan Uan. A fence runs between these two lochs and this can usefully be followed. Pass right around the northern end of Loch nan Uan and come south for a few hundred metres to a point about halfway down the loch. From here ascend steeply up the grass and heather slopes to the east. It is a stiff climb. A path has tried to establish itself here but without a lot of success; only higher up this steep section,

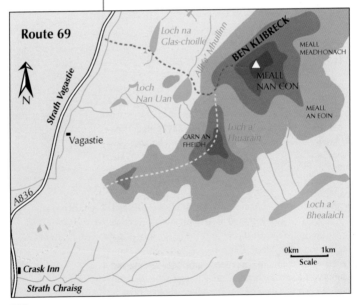

where there is a band of greasy rocks, does the path become clear.

This brings you to the lowest point of the col on the north–south ridge between Ben Klibreck and a subsidiary top at 808m. In fact, before you quite reach the top of this col, you come to a path that leads off to the ridge of A' Chioch. Follow this path northeast over the grassy ridge, then veer round to the east, crossing another small col before climbing quite steeply over blocks and scree to reach **Meall nan Con**, which is the highest point on Ben Klibreck. When it feels as if you've reached the top, you have, and the trig point and stone enclosure appear just a few metres further on at 58529 29901 (2hrs 45mins).

Return by the same route, making sure you locate the correct point of descent from the col to Loch nan Uan (GR 57543 29137).

A longer but altogether gentler approach can be made from further up the road at Vagastie House, or further south still at the Crask Inn. Easier-angled slopes can be followed from these starting points to reach the main ridge above Loch nan Uan.

Ben Klibreck across the Loch na Glas Choile (the ascent line to the col is on the right)

STRATH MORE

ROUTE 70

Ben Hope (927m)

Pronunciation: Ben Hope
Translation: Hill of the Bay (Norse origin)

Distance:	7km
Ascent:	920m
Time:	3hrs 15mins
Maps:	OS sheet 9; Explorer map 447; Area Map 11
Parking:	roadside at foot of hill at 46190 47670
Start:	the start of the path is signposted
Hostel:	YHA, Tongue
B&B/hotel:	Durness; Lairg
Camping:	Durness; Lairg
Access:	Strathmore Estate, tel: 01549 411248

Although this most northerly of the Munros sits right by the roadside and is much frequented – indeed it has a substantial path running all the way up – it nevertheless has an air of isolation and remoteness which is rarely found on other hills. This is partly induced by the long drive to get to it (unless you happen to live in Durness) and partly by the bleakness and wildness of the wind- and rain-ravaged landscape hereabouts.

There is a parking area by the roadside a few metres up from a barn. The path starts, appropriately enough, behind the Ben Hope signpost. Climb quite steeply from the parking area up the valley of a small burn. After a few hundred metres the well-worn path divides; either branch will take you to the same destination. The path curves round towards the east and rises rapidly, eventually

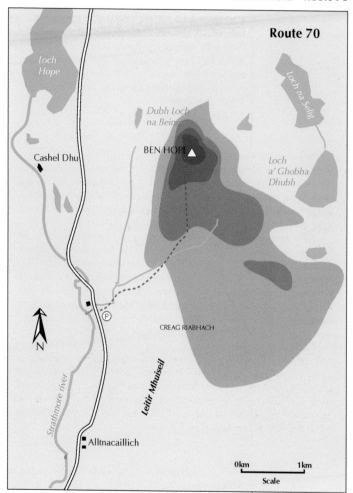

Route 70

Loch Hope

Loch na Seilg

Dubh Loch na Beinn

BEN HOPE

Loch a' Ghobha Dhubh

Cashel Dhu

CREAG RIABHACH

N

Strathmore river

Leitir Mhuiseil

Alltnacaillich

0km   1km
Scale

finding a break in the steep, craggy west flank of the mountain, and at this point it veers back to the north.

There is a short grassy section followed by scree and stones. From this point on, cairns begin to appear and

283

these decorate the path all the way to the summit. Soon the angle relents, and towards the top the path moves close to the edge of the western crags. For the last couple of hundred metres, however, it veers away to the north-east until **Ben Hope**'s summit cairn and trig point are reached towards the back of the broad top at 47753 50139 (2hrs 10mins).

Return by the same route.

Finished your last Munro?

Welcome to the select but growing band of mountaineers who have 'done the Munros'. Over 2500km of walking (and possibly some cycling) are behind you, and over 157,000 vertical metres of climbing – that's equivalent to starting at sea level and climbing Mount Everest nearly 18 times. I hope you agree that it was a goal worth pursuing.

There is no prize for completing the round, no fame or fortune to be won, just the satisfaction of having done it. And yet the rewards are without price: you'll have built for yourself an album of unforgettable memories. You have explored extraordinary places, admired incredible sights, encountered wonderful creatures. You have overcome difficulties along the way. And hopefully at the end of the day, no matter how much you struggled to climb the next hill, or were beaten by Highland storms, you will have emerged stronger in body, and with heart and mind both greatly enlarged.

Congratulations!

APPENDIX 1
Bibliography

Barton, B. and Wright, B., *A Chance in a Million? Scottish Avalanches* (Scottish Mountaineering Trust, 2000)

Bennet, D.J. (ed), *Munro's Tables* (Scottish Mountaineering Trust, 1997)

British Geological Survey (various authors), *British Regional Geology Series*, 'Volume 2: the Northern Highlands', 'Volume 3: The Tertiary Volcanic Districts', 'Volume 4: The Grampian Highlands' (HMSO, London)

Brown, H., *Hamish's Mountain Walk* (Baton Wicks, 1996)

Daiches, D., *Bonnie Prince Charlie* (Penguin Books, 2002)

Dalley, S. and Dalley, J. (ed), *The Independent Hostel Guide* (The Backpackers Press, 2002)

Darling, F. and Boyd, M., *The Highlands and Islands* (Collins, Fontana New Naturalist Series, 1964)

Dixon, C. and Dixon, J., *Plants and People in Ancient Scotland* (Tempus, 2000)

Drummond, P., *Scottish Hill and Mountain Names* (Edinburgh, Scottish Mountaineering Trust, 1991)

Lusby, P. and Wright, J., *Scottish Wild Plants* (Mercat Press, 1997)

Mackenzie, W.C., *Scottish Place Names*, Kegan Paul (Trench and Trubner, London, 1931)

Macleod, A. (translation), *The Songs of Duncan Ban Macintyre* (Oliver and Boyd for the Scottish Gaelic Texts Society, 1952)

Mitchell, I., *Scotland's Mountains Before the Mountaineers* (Luath Press, 1998)

Moran, M., *The Munros in Winter* (David and Charles, 1986)

Moran, M., *Scotland's Winter Mountains* (David and Charles, 1988)

Murray, W.H., *Scotland's Mountains* (Scottish Mountaineering Trust, 1987)

Nicolaisen, W., *Scottish Place-names, their Study and Significance* (Batsford, London, 1976)

Ross, D., *Scottish Place Names* (Birlinn, 2001)

Watson, W.J., *The History of the Celtic Place-names of Scotland* (Birlinn, 1993 (first published William Blackwood and Sons, Edinburgh, 1926))

APPENDIX 2
Contact Details

Avalanche Warnings Internet: sais.gov.uk and posted in all major winter resorts

Backpackers Club c/o P Maguire, 29 Lynton Drive, High Lane, Stockport, Cheshire SK6 8JE

Caledonian MacBrayne (west coast ferries): tel: 01475 650100 or 0990 650000

Forest Enterprise (Scotland): 1 Highlander Way, Inverness Business Park, Inverness IV2 7GB tel: 01463 232045 Internet: www.forestry.gov.uk

Harvey Maps 12–16 Main Street, Doune, Perthshire FK16 6BJ tel: 01786 841202 Internet: www.harveymaps.co.uk

Hillphones Internet: www.hillphones.info

Independent Backpackers Hostels Scotland c/o Pete Thomas, Croft Bunkhouse, Portnalong, Isle of Skye, IV47 8SL tel: 01478 640254 Internet: www.hostel-scotland.co.uk

List of Munroists if you wish to have your name added to the 'official' list of Munroists, notification of completion can be made to the Clerk of the List, currently David A. Kirk, Greenhowe Farmhouse, Banchory-Devenish, Aberdeenshire, AB12 5YJ. The Mountaineering Council of Scotland will update you of new contact details if there is a change of Clerks.

Mountaineering Council of Scotland The Old Granary, West Mill Street, Perth, PH1 5QP tel: 01738 638227 Internet: www.mountaineering-scotland.org.uk

National Trust for Scotland Wemyss House, 28 Charlotte Square, Edinburgh EH2 4ET tel: 0131 2439300 Internet: www.nts.org.uk

Ordnance Survey Romsey Road, Southampton SO16 4GU tel: 08456 050505 Internet: www.ordnancesurvey.co.uk or www.ordsvy.gov.uk

Police Stations

Aviemore	tel: 01479 810222
Fort William	tel: 01397 702361
Inverness	tel:01463 715555
Portree and Lochalsh	tel: 01478 612888
Strathclyde	tel: 0141 5322000
Tayside	tel: 01764 662212

Rail enquiries tel: 0845 7484950

Sabhal Mor Ostaig the Gaelic College, Slèite, Isle of Skye 1V44 8RQ tel: 01471 888240 Internet: www.smo.uhi.ac.uk/smo/cg

Scottish Natural Heritage currently 12 Hope Terrace, Edinburgh tel: 0131 4474784 (but shortly moving to Inverness) Internet: www.snh.org.uk

Scottish Tourist Board tel: 0845 2255121 Internet: www.visitscotland.com

Scottish Youth Hostels Association 7 Glebe Crescent, Stirling, FK8 2JA tel: 01786 891400 Central Reservations Service tel: 08701 55 32 55 Internet: www.syha.org.uk

Weather forecasts
Met Office Area Forecasts for Outdoor Pursuits (updated daily at 0600 and 1800):

West Highlands	tel: 09068 500 441
East Highlands	tel: 09068 500 442

The Weather Centre Lauriston. 'Walk and Climb' weather forecast updated daily approx 4.00pm tel: 09063 666070

APPENDIX 3
Index of Munros (alphabetical)

Munro	Volume	Page
A' Bhuidheanach Bheag	1	
A' Chailleach (Fannaichs)	2	241
A' Chailleach (Monadhliath)	2	81
A' Chralaig	2	143
A' Ghlas-bheinn	2	149
A' Mhaighdean	2	257
A' Mharconaich	1	
Am Basteir	2	198
Am Bodach	1	
Am Faochagach	2	251
An Caisteal	1	
An Coileachan	2	245
An Gearanach	1	
An Riabhachan	2	167
An Sgarsoch	2	60
An Socach (Glen Affric)	2	153
An Socach (Glen Ey/Glenshee)	1	
An Socach (Loch Mullardoch)	2	164
An Stuc	1	
Angels' Peak, The (Sgor an Lochain Uaine)	2	54
Aonach air Chrith	2	130
Aonach Beag (Loch Ossian)	1	
Aonach Beag (Lochaber)	1	
AONACH EAGAICH, THE	1	
Aonach Meadhoin (Glenshiel)	2	139
Aonach Mor	1	
BEINN A' BHEITHIR	1	
Beinn a' Bhuird	2	39
Beinn a' Chaorainn (Glen Derry)	2	43
Beinn a' Chaorainn (Laggan)	2	90
Beinn a' Chlachair	1	
Beinn a' Chlaidheimh	2	257
Beinn a' Chleibh	1	

Note: Appendices 3 and 4 cover volumes 1 and 2, and include all recognised Munros. Appendix 3 also includes ranges (shown in capital letters). Routes and ranges in volume 2 are shown in bold.

Munro	Volume	Page
Beinn a' Chochuill	1	
BEINN A' CHREUCHAIN	1	
Beinn a' Chroin	1	
BEINN A' GHLO	1	
Beinn Achaladair	1	
BEINN ALLIGIN	2	225
Beinn an Dothaidh	1	
Beinn Bheoil	1	
Beinn Bhreac	**2**	**43**
Beinn Bhrotain	**2**	**57**
Beinn Bhuidhe (Glen Fyne)	1	
Beinn Chabhair	1	
Beinn Dearg (Atholl)	1	
Beinn Dearg (Inverlael)	**2**	**268**
Beinn Dorain	1	
Beinn Dubhchraig	1	
Beinn Eibhinn	1	
BEINN EIGHE	2	234
Beinn Eunaich	1	
Beinn Fhada (Ben Attow)	**2**	**149**
Beinn Fhionnlaidh	1	
Beinn Fhionnlaidh (Glen Affric)	**2**	**157**
Beinn Ghlas (Lawers)	1	
Beinn Heasgarnich	1	
Beinn Ime	1	
Beinn Iutharn Mhor	**2**	**63**
Beinn Liath Mhor (Coulin)	**2**	**189**
Beinn Liath Mhor Fannaich	**2**	**245**
Beinn Mhanach	1	
Beinn Mheadhoin	**2**	**46**
Beinn na Lap	1	
Beinn nan Aighenan	1	
Beinn Narnain	1	
Beinn Sgritheall	**2**	**122**
Beinn Sgulaird	1	
Beinn Tarsuinn	**2**	**257**
Beinn Teallach	**2**	**90**
Beinn Tulaichean	1	

Munro	Volume	Page
Beinn Udlamain	1	
Ben Alder	1	
Ben Avon (Leabaidh an Daimh Bhuidhe)	**2**	**39**
Ben Challum	1	
Ben Chonzie	1	
Ben Cruachan	1	
Ben Hope	**2**	**282**
BEN KLIBRECK	**2**	**279**
Ben Lawers	1	
Ben Lomond	1	
Ben Lui	1	
Ben Macdui	**2**	**48**
Ben More (Crianlarich)	1	
Ben More (Mull)	1	
Ben More Assynt	**2**	**275**
Ben Nevis	1	
Ben Oss	1	
Ben Starav	1	
Ben Vane	1	
Ben Vorlich (Callander)	1	
Ben Vorlich (Inveruglas)	1	
BEN WYVIS	**2**	**254**
Bidean nam Bian	1	
Bidein a' Choire Sheasgaich	**2**	**174**
Bidein a' Ghlas Thuill	**2**	**264**
Binnein Beag	1	
Binnein Mor	1	
Bla Bheinn (or Blaven)	**2**	**222**
Braeriach	**2**	**71**
Braigh Coire Chruinn-bhalgain	1	
Broad Cairn	1	
Bruach na Frithe	**2**	**198**
BUACHAILLE ETIVE BEAG	1	
BUACHAILLE ETIVE MOR	1	
Bynack More	**2**	**67**
Cac Carn Beag (Lochnagar)	1	
Cairn Bannoch	1	
Cairn Gorm	**2**	**67**

Munro	Volume	Page
Cairn of Claise	1	
Cairn Toul	2	54
Cairnwell, The	1	
Carn a' Gheoidh	1	
Carn a' Chlamain	1	
Carn a' Choire Bhaidheach	1	
Carn a' Mhaim	2	48
Carn an Fhidhleir	2	60
Carn an Righ	1	
Carn an t-Sagairt Mor	1	
Carn an Tuirc	1	
Carn Aosda	1	
Carn Bhac	2	63
Carn Dearg	2	81
Carn Dearg (Ben Alder)	1	
Carn Dearg (Loch Ossian)	1	
Carn Eige	2	157
Carn Ghluasaid	2	146
Carn Gorm (Glen Lyon)	1	
Carn Liath	1	
Carn Liath	2	86
Carn Mairg	1	
Carn Mor Dearg	1	
Carn na Caim	1	
Carn nan Gabhar	1	
Carn nan Gobhar (Lapaich)	2	167
Carn nan Gobhar (Strathfarrar)	2	171
Carn Sgulain	2	81
Chno Dearg	1	
Ciste Dhubh	2	139
Cona' Mheall (Inverlael)	2	268
Conival (Inchnadamph)	2	275
Craig Leacach	1	
Creag a' Mhaim	2	130
Creag Meagaidh	2	86
Creag Mhor	1	
Creag nan Damh	2	130
Creag Pitridh	1	

Munro	Volume	Page
Creise	1	
Cruach Ardrain	1	
Derry Cairngorm	2	48
Devil's Point, The	2	54
Driesh	1	
Druim Shionnach	2	130
Eididh nan Clach Geala	2	268
Fionn Bheinn	2	249
Gairich	2	109
Garbh Chioch Mhor	2	102
Geal Charn (Ardverikie)	1	
Geal Charn (Drumochter)	1	
Geal Charn (Monadhliath)	2	84
Geal Charn (opposite Ben Alder)	1	
Glas Bheinn Mhor	1	
Glas Leathad Mor	2	254
Glas Maol (Glenshee)	1	
Glas Tulaichean	1	
Gleouraich	2	110
GREY CORRIES, THE	1	
Gulvain	2	96
Inaccessible Pinnacle (Sgurr Dearg)	2	209
Ladhar Bheinn	2	119
LIATHACH	2	229
Luinne Bheinn	2	115
Lurg Mhor	2	174
Mam Sodhail	2	157
MAMORES, THE	1	
Maoile Lunndaidh	2	181
Maol Chean-dearg (Torridon)	2	186
Maol Chinn-dearg (Glenshiel)	2	130
Mayar	1	
Meall a' Bhuiridh	1	
Meall a' Choire Leith	1	
Meall a' Chrasgaidh	2	241
Meall Buidhe (Glen Lyon)	1	
Meall Buidhe (Knoydart)	2	115
Meall Chuaich	1	

Munro	Volume	Page
Meall Corranaich	1	
Meall Dearg (Glencoe)	1	
Meall Garbh (Glen Lyon)	1	
Meall Garbh (Lawers)	1	
Meall Ghaordaidh	1	
Meall Glas	1	
Meall Gorm (Fannaichs)	**2**	**245**
Meall Greigh	1	
Meall na Aighean	1	
Meall na Teanga	**2**	**99**
Meall nan Ceapraichean	**2**	**268**
Meall nan Con	**2**	**279**
Meall nan Eun	1	
Meall nan Tarmachan	1	
Monadh Mor	**2**	**57**
Moruisg	**2**	**184**
Mount Keen	1	
Mullach an Rathain (Liathac)	**2**	**229**
Mullach Clach a' Bhlair	**2**	**75**
Mullach Coire Mhic Fhearchair	**2**	**257**
Mullach Fraoch-choire	**2**	**143**
Mullach na Dheiragain	**2**	**153**
Mullach nan Coirean	1	
Na Gruagaichean	1	
Ruadh Stac Mor	**2**	**257**
Ruadh Stac Mor (Beinn Eighe)	**2**	**234**
Saddle, The	**2**	**125**
Sail Chaorainn	**2**	**146**
Saileag	**2**	**139**
Scheihallion	1	
Seana Bhraigh	**2**	**272**
Sgairneach Mhor	1	
Sgiath Chuil	1	
Sgor Gaibhre	1	
Sgor Gaoith	**2**	**79**
Sgor na h-Ulaidh	1	
Sgorr Dhearg	1	
Sgorr Dhonuill	1	

Munro	Volume	Page
Sgorr nam Fiannaidh	1	
Sgorr Ruadh	2	189
Sgurr a' Bhealaich Dheirg	2	139
Sgurr a' Chaorachain	2	178
Sgurr a' Choire Ghlais	2	171
Sgurr a' Ghreadaidh	2	202
Sgurr a' Mhadaidh	2	202
Sgurr a' Mhaim	1	
Sgurr a' Mhaoraich	2	113
Sgurr Alasdair	2	215
Sgurr an Doire Leathain	2	130
Sgurr an Lochain	2	130
Sgurr Ban (Fisherfield)	2	257
Sgurr Breac	2	241
Sgurr Choinnich	2	178
Sgurr Choinnich Mor	1	
Sgurr Dubh Mor	2	218
Sgurr Eilde Mor	1	
Sgurr Fhuaran	2	135
Sgurr Fhuar-thuill	2	171
Sgurr Fiona	2	264
Sgurr Mhic Choinnich	2	209
Sgurr Mhor (Beinn Alligin)	2	225
Sgurr Mor (Fannaichs)	2	245
Sgurr Mor (Glen Kingie)	2	106
Sgurr na Banachdich	2	206
Sgurr na Carnach	2	135
Sgurr na Ciche	2	102
Sgurr na Ciste Duibhe (Five Sisters)	2	135
Sgurr na Lapaich	2	167
Sgurr na Ruaidhe	2	171
Sgurr na Sgine	2	125
Sgurr nan Ceannaichean	2	184
Sgurr nan Ceathreamhnan	2	153
Sgurr nan Clach Geala	2	241
Sgurr nan Coireachan (Glen Dessary)	2	102
Sgurr nan Coireachan (Glenfinnan)	2	92
Sgurr nan Conbhairean	2	146

Munro	Volume	Page
Sgurr nan Each	2	241
Sgurr nan Eag	2	218
Sgurr nan Gillean	2	194
Sgurr Thuilm	2	93
Slioch	2	238
Spidean a' Choire Leith	2	229
Spidean Coire nan Clach	2	234
Spidean Mialach	2	110
Sron a' Choire Ghairbh	2	99
Stob a' Choire Mheadhoin	1	
Stob a' Choire Odhair	1	
Stob Ban (Grey Corries)	1	
Stob Ban (Mamores)	1	
Stob Binnein	1	
Stob Choire Claurigh	1	
Stob Coir'an Albannaich	1	
Stob Coire a' Chairn	1	
Stob Coire an Laoigh	1	
Stob Coire Easain	1	
Stob Coire Raineach	1	
Stob Coire Sgreamhach	1	
Stob Coire Sgriodain	1	
Stob Dearg (Glencoe)	1	
Stob Diamh	1	
Stob Dubh (Glencoe)	1	
Stob Ghabhar	1	
Stob na Broige	1	
Stob Poite Coire Ardair	2	86
Stuc a' Chroin	1	
Stuchd an Lochain	1	
Toll Creagach	2	162
Tolmount	1	
Tom a' Choinich	2	162
Tom Buidhe	1	
Tom na Gruagaich	2	225

APPENDIX 4

Index of Munros (by height)

	Height order	Height (m)	Volume	Page
Ben Nevis	1	1343	1	
Ben Macdui	**2**	**1309**	**2**	**48**
Braeriach	**3**	**1296**	**2**	**71**
Cairn Toul	**4**	**1291**	**2**	**54**
Angels' Peak, The (Sgor an Lochain Uaine)	**5**	**1258**	**2**	**54**
Cairn Gorm	**6**	**1245**	**2**	**67**
Aonach Beag (Lochaber)	7	1234	1	
Aonach Mor	8	1221	1	
Carn Mor Dearg	9	1220	1	
Ben Lawers	10	1214	1	
Beinn a' Bhuird	**11**	**1197**	**2**	**39**
Carn Eige	**12**	**1183**	**2**	**157**
Beinn Mheadhoin	**13**	**1182**	**2**	**46**
Mam Sodhail	**14**	**1181**	**2**	**157**
Stob Choire Claurigh	15	1177	1	
Ben More (Crianlarich)	16	1174	1	
Ben Avon (Leabaidh an Daimh Bhuidhe)	**17**	**1171**	**2**	**39**
Stob Binnein	18	1165	1	
Beinn Bhrotain	**19**	**1157**	**2**	**57**
Derry Cairngorm	**20**	**1155**	**2**	**48**
Cac Carn Beag (Lochnagar)	21	1155	1	
Sgurr nan Ceathreamhnan	**22**	**1151**	**2**	**153**
Bidean nam Bian	23	1150	1	
Sgurr na Lapaich	**24**	**1150**	**2**	**167**
Ben Alder	25	1148	1	
Geal Charn (opposite Ben Alder)	26	1132	1	
Binnein Mor	27	1130	1	
Ben Lui	28	1130	1	
Creag Meagaidh	**29**	**1130**	**2**	**86**
An Riabhachan	**30**	**1129**	**2**	**167**
Carn nan Gobhar	31	1129	1	
Ben Cruachan	32	1126	1	
A' Chralaig	**33**	**1120**	**2**	**143**

	Height order	Height (m)	Volume	Page
An Stuc	34	1118	1	
Meall Garbh (Lawers)	35	1118	1	
Sgor Gaoith	**36**	**1118**	**2**	**79**
Aonach Beag (Loch Ossian)	37	1116	1	
Stob Coire an Laoigh	38	1116	1	
Stob Coire Easain	39	1115	1	
Monadh Mor	**40**	**1113**	**2**	**57**
Tom a'Choinich	**41**	**1112**	**2**	**162**
Carn a'Choire Bhaidheach	42	1110	1	
Sgurr Mor (Fannaichs)	**43**	**1110**	**2**	**245**
Sgurr nan Conbhairean	**44**	**1109**	**2**	**146**
Meall a'Bhuiridh	45	1108	1	
Stob a'Choire Mheadhoin	46	1105	1	
Beinn Ghlas (Lawers)	47	1103	1	
Beinn Eibhinn	48	1102	1	
Mullach Fraoch-choire	**49**	**1102**	**2**	**143**
Creise	50	1100	1	
Sgurr a'Mhaim	51	1099	1	
Sgurr Choinnich Mor	52	1094	1	
Sgurr nan Clach Geala	**53**	**1093**	**2**	**241**
Bynack More	**54**	**1090**	**2**	**67**
Stob Ghabhar	55	1090	1	
Beinn a' Chlachair	56	1087	1	
Beinn Dearg (Inverlael)	**57**	**1084**	**2**	**268**
Schiehallion	58	1083	1	
Sgurr a' Choire Ghlais	**59**	**1083**	**2**	**171**
Beinn a' Chaorainn (Glen Derry)	**60**	**1082**	**2**	**43**
Beinn a' Chreachain	61	1081	1	
Beinn Heasgarnich	62	1078	1	
Ben Starav	63	1078	1	
Beinn Dorain	64	1076	1	
Stob Coire Sgreamhach	65	1072	1	
Braigh Coire Chruinn-bhalgain	66	1070	1	
An Socach (Loch Mullardoch)	**67**	**1069**	**2**	**164**
Meall Corranaich	68	1069	1	
Glas Maol (Glenshee)	69	1068	1	
Sgurr Fhuaran	**70**	**1067**	**2**	**135**
Cairn of Claise	71	1064	1	

	Height order	Height (m)	Volume	Page
Bidein a' Ghlas Thuill	72	**1062**	2	**264**
Sgurr Fiona	73	**1060**	2	**264**
Na Gruagaichean	74	1055	1	
Spidean a' Choire Leith	75	**1055**	2	**229**
Stob Poite Coire Ardair	76	**1053**	2	**86**
Toll Creagach	77	**1053**	2	**162**
Sgurr a' Chaorachain	78	**1053**	2	**178**
Beinn a' Chaorainn (Laggan)	79	**1052**	2	**90**
Glas Tulaichean	80	1051	1	
Geal Charn (Ardverike)	81	1049	1	
Sgurr Fhuar-thuill	82	**1049**	2	**171**
Carn an t-Sagairt Mor	83	1047	1	
Creag Mhor	84	1047	1	
Glas Leathad Mor	85	**1046**	2	**254**
Chno Dearg	86	1046	1	
Cruach Ardrain	87	1046	1	
Beinn Iutharn Mhor	88	**1045**	2	**63**
Meall nan Tarmachan	89	1044	1	
Stob Coir'an Albannaich	90	1044	1	
Carn Mairg	91	1042	1	
Sgurr na Ciche	92	**1040**	2	**102**
Meall Ghaordaidh	93	1039	1	
Beinn Achaladair	94	1038	1	
Carn a' Mhaim	95	**1037**	2	**48**
Sgurr a' Bhealaich Dheirg	96	**1036**	2	**139**
Gleouraich	97	**1035**	2	**110**
Carn Dearg (Ben Alder)	98	1034	1	
Am Bodach	99	1032	1	
Beinn Fhada (Ben Attow)	100	**1032**	2	**149**
Ben Oss	101	1029	1	
Carn an Righ	102	1029	1	
Carn Gorm (Glen Lyon)	103	1029	1	
Sgurr a' Mhaoraich	104	**1027**	2	**113**
Sgurr na Ciste Duibhe (Five Sisters)	105	**1027**	2	**135**
Ben Challum	106	1025	1	
Sgorr Dhearg	107	1024	1	
Mullach na Rathain (Liathac)	108	**1023**	2	**229**
Stob Dearg (Glencoe)	109	1022	1	

	Height order	Height (m)	Volume	Page
Aonach air Chrith	**110**	**1021**	**2**	**130**
Ladhar Bheinn	**111**	**1020**	**2**	**119**
Beinn Bheoil	112	1019	1	
Carn an Tuirc	113	1019	1	
Mullach Clach a' Bhlair	**114**	**1019**	**2**	**75**
Mullach Coire Mhic Fhearchair	**115**	**1019**	**2**	**257**
Garbh Chioch Mhor	**116**	**1013**	**2**	**102**
Cairn Bannoch	117	1012	1	
Beinn Ime	118	1011	1	
Beinn Udlamain	119	1011	1	
Ruadh Stac Mor (Beinn Eighe)	**120**	**1010**	**2**	**234**
Saddle, The	**121**	**1010**	**2**	**125**
Sgurr an Doire Leathain	**122**	**1010**	**2**	**180**
Sgurr Eilde Mor	123	1010	1	
Beinn Dearg (Atholl)	124	1008	1	
Maoile Lunndaidh	**125**	**1007**	**2**	**181**
An Sgarsoch	**126**	**1006**	**2**	**60**
Carn Liath	**127**	**1006**	**2**	**86**
Beinn Fhionnlaidh (Glen Affric)	**128**	**1005**	**2**	**157**
Beinn an Dothaidh	129	1004	1	
Devil's Point, The	**130**	**1004**	**2**	**54**
Sgurr an Lochain	**131**	**1004**	**2**	**130**
Sgurr Mor (Glen Kingie)	**132**	**1003**	**2**	**106**
Sail Chaorainn	**133**	**1002**	**2**	**146**
Sgurr na Carnach	**134**	**1002**	**2**	**135**
Aonach Meadhoin (Glenshiel)	**135**	**1001**	**2**	**139**
Meall Greigh	136	1001	1	
Sgorr Dhonuill	137	1001	1	
Sgurr Breac	**138**	**999**	**2**	**241**
Sgurr Choinnich	**139**	**999**	**2**	**178**
Stob Ban (Mamores)	140	999	1	
Ben More Assynt	**141**	**998**	**2**	**275**
Broad Cairn	142	998	1	
Stob Diamh	143	998	1	
A' Chailleach (Fannaichs)	**144**	**997**	**2**	**241**
Glas Bheinn Mhor	145	997	1	
Spidean Mialach	**146**	**996**	**2**	**110**
An Caisteal	147	995	1	

	Height order	Height (m)	Volume	Page
Carn an Fhidhleir	**148**	**994**	**2**	**60**
Sgor na a' Ulaidh	149	994	1	
Spidean Coire nan Clach	**150**	**993**	**2**	**234**
Sgurr na Ruaidhe	**151**	**993**	**2**	**171**
Sgurr Alasdair	**152**	**992**	**2**	**215**
Carn nan Gobhar (Lapaich)	**153**	**992**	**2**	**167**
Carn nan Gobhar (Strathfarrar)	**154**	**992**	**2**	**171**
Sgairneach Mhor	155	991	1	
Beinn Eunaich	156	989	1	
Sgurr Ban (Fisherfield)	**157**	**989**	**2**	**257**
Conival (Inchnadamph)	**158**	**987**	**2**	**275**
Craig Leacach	159	987	1	
Druim Shionnach	**160**	**987**	**2**	**130**
Gulvain	**161**	**987**	**2**	**96**
Sgurr Mhor (Beinn Alligin)	**162**	**986**	**2**	**225**
Lurg Mhor	**163**	**986**	**2**	**174**
Inaccessible Pinnacle (Sgurr Dearg)	**164**	**986**	**2**	**209**
Ben Vorlich (Callander)	165	986	1	
An Gearanach	166	982	1	
Mullach na Dheiragain	**167**	**982**	**2**	**153**
Maol Chinn-dearg (Glenshiel)	**168**	**981**	**2**	**130**
Meall na Aighean	169	981	1	
Stob Coire a'Chairn	170	981	1	
Slioch	**171**	**980**	**2**	**238**
Beinn a'Chochuill	172	980	1	
Cona' Mheall (Inverlael)	**173**	**980**	**2**	**268**
Ciste Dhubh	**174**	**979**	**2**	**139**
Stob Coire Sgriodain	175	979	1	
Beinn Dubhchraig	176	978	1	
Meall nan Ceapraichean	**177**	**977**	**2**	**268**
Stob Ban (Grey Corries)	178	977	1	
A' Mharconaich	179	975	1	
Carn a Gheoidh	180	975	1	
Carn Liath	181	975	1	
Stuc a' Chroin	182	975	1	
Beinn Sgritheall	**183**	**974**	**2**	**122**
Ben Lomond	184	974	1	
Sgurr a' Ghreadaidh	**185**	**973**	**2**	**202**

	Height order	Height (m)	Volume	Page
Meall Garbh (Glen Lyon)	186	968	1	
A' Mhaighdean	**187**	**967**	**2**	**257**
Sgorr nam Fiannaidh	188	967	1	
Ben More (Mull)	189	966	1	
Sgurr na Banachdich	**190**	**965**	**2**	**206**
Sgurr nan Gillean	**191**	**964**	**2**	**194**
Carn a' Chlamain	192	963	1	
Sgurr Thuilm	**193**	**963**	**2**	**93**
Meall nan Con	**194**	**961**	**2**	**279**
Sgorr Ruadh	**195**	**962**	**2**	**189**
Stuchd an Lochain	196	960	1	
Beinn Fhionnlaidh	197	959	1	
Meall Glas	198	959	1	
Bruach na Frithe	**199**	**958**	**2**	**198**
Stob Dubh (Glencoe)	200	958	1	
Tolmount	201	958	1	
Beinn nan Aighenan	202	957	1	
Carn Ghluasaid	**203**	**957**	**2**	**146**
Tom Buidhe	204	957	1	
Saileag	**205**	**956**	**2**	**139**
Sgurr nan Coireachan (Glenfinnan)	**206**	**956**	**2**	**92**
Stob na Broige	207	956	1	
Sgor Gaibhre	208	955	1	
Beinn Liath Mhor Fannaich	**209**	**954**	**2**	**245**
Am Faochagach	**210**	**954**	**2**	**251**
Beinn Mhanach	211	953	1	
Meall Dearg (Glencoe)	212	953	1	
Sgurr nan Coireachan (Glen Dessary)	**213**	**953**	**2**	**102**
Meall Chuaich	214	951	1	
Meall Gorm (Fannaichs)	**215**	**949**	**2**	**245**
Beinn Bhuidhe (Glen Fyne)	216	948	1	
Sgurr Mhic Choinnich	**217**	**948**	**2**	**209**
Creag a'Mhaim	**218**	**947**	**2**	**130**
Driesh	219	947	1	
Beinn Tulaichean	220	946	1	
Carn Bhac	**221**	**946**	**2**	**63**
Meall Buidhe (Knoydart)	**222**	**946**	**2**	**115**
Sgurr na Sgine	**223**	**946**	**2**	**125**

	Height order	Height (m)	Volume	Page
Bidein a' Choire Sheasgaich	**224**	**945**	**2**	**174**
Carn Dearg	**225**	**945**	**2**	**81**
Stob a' Choire Odhair	226	945	1	
An Socach (Glen Ey/Glenshee)	227	944	1	
Sgurr Dubh Mor	**228**	**944**	**2**	**218**
Ben Vorlich (Inveruglas)	229	943	1	
Binnein Beag	230	943	1	
Beinn a' Chroin	231	942	1	
Carn Dearg (Loch Ossian)	232	941	1	
Carn na Caim	233	941	1	
Luinne Bheinn	**234**	**939**	**2**	**115**
Mount Keen	235	939	1	
Mullach nan Coirean	236	939	1	
Beinn Sgulaird	237	937	1	
Beinn Tarsuinn	**238**	**937**	**2**	**257**
A' Bhuidheanach Bheag	239	936	1	
Sron a' Choire Ghairbh	**240**	**935**	**2**	**99**
Beinn na Lapp	241	935	1	
Am Basteir	**242**	**934**	**2**	**198**
Meall a'Chrasgaidh	**243**	**934**	**2**	**241**
Beinn Chabhair	244	933	1	
Cairnwell, The	245	933	1	
Fionn Bheinn	**246**	**933**	**2**	**249**
Maol Chean-dearg (Torridon)	**247**	**933**	**2**	**186**
Meall Buidhe (Glen Lyon)	248	932	1	
Beinn Bhreac	**249**	**931**	**2**	**43**
Ben Chonzie	250	931	1	
A' Chailleach (Monadhliath)	**251**	**930**	**2**	**81**
Bla Bheinn (or Blaven)	**252**	**928**	**2**	**222**
Mayar	253	928	1	
Meall nan Eun	254	928	1	
Moruisg	**255**	**928**	**2**	**184**
Eididh nan Clach Geala	**256**	**928**	**2**	**268**
Ben Hope	**257**	**927**	**2**	**282**
Seana Bhraigh	**258**	**927**	**2**	**272**
Beinn Liath Mhor (Coulin)	**259**	**926**	**2**	**189**
Beinn Narnain	260	926	1	
Geal Charn (Monadhliath)	**261**	**926**	**2**	**84**

	Height order	Height (m)	Volume	Page
Meall a' Choire Leith	262	926	1	
Stob Coire Raineach	263	925	1	
Creag Pitridh	264	924	1	
Sgurr nan Eag	**265**	**924**	**2**	**218**
An Coileachan	**266**	**923**	**2**	**245**
Sgurr nan Each	**267**	**923**	**2**	**241**
Tom na Gruagaich	**268**	**922**	**2**	**225**
An Socach (Glen Affric)	**269**	**921**	**2**	**153**
Sgiath Chuil	270	921	1	
Carn Sgulain	**271**	**920**	**2**	**81**
Gairich	**272**	**919**	**2**	**109**
A' Ghlas-bheinn	**273**	**918**	**2**	**149**
Creag nan Damh	**274**	**918**	**2**	**130**
Ruadh Stac Mor	**275**	**918**	**2**	**257**
Sgurr a' Mhadaidh	**276**	**918**	**2**	**202**
Carn Aosda	277	917	1	
Meall na Teanga	**278**	**917**	**2**	**99**
Geal Charn (Drumochter)	279	917	1	
Beinn a' Chlaidheimh	**280**	**916**	**2**	**257**
Beinn a' Chleibh	281	916	1	
Beinn Teallach	**282**	**915**	**2**	**90**
Ben Vane	283	915	1	
Sgurr nan Ceannaichean	**284**	**915**	**2**	**184**

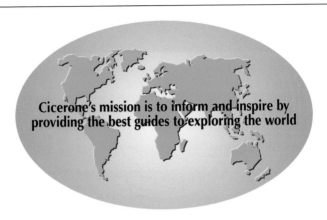

Cicerone's mission is to inform and inspire by providing the best guides to exploring the world

Since its foundation over 30 years ago, Cicerone has specialised in publishing guidebooks and has built a reputation for quality and reliability. It now publishes nearly 300 guides to the major destinations for outdoor enthusiasts, including Europe, UK and the rest of the world.

Written by leading and committed specialists, Cicerone guides are recognised as the most authoritative. They are full of information, maps and illustrations so that the user can plan and complete a successful and safe trip or expedition – be it a long face climb, a walk over Lakeland fells, an alpine traverse, a Himalayan trek or a ramble in the countryside.

With a thorough introduction to assist planning, clear diagrams, maps and colour photographs to illustrate the terrain and route, and accurate and detailed text, Cicerone guides are designed for ease of use and access to the information.

If the facts on the ground change, or there is any aspect of a guide that you think we can improve, we are always delighted to hear from you.

Cicerone Press
2 Police Square Milnthorpe Cumbria LA7 7PY
Tel:01539 562 069   Fax:01539 563 417
e-mail:info@cicerone.co.uk   web:www.cicerone.co.uk

CICERONE